Women in Archaeology

Women in Archaeology

Edited by Cheryl Claassen

University of Pennsylvania Press

Philadelphia

Library of Congress Cataloging-in-Publication Data
Women in archaeology / edited by Cheryl Claassen.
        p.   cm.
    Includes bibliographical references and index.
    ISBN 0–8122–3277–1. — ISBN 0–8122–1509–5 (pbk.)
    1. Women archaeologists—United States—Biography.   2. Women
archaeologists—United States.   I. Claassen, Cheryl, 1953–   .
CC110.W66   1994
930.1′082—dc20   94–8818
                                                          CIP

Contents

List of Tables   vii

List of Figures   ix

1. Introduction   1
   Cheryl Claassen

2. Creating Their Own Niches: Career Styles Among
   Women in Americanist Archaeology Between the Wars   9
   Mary Ann Levine

3. Ladies of the Expedition: Harriet Boyd Hawes and
   Edith Hall at Work in Mediterranean Archaeology   41
   Diane L. Bolger

4. Dorothy Hughes Popenoe: Eve in an Archaeological
   Garden   51
   Rosemary A. Joyce

5. Blue Corn Girls: A Herstory of Three Early Women
   Archaeologists at Tecolote, New Mexico   67
   Robert W. Preucel and Meredith S. Chesson

6. Marian E. White: Pioneer in New York Archaeology   85
   Susan J. Bender

7. Early Women in Southeastern Archaeology: A
   Preliminary Report on Ongoing Research   96
   *Nancy Marie White, Rochelle A. Marrinan, and
   Hester A. Davis*

8. Madeline Kneberg Lewis: An Original Southeastern
   Archaeologist   110
   Lynne P. Sullivan

9. Down in the Field in Louisiana: An Historical Perspective
   on the Role of Women in Louisiana Archaeology   120
   Susan J. Wurtzburg

10. Cowgirls with the Blues? A Study of Women's Publication
    and the Citation of Women's Work in *Historical
    Archaeology*   138
    Mary Beaudry and Jacquelyn White

11. Women in Mesoamerican Archaeology: Why Are the
    Best Men Winning?   159
    Anabel Ford

12. Male Hunting Camp or Female Processing Station?
    An Evolution Within a Discipline   173
    Tracy Sweely

13. Women in Contract Archaeology   182
    *Barbara Avery Garrow, Patrick H. Garrow, and
    Pat A. Thomas*

14. Academic Alternatives: Gender and Cultural Resource
    Management in Arizona   202
    Stephanie M. Whittlesey

15. Women and Archaeology in Australia   210
    Wendy Beck

   References Cited   219
   Index   245
   Contributors   251

Tables

Chapter 10

Table 1. Membership in the Society for Historical Archaeology,
      1987–1991.   141
Table 2. Content analysis of *Historical Archaeology*.   143

Chapter 11

Table 1. Proportion of ladder faculty at teaching colleges
      and research universities.   161
Table 2. Students continuing in postgraduate studies.   162

Chapter 13

Table 1. Staff levels and qualifications.   186
Table 2. Employees by level and gender.   187
Table 3. Employees by level, gender, and mean age.   189
Table 4. Employee publications by education and gender.   192
Table 5. Applicant publications by education and gender.   193
Table 6. Gender of SOPA members by region.   194
Table 7. 1992 SOPA emphases by gender.   195

Chapter 14

Table 1. Ranking of primary job responsibilities.   204
Table 2. Education (degree) by annual salary and gender.   206
Table 3. Reasons for choosing nonacademic career paths
      by gender.   207

Figures

Chapter 3

Figure 1. Harriet Boyd Hawes sorting sherds, 1902.   46

Chapter 4

Figure 1. Dorothy Popenoe, excavation 5 at Playa de
           los Muertos.   52
Figure 2. Photograph by Dorothy Popenoe of objects from
           burials at Playa de los Muertos.   65

Chapter 5

Figure 1. Frances Watkins with A. V. Kidder and Charles
           Amsden (?) at Tecolote ruin.   76
Figure 2. Church, Tecolote Village.   79
Figure 3. Women's living quarters, Tecolote village.   80
Figure 4. Eva Horner and unidentified workman
           excavating 300 series mound.   81

Chapter 8

Figure 1. WPA laboratory, University of Tennessee.   111
Figure 2. Madeline Kneberg and Thomas M. N. Lewis, at
           Frank H. McClung Museum.   113
Figure 3. Cartoon from *Proceedings of the Sixteenth
           Southeastern Archaeological Conference*.   118

Chapter 11

Figure 1. Mesoamerican archaeologists, top 30 institutions   163
Figure 2. Faculty positions in Mesoamerican archaeology.   164
Figure 3. Ph.D.s in Mesoamerican archaeology, 1979–1989.   165
Figure 4. Profile of respondents' personal data.   168

Chapter 12

Figure 1. Number of skills possessed by fieldworkers.   179

Chapter 13

Figure 1. Employees by year of first hire by gender.   185
Figure 2. Employees by age at initial hire.   188
Figure 3. Experience of applicants and employees at initial
          hire.   190
Figure 4. Education by level of employees and applicants.   191

Chapter 1
Introduction

Cheryl Claassen

Why a book of articles specifically about women archaeologists? Life experiences moderate choices throughout one's life. Of significance to the discipline of archaeology are the choices of career, school, mentor, and specialization. Within the practice of science, life experiences have been shown to influence choices at all steps of the scientific cycle— problem selection, hypothesis, explanation, theory, method, technique, even bibliography. Gender is a significant element in life experience, one that is currently undergoing a great deal of scrutiny in archaeology. These authors explore the relationship between gender and choices made in the work of archaeology.

Numerous articles have demonstrated the link between gender and the pursuit of college and graduate schooling and gender and career choice. Garrow et al. (this volume) discuss gender and mentors in archaeology and numerous studies demonstrate the positive influences women mentors bring to women and men students. Gender influences fieldwork opportunities (Bender 1991; Preucel and Chesson, this volume; Wurtzburg, this volume) and excavation skills (Sweely, this volume). Gender influences role choice in archaeology with a greater proportion of women choosing laboratory specialties and, in the past, laboratory/museum jobs and analytical methods such as floral, lithic edgewear, faunal, bead, and ceramic analyses. Gender has been shown to be a significant factor in the acquisition of technical skills such as those provided by physics, chemistry, and astronomy. The type of analysis a woman feels competent to do governs her choice of research problem as does her mentor, geographical location (more often cited by women than by men to explain a number of phenomena), fieldwork opportunities, peer group, and role models, all influenced by gender. Beaudry (this volume) provides information on the citation of women's writing that strongly suggests gender even influences who gets cited, as well as the contents of bibliographies, lists of recent research, and lists of recent publications.

It can no longer be doubted that gender directly and significantly influences the state of knowledge in archaeology, our perception of our knowledge both about our own history and about the past for various regions and ethnic groups. This statement about gender is not meant to include the alterations brought to concepts of the past by a gendered prehistory. Instead I implicate the alterations brought to the presented past by the exclusion of data, hypotheses, explanations, and practitioners or the usurping of those perspectives by others.

So, a book about women archaeologists will offer us insight into the making of archaeological science. It serves other purposes as well. The biographies and surveys included here and recently published elsewhere about women working in archaeology indicate omissions and flaws in some accounts of the history of archaeology and, perhaps more important, reveal sources of data and ideas that lie largely untapped simply because the reports were penned by women. The articles provide information of use to historians and sociologists of science and indicate the successes or failures of affirmative action policies and laws. They indicate the necessity for rewriting academic and private sector employment policies, redefining professionalism, and modifying tenure procedures and expectations.

Biographies and Surveys

Eight articles in this collection are based on biographical information about early women archaeologists. Gacs et al. (1989:xv–xvi) make several points about the role of biographies in scholarship. Biographies tell us something about the state of archaeology during the period of that career. In addition, we can study the professionalization of archaeology by looking at particular biographies of individuals recognized as professionals and ever widening the sample size: "Biographies demonstrate some of the ways in which person, discipline, and society articulate in particular ways at particular times, to create science and scholarship" (Gacs et al. 1989:xvi).

Forty-one women are discussed in some detail in this volume, 29 of whom were at work as archaeologists before 1940. In 12 cases, the information was derived through interviews and represents information never presented before: Bettye Broyles, Hester Davis, Madeline Kneberg, Yulee Lazarus, Martha Rolingson, Christine Adcock Wimberly (White et al.), Frances French, Paula Johnson, Rita Krouse (Wurtzburg), Frederica de Laguna, Doris Stone, and Mildred Wedel (Levine). Biographies are offered in this volume for Marian White

(Bender), Madeline Kneberg (Sullivan, White et al.), and Dorothy Popenoe (Joyce).

Substantial information is given for most of the women included herein. These women are Edith Hall, Harriet Boyd Hawes (Bolger), Katharine Bartlett, Elizabeth Campbell, Florence Ellis, Dorothy Cross Jensen, Dorothy Keur, Frederica de Laguna, Marjorie Lambert, Mary Butler Lewis, Ann Morris, Tatiana Proskouriakoff, Jean Pinkley, Anna Shepard, Doris Stone, Frances Watkins, and Mildred Wedel (Levine), Bettye Broyles, Hester Davis, Yulee Lazarus, and Martha Rolingson (White et al.), Caroline Dormon, Margaret Drew, Jo Evans, Frances French, Paula Johnson, Rita Krouse, and Lanier Simmons (Wurtzburg), and Eva Horner (Preucel and Chesson). Isabel Kelly and Frances Watkins are covered in two articles, those by Preucel and Chesson and Levine. Some information is provided about Margaret Ashley, Adelaide Bullen, Marion Heimlich, Catherine McCann, and Christine Adcock Wimberly (in White et al.), Mary Hemenway, and Zelia Nuttall (Levine).

There have been surveys on a number of different facets of women working in archaeology (Levine 1991). Preceding this publication, studies utilizing survey questionnaires had been carried out for women in archaeology in general (Wildesen 1980, Kramer and Stark 1988, Stark 1991), in the U. S. Forest Service (McLemore and Reynolds 1979), success at the National Science Foundation (Yellen 1983, 1991), in museums (Parezo 1989), in Canadian archaeology (Kelley and Hill 1991), in anthropology couples (Nelson and Crooks 1991), in Asian archaeology (Nelson 1991), in Arizona archaeology (Whittlesey 1991) and women's representation in *American Antiquity* and *Historical Archaeology* (Victor and Beaudry 1992). In this collection one may find the first surveys of women in Cultural Resource Management—900 applicants and employees of Garrow and Associates (Garrow et al.), skills of women and men field laborers (Sweely), and women in Louisiana CRM (Wurtzburg). Several other surveys add to the data base previously described: more on women's representation in the journal *Historic Archaeology*, on women Mesoamericanists (Ford), and women in Australian CRM (Beck).

The overlaps and connections among these articles will be apparent to the reader of more than one chapter. The biographies and life annotations contained in Part I give faces to the statistics presented in the surveys of Part II. The assessments of archaeology today (Part II) identify problems and situations—family commitments, geographical constraints, underemployment and underutilization—and successes that are no different from those of forty or even eighty years ago. The articles also indicate ways women's situation in archaeology has changed (women field crews and supervisors are more common) or has taken on new dimensions—women dominate some research specialties. In earlier years fewer women attempted to enter the professional ranks of archaeology, while today many enter but find their progress to be slow. The professional sacred terrain has turned out not to be the field, but rather the academy.

One theme running throughout this volume is how women adapt in whatever way necessary to participate in archaeology. A number of studies have found, in fact, that women have a greater diversity of types of employers than do men archaeologists (Whittlesey), that more women work in museums and have titles of research associates than do men (Ford), and that women are more likely to seek non-academic employment (Whittlesey). These generalizations have been generated by studies of women participating in archaeology both before and after 1960. Dincauze (1992) called for a "serious exploration of career styles in archaeology," which has been answered by Mary Ann Levine and further illustrated by the annotations in papers by White et al. and Wurtzburg. Those career styles continue today and continue to proliferate. In each paper one can read how particular women strategized or conceded to practice archaeology and how nameless women continue to do so. For the 41 women discussed in Part I, only 10 ever held positions in academic departments. Several of those who did had short affiliations and assumed some other role during much of their careers as is the case with many contemporary women archaeologists. In fact, few women archaeologists have been academics; most women archaeologists today who are employed, are employed in contract work as laborers or in cultural resource management. Several papers address their responsibilities, salaries, job satisfaction, and research efforts (Beck; Garrow et al.; Sweely; Wurtzburg; Whittlesey).

Influencing women's roles within archaeology are marriage, children, and mobility. Personal responsibilities have taken their toll on women far more often than on men, suggestion supported in the studies by Whittlesey and Ford, and in the lives of Hawes, Hall, Wedel, and Simmons. Comparative statistics from the 1960s and 1989–92 indicate that more women academics are married now than in the 1960s, and more have children now. From the frequently reported sense of restriction in mobility, women have adopted the strategy of digging and undertaking research close to home. Dorothy Popenoe worked in Honduras because she lived in Honduras. Marian White, Dorothy Jensen, Mary Lewis worked in the Northeast because they lived in the Northeast. Dormon, Drew, Krouse, Johnson, and Simmons worked in Louisiana because they lived in Louisiana. The same can be said of most of the women working in the Southwest, Southeast, and the Northeast. De Laguna, Hawes, Hall, Proskouriakoff, Stone, and McCann are the exceptions to this strategy, as are the women of Ford's study.

Women have always been a minority in academia. Many of the 41 women discussed here appear to have worked in virtual isolation from other women and even from more than one or two other professional archaeologists. Today women constitute only 15 percent of the archaeologists in the top 30 academic departments (Ford). Hundreds of women are working in small contract companies or have only research affiliations with departments and museums. This century of isolation has taken its toll scholastically in dozens of ways. Ideas are underdeveloped, unheard, easily misappropriated. Graduate student women have few role models or women mentors (Garrow) and receive fewer teaching and research assistantships, even though they are often in the majority in graduate programs, because male faculty tend to hire male students (Ford) exacerbating their higher dropout rate between Ph.D. and employment as archaeologists. Social and academic networks for women archaeologists are poorly developed. More women are employed at teaching universities or not affiliated at all handicapping their research programs. Few of the women discussed by name in this collection or surveyed anonymously were ever in a position to influence student archaeologists. Garrow et al. stress the important role that the lack of women mentors is playing in the training of today's archaeologists while a number of biographies show non-academic employment to be equivalent to professional invisibility.

Nearly invisible from even this collection are women of color and lower-class/working-class women. Approximately 160 black women who qualified for Works Progress Administration employment in the late 1930s excavated at four mound sites in Georgia and Alabama: Irene, Macon, Swift Creek, and Whitesburg Bridge (White et al., this volume; Claassen 1993). At the Irene and Swift Creek sites they were the total labor force and were supervised by white college educated men, while a mixed black crew excavated at Whitesburg Bridge. By 1940 poor white women were part of mixed sex, mixed race excavation crews in North Carolina (Claassen 1993). A class and race based definition of femininity encouraged educated white supervisors to seek poor women as unskilled laborers in the field as early as 1935 but repelled educated white women from the field in the United States until the late 1960s and continues to keep them out of the field in the Mediterranean area today. As far as is known, none of the women who worked on New Deal projects attempted to continue in archaeology and it is rarely the case that participants in recent government sponsored make-work or work training projects attempt to stay in archaeology. It is hoped that future research will provide information on the large numbers of poor women who have dug up our data for us since 1935 in this country (e.g., WPA, NYA, CETA government programs) and processed it in the laboratories. White women of different classes have also played vital roles in amateur archaeological societies (Wurtzburg, this volume; Claassen 1993), roles which are usually documented only at the local level. All classes of women have worked at archaeology.

Future Research

A sociological approach to archaeology has provided many insights into the making of archaeological science and perceptions of prehistory. Biographies reveal interesting roles for luck, determination, and choice in the making of an archaeologist. On the level of the individual practitioner, however, uncovering patterns in who becomes an archaeologist and how the pursuit of knowledge is shaped by variables like gender, class, and educational background, is a slow process. Surveys offer a better chance for exposing patterns but cannot give us insight into past communities of archaeologists. There are at least two other sources of large data bases for those past communities of archaeologists that are so far untapped. These are (1) close scrutiny of archaeological educators and their interactions with students, and (2) biographies of departments, with a focus on those students who graduated and those who did not. Patterns in mentoring, field opportunities, overt and covert policies and practices will be readily apparent as will be the role of gender.

One underdeveloped example in which the reader can readily see the potential for both types of studies is the record of women graduates of Harvard University's Department of Anthropology, Archaeology Wing. The first woman admitted to the Department of Anthropology at Harvard University who also graduated was Marie Wormington, who entered the program in 1937 and matriculated in 1954. From 1954 through 1992, 30 women have received the Ph.D. from this department. I detect a strong role for class (assumed from her undergraduate institution) in the admission to candidacy and successful completion of the degree. Of the 30 women specializing in archaeology to have completed the doctorate, 18 had received Ivy League B.A. degrees. Of those who did not, three entered with a master's degree (thereby proving themselves capable?), and five had graduated from well respected undergraduate departments (UCLA, Berkeley, Wisconsin, Cornell, Michigan). The remaining four women probably represented a different social class from the others (and consequently the only "risks"?), to judge from their undergraduate institutions, as may have the master's degree admissions. While few would doubt the role for class in undergraduate admissions at Harvard, it appears to play quite a significant role in determining which women graduate with the Ph.D. Data on who was admitted but did not complete the doctorate degree are not currently available.

Those senior faculty in the Department of Anthropology at Harvard most often chairing committees of women have been Stephen Williams (7), Gordon Willey (6), and Hallam Movius (4). Of the other senior faculty, Carl Lamberg-Karlovsky and J. O. Brew chaired two committees, David Pilbeam one, and Phillip Phillips, Kwang-Chih Chang, Ofer Bar-Yosef, and Nicholas van der Merwe none. From stories and personal experience, I would have predicted quite different numerical associations.

The junior faculty are rarely present for more than seven years and thus cannot usually fulfill chair obligations. (Eight years is the average completion time for women candidates.) Consequently the three women archaeologists employed by the department as teaching faculty in its history, Maria Gimbutas, Ruth Tringham, and Rosemary Joyce, never saw a woman candidate through to completion. Junior faculty Peter Wells and Jeremy Sabloff chaired two and Michael Moseley and Jon Ericson chaired one successful woman's committee, while Geoffrey Conrad, Izumi Shimada, and Robert Preucel chaired none. How these mentors were able to assist the careers of the 30 women in this 55-year period will prove to be a very interesting study.

We have no understanding of the crucial issues for women in countries other than a few in the English-speaking world. Gero (1983) provides some intriguing data on women publishing in South American countries and the role of class in those statistics. In volumes 1 and 2 of the Mexican journal *Arqueologia* the editor is a woman and production editors are a woman and a man. Of the eleven articles in Volume 1, five have women as senior authors and three other women are junior authors. Only two of the nine articles in volume 2 were penned by women, however.

During the fall 1990 and fall 1991 semesters I taught at a major private university in Mexico where the four archaeologists were all unmarried women, the three cultural anthropologists were married and unmarried men, and the vast majority of students were women specializing in archaeology—three enigmas from a United States perspective. Several of those students expressed to me their perception that being an archaeologist meant they would not be able to marry and thus they were planning to seek "non-archaeological" museum positions. The large number of women students was apparently the result of upper class expectations that women would marry so it did not matter what career they chose, while men were expected to train in a "practical" career. A recent bibliography of ethnoarchaeology and experimental archaeology in Mexico (Claassen 1991) revealed that both endeavors are very rarely participated in by women employed in or trained in archaeology in Mexico, in contrast to a large number of women participating in both who reside in and/or were trained in the United States. These topics are just a few that promise much insight into the professionalization of women archaeologists cross-culturally.

The stories laid out before the reader or alluded to in statistics give us the evidence we need to understand why women do not go into academics, why academically inclined women do not choose archaeology, why women who choose archaeology do not stay in it, why women who stay in it may not engage in fieldwork or submit articles for publication or grant proposals, and why some women can do it all. They also give us the evidence we need to reshape the disciplinary reward system, eliminate tenure or drastically modify it, modify curriculum and disciplinary history, rethink the objectivity of science and the definition of a professional archaeologist, and, as a result, undertake what many women would call a feminist archaeology.

Chapter 2
Creating Their Own Niches: Career Styles Among Women in Americanist Archaeology Between the Wars

Mary Ann Levine

Historiography is a highly selective enterprise and as such has silenced the voices of many people. In archaeology, the people to whom a written history has been denied include women. Patterson (1986:7) notes that "extant histories of archeology are narrowly professional, usually narratives of the adventures of men and ideas." In a citation analysis of standard disciplinary histories Kehoe (1989:105) calculated that 6 percent of all persons cited by Daniel (1967) and only 2 percent of all those cited by Willey and Sabloff (1974) are women. Although Reyman (1992b:76) does note some improvement in Willey and Sabloff's (1980) second edition, few women are discussed at length. In general, such written histories of archaeology neither consider the scientific contributions of women nor examine the role that women played in shaping the discipline.

It is only in the last decade that archaeologists have expressed any outward interest concerning women in archaeology. Since the 1980s, scholars have made strides toward redressing this neglect (a detailed review of research undertaken in the last decade is available in Levine 1991:180–183). Until the 1980s, discussions concerning women's experiences in archaeology existed in oral traditions, outside the pages of written texts. A vibrant tradition of oral history concerning women's participation in the discipline emerged through the alliances forged by informal networks of communication often referred to as "old-girl networks." Despite the importance of this medium, we can no longer afford to have the history of women in our discipline exist in this form only. Because we are only beginning to uncover and document the history of the "people without history" (Wolf 1982:x), there are many issues concerning the presence and contributions of women in Americanist archaeology that are under-studied and merit our immediate consideration.

One topic attracting increasing scholarly attention is the history of women in Americanist archaeology from the 1920s to the present. This chapter contributes to this small but steadily growing body of literature by examining one issue that has not received sufficient attention, the diversity of women's experiences for that time period. Dincauze (1992) has alerted us to the need to explore the differences in professional styles among female archaeologists, having herself noticed the diverse routes to achievement that women have taken in archaeology. In this article I call attention to the diversity in women's career trajectories and experiences in the discipline by specifically discussing the range of professional styles exhibited in the lives of female archaeologists who created niches of their own in the years between the wars. For the purposes of this paper, I do not explore women in classical studies, but rather examine women's experiences in Americanist archaeology.

I discuss diversity as evidence for strategizing among women as the profession was feminized. Because this diversity must be seen within the broader framework of the feminization of the profession, a brief history of women in Americanist archaeology from the late nineteenth century to World War II is offered. Although temporal constraints serve to focus analyses, they are arbitrary and not absolute by nature. With that in mind, I first chronicle the role of women in Americanist archaeology prior to World War I, then turn to the inter-war years and examine women in academia and as museum curators to provide the context necessary to discuss women who followed professional pathways that led them outside of these two traditional routes. Drawing from biographical data collected for eight women, I then discuss alternative career styles, which include, for example, working as museum research associates, writing for the public, working for the Park Service, working in a laboratory, and itinerancy.

In documenting and giving voice to this silenced past I suggest that the history of women in Americanist archaeology is not reducible to one homogeneous story. In our efforts to reinstate women as active participants in the development of archaeology we cannot essentialize the history of women in the profession to a single female experience. Experiences that defy easy categorization should not be considered as noise that disrupts a perceived pattern, but rather as vital information for exposing the complexity in the interaction between gender and science. In exploring this issue, I hope to help fill some voids in our standard written histories of archaeology.

The Feminization of Americanist Archaeology to World War II

The First Generation

Although women are absent from much of the literature on the early history of Americanist archaeology, they have been contributing to the development of archaeology for over a century. In the 1880s, female anthropologists began to hold marginal positions in museums (Rossiter 1982:58). Women participated in anthropology as loosely affiliated field workers who were generally unpaid but permitted to publish in museum proceedings, or as financial patrons for particular museums (Rossiter 1982:58–59). For example, Mary Hemenway (1820–1894), a philanthropist, donated the substantial collection of materials unearthed by the Hemenway Southwestern Archaeological Expedition to Harvard's Peabody Museum. As possibly the first avowedly scientific research into that area's prehistory (see Woodbury and Woodbury 1988:46), Hemenway's Expedition helped establish the Southwest as a distinct culture area (McChesney 1991:282). Zelia Nuttall (1857–1933), a Mesoamerican archaeologist, acted as an Honorary Assistant at Harvard's Peabody Museum and frequently published through that institution. Her most significant contribution to Americanist archaeology centers on having rediscovered and authenticated several codices and manuscripts (Chiñas 1988:269). Both women were members of the Women's Anthropological Society of America (est. 1885), an organization established as an alternate to the sexist practices of the all-male Anthropological Society of Washington (McGee 1889; Rossiter 1982: 80).

While their contributions to archaeology differed, Mary Hemenway and Zelia Nuttall had much in common. Neither woman carried out extensive fieldwork nor received formal training in archaeology. They both contributed to archaeology as single women and they were both sufficiently affluent to make their chosen careers possible. Women such as Hemenway and Nuttall were active in Americanist archaeology prior to World War I and made notable contributions to the development of the discipline, but their involvement was limited and circumscribed. Male organizations such as the Anthropological Society of Washington marginalized women from the mainstream of professional life in anthropology. The first generation of women in Americanist archaeology were excluded from both formal and informal networks of communication and were afforded few career opportunities. The range of career styles for female archaeologists during the late nineteenth century and early twentieth century was exceedingly narrow (additional information on women in the late nineteenth century and early twentieth century is available in Levine [in preparation]).

The next generation of female archaeologists includes women born early in the twentieth century who launched their careers in the inter-war years, the 1920s and 1930s. Beginning in the 1920s, the range of professional pathways for women in archaeology widened while the education opportunities and socio-economic backgrounds of women expanded. Although women in this second generation also faced size-able obstacles to advancement and recognition, they achieved greater visibility in academic and museum settings. To explore this point further I provide brief vignettes for women active in these two settings during the inter-war years.

Women were awarded Ph.D.s for their research in cultural anthro-pology as early as 1914 (Anonymous 1955:703), but it was not until the 1930s that women earned doctorates in anthropology for their re-search in archaeology. The 1930s also witnessed female archaeologists securing academic posts for the first time. My research suggests that the first cohort of women who obtained academic employment were Frederica de Laguna, Florence Hawley Ellis, Dorothy Cross Jensen, Dorothy Strouse Keur, and Madeline Kneberg. (See Sullivan or White et al. [both this volume] for a report of Kneberg's contributions to archaeology.)

The Second Generation: Academics

Frederica de Laguna (1906–   )

Frederica de Laguna earned her Ph.D. in 1933 from Columbia University. Her dissertation on Inuit and Paleolithic art was the first archaeology dissertation written by a woman in the anthropology de-partment at Columbia (Anonymous 1955:704). It is highly probable that she produced the earliest archaeology dissertation written by a woman in the United States. She began teaching as a lecturer at Bryn Mawr College in 1938, was promoted to full professor in 1955, and has been associated with the college in the capacity of professor emerita since 1975. De Laguna was elected Fellow of the Society for American Archaeology (SAA) in 1934 and served as President of the American Anthropological Association in 1966–67. She was among the first women anthropologists elected to the National Academy of Sciences. In contrast to the other women in this article, de Laguna specialized in Arctic anthropology. In 1929, she participated in the first professional

archaeological survey of Greenland (de Laguna 1977:25). Her pioneering research in Alaska in the 1930s led to the publication of such
time-honored volumes as *The Archaeology of Cook Inlet, Alaska* (de
Laguna 1934) and *Chugach Prehistory* (de Laguna 1956). A complete
account of de Laguna's subsequent field work and publications is available in McClellan's (1988) biographical account.

Although de Laguna came close to marrying an English engineer
who was planning a career in the coal mines of Wales, she chose to
remain single (de Laguna 1977:22). In her autobiography she (1977:
11) states that "my first week's contact with the Danish scholars in the
National Museum of Denmark in Copenhagen convinced me that
anthropology was what I wanted most in the world. Having once set
foot in Greenland for a stay of almost half a year, I could not turn aside
from that long journey or that vocation, even though I had to give up
the man I loved." In a letter dated July 17, 1929, de Laguna wrote to
her parents and stated that "I can't bear the thought of giving up all my
intellectual work and living in Wales all my life" (de Laguna 1977:160).
She believed that she could not be the kind of wife that her fiancé
wanted and broke their engagement that spring following her departure from Greenland (de Laguna 1977:283). In a letter responding to
my questions on her experiences as a female archaeologist, she wrote,
"I don't believe that my archaeology was any different from that of any
man working in a similar area at the same time (de Laguna, personal
communication 1985).

Florence Hawley Ellis (1906–1991)

Florence Hawley earned her B.A. and M.A. from the University of
Arizona. For her master's thesis she refined existing typologies for
Southwestern prehistoric pottery and called attention to the possible
relationships between the Southwest and Mexico (Hawley 1930). T. T.
Waterman, then temporarily a faculty member at the University of
Arizona, attempted to coax her into publishing her thesis jointly with
him, although he played no role in its preparation whatsoever (Irwin-
Williams 1990:25). From 1928 to 1933, Hawley worked as an Instructor at the University of Arizona. When junior faculty members were
laid off for one year during the Depression, she traveled to the University of Chicago to complete her dissertation on materials from Chetro
Ketl in Chaco Canyon (Frisbie 1974:3–4). For her doctoral thesis,
awarded and published in 1934, she combined dendrochronological
studies of architectural timbers, pottery analyses, and numerical methods to explain the occupational history and abandonment at Chaco
Canyon (Frisbie 1974:4). In archaeology she was among the first re-

searchers to utilize dendrochronology as well as the first scholar to employ the chi-square statistic in archaeological inquiry (Frisbie 1974: 4). Ellis often stated that as a woman she felt it was important to have a specialty that could enhance her employability in case she was unable to get work in archaeology (Cordell 1991a:148). For Ellis, dendrochronology was her chosen special skill (Cordell 1991a:148).

In 1934 she was hired by the University of New Mexico as an assistant professor and in the following year was elected one of 42 fellows of the SAA (Griffin 1985:267). She retired from the university in 1971 and held emerita status until her death in 1991 (Frisbie 1991). In 1936 she married Donovan Senter, an archaeologist, and in 1939 they had a daughter. The couple divorced in 1947 due in part to the perception of professional competition, and in 1950 she married Bruce Ellis, a historian.

Florence Hawley Ellis's teaching load increased during World War II when male faculty members were away at war (Frisbie 1974:7). After the war a survey determined that she continued to carry the heaviest teaching load in the department yet her salary was lower than that of her male counterparts, even those who had less seniority (Irwin-Williams 1990:25). This salary discrepancy persisted and her promotions came more slowly than for her male colleagues (Irwin-Williams 1990:35). Although her teaching responsibilities were weighty, she continued to be very active in the field. Ellis participated in 11 field seasons at Chaco as well as a variety of other archaeological and ethnological field projects. Her research resulted in the production of 300 published monographs, books, and papers, as well as manuscripts (Frisbie 1991:94).

Dorothy Cross Jensen (1906–1972)

Dorothy Cross earned her Ph.D. in Oriental Studies and Anthropology in 1936 from the University of Pennsylvania. As a graduate student she was primarily interested in Near Eastern archaeology and worked as registrar on the Tell Billa and Tepe Gawra excavations in Iraq (Ehrich 1973:407). Her Near Eastern research led to two major publications, including her dissertation (Cross 1937), which is described as a classic (Ehrich 1973:408). She married Paul Jensen before World War II and was widowed in 1957.

Although her research on the Near East has had lasting significance, she is best known for her contributions to Americanist archaeology, particularly New Jersey prehistory. As one of the first women to study New Jersey prehistory, she recast the overwhelming male tenor of

Northeastern archaeology. In 1938 she began simultaneously working as an instructor at Hunter College and as Archaeologist for the New Jersey State Museum. During her 43-year involvement with the New Jersey State Museum she was appointed to numerous positions, including State Archaeologist (Conant 1974:81). She supervised a large Works Progress Administration project from 1936 to 1942 that filled in the apparent spottiness of New Jersey's prehistoric record. The reconnaissance project provided the data for her two-volume work, *Archaeology of New Jersey* (Cross 1941, 1956). In addition to these books written for the professional community, she published more general accounts for the public (Conant 1974:80).

Dorothy Cross Jensen was committed to public education as well as field research and writing. At Hunter College, she taught a variety of courses and acted as subchairperson for anthropology in the department of sociology and anthropology from 1950 to 1957 (Ehrich 1973: 409). She was promoted from instructor to assistant professor in 1947 and became a full professor in 1962, 28 years after having joined the faculty (Ehrich 1973:409). She continued her dual career in teaching and museum work until her death in 1972.

Dorothy Strouse Keur (1904–1989)

Dorothy Strouse, a native of New York City, attended the nearby tuition-free Hunter College. She took classes with Edward Stanford Burgess, a botanist with a keen interest in anthropology (James 1988: 181). As his favorite student, she was delegated to carry his lunch from the cafeteria to his office (James 1988:182). She graduated summa cum laude in 1925 and accepted his offer to fill the post of laboratory assistant for a $150 a month (James 1988:182). However, he made her agree to give half of that back each month so he could buy artifacts for the college (James 1988:182). The president of the nearby American Museum of Natural History encouraged her to attend graduate school, and her decision to do so initiated her long-term involvement in Southwestern archaeology and social anthropological research.

In 1928 she married John Y. Keur, a Dutch biologist, and began teaching at Hunter, while working on her doctoral dissertation at Columbia. She was awarded her Ph.D. in 1941 for her work at Big Bead Mesa in New Mexico and the results of her research were published by the SAA as the first volume in their Memoir series (Keur 1941). In the 1950s, her increasing interest in Holland led her and her husband to carry out several projects including a study of an agrarian village in Holland and an examination of the impact of Dutch colonialism on the

Windward Islands (James 1988:183–184). These projects were funded by Fulbright and Wenner-Gren respectively, and resulted in the publication of two co-authored books.

Although Dorothy Keur was a dedicated researcher and writer, she felt that her primary contribution to anthropology was as an educator. She taught a wide variety of courses in all sub-disciplines and channeled much of her energies into the development of undergraduate courses in anthropology (James 1988:184). She was promoted from instructor to assistant professor in 1940 and received her next promotion in 1947. She became a full professor in 1957, 29 years after having joined the faculty at Hunter. A few years before her death in 1989, she stated that "I really feel that my chief contribution has been in teaching thousands upon thousands of students. . . . For me, this was more rewarding than just having additional publications or becoming famous in one line or another" (quoted in Babcock and Parezo 1988: 143).

Discussion

During the inter-war years, women in archaeology secured academic employment for the first time. Despite this breakthrough, women were still considerably underrepresented in this form of employment, which in archaeology earns power, prestige, and recognition. Although women's infiltration into this male-dominated arena enabled them to achieve many "firsts," these advances came at a cost. Women first encountered barriers long before they entered academia. One male researcher attempted to undermine the publication of Florence Hawley Ellis's master's thesis. Another male professor denigrated Dorothy Keur by having her regularly fetch his lunch and effectively extorted her salary to supply his lab with artifacts. Once in academia, women faced overt gender-based status differentiation. Florence Hawley Ellis's salary was smaller than that of her male counterparts, while her responsibilities were greater than her better paid male colleagues. Florence Hawley Ellis, Dorothy Cross Jensen, and Dorothy Keur all received infrequent promotions. Slower promotion rates kept women at the lower end of the academic ladder longer, undoubtedly resulting in infrequent salary increases. Efforts to obstruct women's climb up the academic ladder probably reduced their chances for recognition as well.

All of these obstacles were intended to keep women from centers of power in the profession. Academic women did devise strategies to try to overcome marginality. Glazer and Slater (1987:211) note that some women sought status through extraordinary efforts and performance, including a willingness to sacrifice traditional relationships for their careers. Frederica de Laguna was clearly willing to forgo marriage and children for her career. Another strategy, innovation, was used by women who were drawn deliberately or by chance to new fields of interest (Glazer and Slater 1987:211). Glazer and Slater describe innovators as those who remove themselves from direct competition with their male colleagues. Frederica de Laguna and Dorothy Cross Jensen may have chosen to work in the Arctic and New Jersey as a creative response to marginalization. Similarly, Florence Hawley Ellis's decision to develop a special skill, tree-ring dating, may be viewed as a strategy to ensure a place for herself in science.

The Second Generation: Museum Curators

As noted elsewhere, female anthropologists such as Zelia Nuttall began to secure marginal positions in museums by the 1880s. From that time onward, the presence of women in museum settings steadily increased. In "Exploring the Museum Field," published by the *Independent Woman* in 1933, Thomas (1933:238) could easily state that "innumerable important posts are held by women in this field." Regrettably, some reasoned that women were well suited for museum work from an almost biologically determined perspective. For example, Williams Henry Fox of the Brooklyn Museum felt that "women are especially suited to museum work by their love of the beautiful, their adaptability and their patience in detail work" (Thomas 1933:238). It is implicit in this statement that he did not regard women as well suited for this vocation for their intellectual capabilities. Before World War II, at least four female archaeologists had already launched successful careers as museum curators or directors: Elizabeth Crozer Camppbell, Frances Watkins, Katharine Bartlett, and Marjorie Ferguson Lambert.

Elizabeth W. Crozer Campbell

Like some of the other women discussed in this article, Elizabeth Crozer Campbell formed part of a husband-wife team. The couple appear to have had one son who accompanied them in the field (Campbell 1929b:19). There is no evidence to suggest that the Campbells ever received formal academic training in archaeology. The couple moved to the California desert in 1925 and immediately developed a keen interest in the prehistoric occupation of that area (Hodge 1935:7). Their interest in collecting, preserving, and properly curating archaeological materials resulted in the establishment of the Desert Branch of the Southwest Museum. For several decades, Elizabeth Campbell held the position of director and with the assistance of her husband embarked on numerous reconnaissance projects in the Californian deserts and other parts of the Great Basin. Their fieldwork is well documented in a series of accounts published independently (E. Campbell 1929a, 1929b, 1931a, 1931b, 1932, 1936, 1949) and jointly (E. Campbell and W. Campbell 1935, 1937, 1940).

In the 1920s and 1930s, the Great Basin was one of the least known areas in American archaeology (Irwin-Williams 1990:13). Mrs. Campbell is the only woman in this study to have developed an expertise in Great Basin archaeology. For her contributions to the culture history of this region, she is remembered as a pioneer in some circles (Warren 1970:5). Yet, as Irwin-Williams (1990:13) points out, her achievements did not receive sufficient attention to warrant an obituary. Biographical details concerning her life as a museum director and field-oriented researcher are scant. In fact, a library search as well as a telephone call to the archivist at the Southwest Museum did not uncover her dates of either birth or death.

Frances E. Watkins

Frances Watkins received her B.A. in 1929 from the University of Denver and earned her Ph.D., presumably in Anthropology, in 1942 at the University of Southern California. After earning her first degree in 1930, she became curator of the Southwest Museum. She held this position throughout most of her professional career. Although she may have interacted with Elizabeth Crozer Campbell within their common institution, I have no information concerning their relationship and in fact, lack many details surrounding Watkins's life as a museum curator. I unsuccessfully attempted to uncover her dates of birth and death through library research and by calling the Southwest Museum.

While at the Museum, Watkins published extensively in *The Masterkey*, a regional journal. The majority of her articles report on recent gifts made to the Museum or describe various collections housed there. Her research interests included crafts and industries of Native American women, and Indian games and baskets. In addition to developing an expertise in museology, she acquired field training as well. In fact, her most significant contributions to the discipline lie in two self-reflexive articles concerning her field experiences: "My Experiences as a Field Archeologist" (Watkins 1930) and "Archeology as a Profession for Women" (Watkins 1931).

In 1929, the Laboratory of Anthropology at Santa Fe, a facility founded by John D. Rockefeller, awarded fellowships to six individuals, three men and three women (Watkins 1930:13). The female recipients were Isabel Kelly, Eva Horner, and Frances Watkins. The scholarship recipients worked at Pecos under the guidance of A. V. Kidder, director for the archaeology section for the Laboratory of Anthropology. Preucel and Chesson (this volume) offer a detailed account of the experiences of these three women at the excavation of Tecolote during the summer of 1929. Watkins (1931:175) maintained that "There have been a great many American women in the field as assistants, secretaries, or relatives of the men in charge of expeditions, but never until the summer of 1929 was an expedition staffed entirely by women sent out by an authorized institution. I had the great good fortune to be one of three feminine directors, and I think that I can safely say that the experiment . . . was a success." The women selected their own equipment, chose their own ruin, hired their own laborers, and "excavated four weeks without masculine supervision" (Watkins 1931:176). Although all members of the expedition were given the same training course, the three men were given a larger ruin to excavate. Watkins (1931:176) states that "The boys worked on a larger ruin, and did about three times as much actual excavation, with excellent mapping while ours was smaller, but every bit of material and information worked out to the farthest degree. Dr. Kidder said that it was the *tidiest little excavation* he had ever seen—and we are still puzzling over his exact meaning" (italics mine).

Katharine Bartlett (1907–)

Katharine Bartlett was born in Denver in 1907 and raised in a family apparently of modest means. Unable to afford the high cost of going to Smith College, she attended the University of Denver (Babcock and Parezo 1988:171), where, like Frances Watkins, she studied with E. B. Renaud. She earned her first degree in 1929, received her master's degree in 1930, and began her sixty-year career with the Museum of Northern Arizona upon graduation. From 1930 to 1952 she was Librarian and Curator of Anthropology and Archaeology and from 1953 to 1975 she was Curator of History (Babcock and Parezo 1988:171). While at the Museum she furthered her education through a 1936–37 Rockefeller Foundation Museum Internship at the Brooklyn Museum (Babcock and Parezo 1988:171). Throughout the 1930s, 1940s, and 1950s, she participated in numerous archaeological field projects and engaged in ethnographic fieldwork among the Hopi in addition to working at the Museum (Babcock and Parezo 1988:171). Her research resulted in more than fifty published articles (Anonymous 1992:5) that ranged from discussions of lithic industries from Arizona for the academic community (Bartlett 1943) to syntheses of Hopi history tailored more to the public (Bartlett 1934, 1936).

Marjorie Ferguson Lambert (1910–   )

Marjorie Ferguson Lambert earned her M.A. degree in Anthropology in 1931 from the University of New Mexico for her work on acculturation at Sandia Pueblo (Cordell 1991b:505). Although her family would have preferred her to become a teacher or librarian, she pursued a career in Southwestern archaeology and became one of the first women in the country to occupy a major curatorial position (Irwin-Williams 1990:27). She worked for the Museum at the University of New Mexico and served as Curator of Archaeology from 1938 to 1959, Curator of Anthropology and Exhibits from 1959 to 1963, and Curator of the Research Division from 1963 to 1969 (Babcock and Parezo 1988:131). After her brief marriage to George Tichy, she wed E. V. "Jack" Lambert in 1950. By all accounts, her second husband was highly supportive of her career (Fox 1976:4; Irwin-Williams 1990:28).

Lambert undertook several field projects and published conscientiously. She has to her credit over 170 articles (see Fox 1976:6–18), the majority appearing in *El Palacio*, a regional journal. Cordell (1991b:505) argues that she is perhaps best known for the research she undertook at Paa-ko from 1935 to 1937. Cordell (1991b:505) describes the published Paa-ko site report as a model even today. At Paa-ko, a large late prehistoric/early historic pueblo, Lambert replaced two male colleagues who had been unsuccessful on two related projects (Irwin-Williams 1990:27). Lambert took on the project for $125 a month, which has been described by Irwin-Williams (1990:27) as a significant salary reduction. When Lambert became director, these colleagues rumored that she would do no better and that native laborers would refuse to work for a woman (Irwin-Williams 1990:27). In the end, the laborers got on well with her and the project was successfully completed (Irwin-Williams 1990:27). Cordell (1991a:148–149) reports that Lambert was underpaid at the Museum of New Mexico and often without appropriate facilities. Although Lambert received support from her husband and some male professionals, not all of her interactions with men were positive. Lambert has reported being accosted in dimly lit hallways and subjected to colleagues who "wanted kisses and other things for the privilege of working with them" (Irwin-Williams 1990:28).

Discussion

The number of women employed in museums increased in the years between the wars, a situation not unlike that previously described for women in academia. In contrast to women who pursued careers as academicians, of the women employed in museums who received university training, not one attended prestigious Ivy League schools. Frances Watkins and Katharine Bartlett attended the University of Denver, and Marjorie Lambert attended Colorado College and the University of New Mexico. Frances Watkins is the only woman in this group to have been awarded a Ph.D.

With the exception of Elizabeth Crozer Campbell, who evidently had the resources necessary to found a museum branch, these women appear to have been of modest means. Two of them (Elizabeth Crozer Campbell and Marjorie Ferguson Lambert) were married and at least one (Elizabeth Crozer Campbell) had children. Surprising to some may be the fact that these female museum workers, many of whom held curatorial posts, were accomplished field archaeologists who published extensively as well. However, obtaining field training was difficult and many women published in regional journals with limited readership.

Museum employment was not free from the sexual discrimination experienced by women in academia. At least one woman, Marjorie Ferguson Lambert, reported having been sexually harassed. She also received lower wages than her male counterparts. Of equal interest is the fact that all four women were based in the West, the majority of them specifically centered in the Southwest. In addition to being based in the Southwest, these women pursued careers in Southwestern archaeology. Women may have formed this enclave deliberately to overcome overt and subtle forms of discrimination.

This comprehensive, though not exhaustive, review of women in academia and as museum curators or directors sheds significant light on women's experiences in archaeology during the inter-war years. During this time, female archaeologists registered important advances, such as an impressive increase in the number of women in the profession who worked in these two settings. The inter-war years also witnessed a broadening of employment opportunities for women in Americanist archaeology. Although women were still underrepresented in these two settings and their work remained under-recognized, women achieved many "firsts" in the years between the wars, especially in higher education. Women's place in archaeology did improve in these years, but this amelioration came at considerable cost to them. These vignettes disclose that female archaeologists recognized early on that their entrance into the profession would require special strategies.

Simply discussing women in academia and as museum curators masks much of this strategizing and fails to account for much of the diversity in women's experiences in archaeology during the inter-war years. Not surprisingly, it is often the case that the most interesting phenomena are those that are not easily pigeonholed. Many women, by chance or by design, followed professional pathways that led them outside of these two routes. Dincauze (1992:136) has stated: "The routes to powerful positions within the profession are the same as they have always been; those routes have not traditionally been the paths women trod. Whether on account of training, personal predilection, or the obstacles of discrimination, women conventionally took other ways, ways that led to some personal fulfillment but less often to professional recognition." I will now provide biographical profiles for eight women who pursued alternative career styles, creating niches of their own in the years between the wars.

Alternative Career Styles

Museum Research Associates

The late nineteenth and early twentieth centuries witnessed the rise of female research associates in many scientific disciplines (Rossiter 1982: 205). The number of women with titles such as "collaborator," "fellow," "research assistant," and "research associate" increased dramatically throughout the 1920s and 1930s (Rossiter 1982:204). By the late 1930s, such research personnel were the most common in biochemistry, astronomy, anthropology, and microbiology (Rossiter 1982: 204–205). Many factors contributed to the increased number of female research associates. Science was becoming increasingly team-oriented at roughly the same time that women were seeking to enter the professions (Rossiter 1982:205). In addition, research opportunities expanded, tempting many faculty members to move and universities to respond by offering professors greater funds as an incentive to stay (Rossiter 1982:205). Faculty used such funds to strengthen their own positions and hire more assistants. Women quickly became excellent candidates for assistantship positions on team projects. According to Rossiter (1982:205) women were available and were willing to work harder for lower salaries than men. Although such positions created certain opportunities for women in a depressed job market, it is important to stress that research associate positions generally offered poor

wages, if any at all, an uncertain future, and few prospects for advancement. However, to many women, accepting an unpaid research asso-
ciateship was one strategy to secure a place for themselves in the
profession. Research associateships were courtesy appointments that
offered institutional affiliation to otherwise unemployed or under-
employed researchers (Mason 1992:94). Since Rossiter (1982:205) reports that female research associates figured prominently in anthropology in general, it is not surprising to discover that many women
archaeologists of the 1920s, 1930s, and 1940s worked in this capacity as
well. Mary Butler Lewis, Tatiana Proskouriakoff, and Doris Zemurray
Stone are among those women who followed this professional pathway.

Mary Butler Lewis (1903–1970)

Mary Butler was born in 1903 and received her B.A. from Vassar
College in 1925 (T. Williams 1989:3). After attending the Sorbonne for
a year and teaching French for two years, she studied at Radcliffe
College and earned her M.A. there in 1930 (T. Williams 1989, Appendix A). She earned a doctorate in 1936 from the University of Pennsylvania for her analysis of Piedras Negras pottery. Her dissertation data
were collected during several expeditions to Guatemala (Keur 1971:
255). She was the first female archaeologist to be awarded a Ph.D. from
the Department of Anthropology at the University of Pennsylvania
(Anonymous 1955:748) and part of the first cohort of female archaeologists to earn Ph.D.s in the United States. Butler's areas of professional interest included northeastern and central U.S. prehistory as
well as Mesoamerican archaeology.

Although Butler taught briefly at Hunter College, Vassar, and Bryn
Mawr, her professional career was firmly rooted in the Museum of the
University of Pennsylvania. At the museum, Butler served as Assistant
of the American Section from 1930 to 1939 and worked as a Research
Associate from 1940 until her death in 1970 (Keur 1971:155). Through
funding from the American Philosophical Association, she continued
to direct archaeological fieldwork in Guatemala during her early years
at the museum. Her interest in Mesoamerica resulted in a spate of
publications (Butler 1931, 1934, 1935a, 1935b, 1936a, 1936b, 1937),
many of which reported on pottery.

In the 1940s, Butler's research shifted from Mesoamerican archaeology to northeastern U.S. prehistory. During this time, Northeastern
archaeology was a field heavily dominated by men. At least one prominent northeastern archaeologist prohibited women from working on
his crews (Bender 1991:215). Bender reasons that Butler was able to
secure the credentials to direct fieldwork in the Northeast because she

had received her field training outside the region, working locally only when she could assume a leadership position. Butler directed one of the earliest surveys of the Hudson Valley in New York state. The Carnegie Corporation had originally agreed to fund the Hudson Valley Archaeological Survey for 5 years (T. Williams 1989:1). In 1941, the Corporation discontinued support of Butler's project after the completion of only 2 field seasons and decided to invest its money in the war effort (T. Williams 1989:10). Butler's field crew, which was 25–30 percent women (T. Williams 1989, Appendix D), succeeded in investigating 45 sites. In 1940, she published a brief summary of her fieldwork and presented a paper at the Eastern States Archaeological Federation (Chilton 1991:6). Final site reports were never published. Butler struggled to have her contributions to New York State prehistory recognized; the New York State Archaeologist from 1949 to 1971 failed to include the results of her survey in his major works (Chilton 1991:2).

In 1942, she married Clifford Lewis and together the couple had two children. Keur (1971:255) states that "Mary placed family first; hence she forwent long and distant trips." Although having children limited her mobility, Butler successfully coped with professional problems as they arose (Keur 1971:255). In 1943 Butler responded to an emergency plea to supervise an excavation in the nearby town of Broomall, Pennsylvania (Keur 1971:255). Keur (1971:255) states that "she bundled up her eleven-week-old daughter in the car and went forth to the dig—carrying on efficiently as director, and giving the baby her bottle at the coffee break and lunch hour." Butler's research in local prehistory resulted in several publications (Butler 1936c, 1936d, 1936e, 1941, 1947a, 1947b). Interestingly enough, her decision to concentrate on nearby prehistory as a result of marriage and children is a survival strategy noted by other female archaeologists as well (see Dincauze 1991:10). Dincauze terms the strategy 'backyard archaeology' and suggests that women center their professional activities near family and home institutions because it allows them to rely on support networks of friends and close relatives (in Bender 1991:214). At the time of her death Mary Butler was involved in the restoration of the 18th century Mortenson House in Norwood, a community just outside Philadelphia (Keur 1971:255).

Tatiana Proskouriakoff (1901–1985)

Tatiana Proskouriakoff was born in Tomsk, Siberia, in 1909. Her father was a chemist, her mother a physician, and her grandfather an instructor of natural science who wrote articles on Siberian archaeology (Graham 1990:7). The family moved to Pennsylvania in 1916. Proskouriakoff attended the University of Pennsylvania for one year, but received her B.S. in architecture from Pennsylvania State College in 1930 (Graham 1990:7). She entered the job market during a time of prevailing economic depression when few new buildings were being constructed (Marcus 1988:297). Unable to find a job that would allow her to design new structures, she responded to a job advertisement posted by the Museum of the University of Pennsylvania (Marcus 1988:297). Linton Satterthwaite needed someone to create architectural reconstructions of structures uncovered at Piedras Negras (Marcus 1988:297). Proskouriakoff accepted this employment opportunity and thus launched her career as a Mesoamerican archaeologist. Her distinguished career spanned a half century and focused primarily on Mayan art, architecture, and hieroglyphic writing.

From 1934 to 1938 Proskouriakoff produced an architectural restoration of Structure P-7 and a perspective drawing of the acropolis from the site of Piedras Negras (Marcus 1988:298). She joined the 1936 expedition to that site with travel and expenses paid but no salary (Graham 1990:7). After another season at the site, Satterthwaite threatened to "fire" her since he could not agree to continue "employing" her without remuneration (Graham 1990:7). Fortunately, Sylvanus Morley at the Carnegie Institution raised money to finance Proskouriakoff's trip to join the Institution's team in Copán in 1939 and Chichén Itzá in 1940 (Marcus 1988:298). Proskouriakoff's efforts resulted in a Carnegie Institution publication entitled *An Album of Maya Architecture* (Proskouriakoff 1946).

In 1943, A. V. Kidder, head of the Carnegie's Division of Historical Research, promoted Proskouriakoff from draftsperson and illustrator to staff member (Graham 1990:8). She participated on the Mayapán project (1950–1955), the Institution's last archaeological endeavor, in the capacity of surveyor and excavator (Graham 1990:8). Although all staff members were to be retired at the project's end, Kidder persuaded the Institution to retain her and two others at reduced salary (Graham 1990:8). The Carnegie stopped funding archaeological research in 1958 (Marcus 1988:298). While still associated with the Carnegie team, Proskouriakoff (1950) produced her next monograph, *A Study of Classic Maya Sculpture,* which presented a method for estimating the age of stone monuments lacking inscribed dates. Marcus (1988:298) states that this work "remains the definitive treatment in the field."

In 1958, Proskouriakoff joined Harvard's Peabody Museum staff as a Research Associate. She retired from her position as Honorary Curator of Maya art at the Peabody Museum in 1977. At the Peabody, she pursued her interest in hieroglyphic texts from Piedras Negras. Her study of Piedras Negras stelae challenged the idea that inscriptions contained only calendrical and astronomical information and demonstrated that the Maya were in fact recording their own political and dynastic histories (Marcus 1988:299). For this path-breaking research (Proskouriakoff 1960), a special committee of the American Anthropological Association awarded her the fifth A. V. Kidder Medal (Marcus 1988:299). This research continues to be highly lauded by contemporary archaeologists and considered by many to be the most significant of her many contributions to the discipline (Marcus 1988:299; Graham 1990:8).

After the completion of this research, Proskouriakoff embarked upon a 15-year study of approximately 1000 jade pieces that had lain unstudied almost 70 years in the Peabody (Graham 1990:8). Her ambitious efforts resulted in the publication of an illustrated and descriptive catalogue entitled *Jades from the Cenote of Sacrifice* (Proskouriakoff 1974). Before her death in 1985, Proskouriakoff sought to reconstruct the political histories of Classic Maya cities (Marcus 1988:299). According to Graham (1990:8) she was able to complete the essentials of this last major research project before the onset of her final illness.

Evidently, Tatiana Proskouriakoff never married. Graham (1990:9) states the following: "Friends she had, and a few of her close friendships meant enough to have stirred occasional yearnings for a more social or companionable existence, as against the cloistered life of the scholar." Her accomplishments gained her Pennsylvania State University's nomination of Women of the Year for 1971, honorary degrees from Tulane University and Pennsylvania State University, and the Order of the Quetzal, the highest honor awarded to a foreigner by Guatemala (Marcus 1988:300; Graham 1990:9). Despite her many accomplishments, Proskouriakoff frequently received inadequate financial compensation for her work. Through her near 80 publications, many reporting on pioneering breakthroughs in Mayan archaeology and epigraphy, Proskouriakoff is revealed as a meticulous, disciplined, and insightful researcher.

Doris Zemurray Stone (1909–   )

Doris Zemurray was born in 1909 in New Orleans in fortunate circumstances. She received her B.A. from Radcliffe College in 1930. In that same year she was appointed to the position of Associate in Archaeology at Tulane University's Middle American Research Institute, which her father helped to found. From 1954 onward she concurrently functioned as a Research Associate in Central American Archaeology and in Ethnology at Harvard's Peabody Museum. She served as a trustee of Radcliffe during the periods from 1941 to 1953 and 1968 to 1980 and is currently an honorary associate in Central American Archaeology at the Peabody. As her professional titles and the contents of her bibliography (more than 150 items) indicate, Doris Stone's main areas of professional specialization were the prehistory and ethnology of Honduras and Costa Rica (see Andrews 1986:viii; S. Williams 1986a).

Stone published for both the professional community and the public, in English and in Spanish (S. Williams 1986b:201). She based her publications on field research as well as collection analyses (S. Williams 1986b:200). Andrews (1986:viii) argues that two volumes (*Archaeology of the North Coast of Honduras* published in 1941 and *The Archaeology of Central and Southern Honduras* which appeared in 1957), largely based on her own research, had an especially profound impact on the discipline. For her contributions to the discipline she received honorary degrees from Tulane and Union, and a citation from Radcliffe at the seventy-fifth anniversary celebration of the college. She also served as chief of the Costa Rican delegation at five International Congresses of Americanists.

At her graduation, she met Roger Thayer Stone, a graduate of Union College (S. Williams 1986b:200). They were married later that summer and spent over fifty years together (S. Williams 1986b:200). Although Stone was not appointed a Research Associate until the 1950s, her experiences in the years between the wars helped define this alternative career style. In a retrospective essay written for her fiftieth college reunion, Stone (1980) exposes some of the difficulties she encountered as a female undergraduate in the 1920s. She states that "Though not a feminist in an active sense, I was both old-fashioned and rebellious, determined to follow a profession in spite of marriage and family." She adds that "In the 1920s, I was required to obtain permission from the president of Harvard to attend classes at the Peabody Museum, and with the permission came the warning that if my deportment was not entirely proper, my association with that austere building would be ended. And never did I attend a class in Harvard Yard, let alone have any acquaintance with the dormitories" (Stone 1980:20). Stone (1980:20) was advised against studying for a Ph.D. and states that "Women simply weren't encouraged to go that far, particularly in anthropology." However, in response to my letter that questioned her about struggles she may have had as a woman pursuing a career in archaeology, she replied that "I am not conscious of any unpleasant experiences. I came around during a very early time span of American archaeologists when there were few students or professors and everyone was interested in his work for the subject's sake. I was lucky to have had as professors some of the 'fathers' of American Anthropology" (Doris Stone, personal communication 1985).

Doris Stone has had a profound impact on both Americanist archaeology and women in archaeology. Patricia Urban (1988:888) notes that "Doris Stone has had a long and varied career, and she served and continues to serve as an inspiration to many, particularly women who sometimes wonder what has changed in the decades since Stone was discouraged from attempting graduate study and fieldwork." Urban (1988:888) respectfully notes that she would not be working in Honduras if Doris Stone had not forged the way.

Beyond the Standard Professional Pathways

A considerable number of women followed professional pathways that led them far outside academia, museum curatorships and research associateships. In this section I discuss the diverse career styles exhibited in the lives of Ann Axtell Morris, Anna O. Shepard, Isabel T. Kelly, Jean Pinkley, and Mildred Mott Wedel.

Ann Axtell Morris (1900–1945)

Ann Axtell was born in 1900 and had already chosen archaeology as her vocation by the age of six, long before she knew what the word archaeology meant (Morris 1933:12). When a house guest asked what she wanted to do when she grew up, she replied: "I want to dig for buried treasure, and explore among the Indians, and paint pictures, and wear a gun, and go to college" (Morris 1933:12). Ann Axtell attended Smith College where she attempted to pursue her interest in Indians via the field of history. She soon noted that "My Indians, the first Americans, were left hanging in thin air attached to textbooks only at the latter end of their story—a story that it seemed to me must be both fascinating and important" (Morris 1933:13). One professor observed that her goals could be more easily realized if she studied archaeology; therefore after graduation, she traveled to France to join the American School of Prehistoric Research (Morris 1933:13). Although she spent a "gorgeous" year excavating a Mousterian site, she did not relinquish her professional interest in Americanist archaeology (Morris 1933:14).

In 1923, she married Earl H. Morris (1889–1956), a Mesoamerican and Southwestern archaeologist. In the early 1930s they had two daughters, Sarah Lane and Elizabeth Ann (Kidder 1957:394). Elizabeth Ann (Ph.D., University of Arizona, 1959) followed in her parents' footsteps to become a Southwestern archaeologist (Woodbury 1988:4). In contrast to those women previously discussed, Ann Axtell Morris did not hold an official title or become directly affiliated with any professional institution. However, she did collaborate with her husband on virtually all of his research for the Carnegie Institution (Anonymous 1946:117). Her contributions to the field rest on both her scholarly work and popular accounts of Mesoamerican and Southwestern archaeology.

At Chichén Itzá she excavated the Temple of the Xtoloc Cenote and meticulously copied the wall art of the Temple of the Warriors (Anonymous 1946:117).She remarked that it was at the "small Temple of the Xtoloc Cenote where I earned my spurs as an excavator" (Morris 1931:164–165). Her research there resulted in the article "Murals from the Temple of the Warriors and Adjacent Structures" in the two volume set co-authored by E. Morris, J. Charlot, and Morris (1931: 347–484). In the Southwest, she recorded and studied pictographs and cave art. Her efforts resulted in a large archive of photos, drawings, and watercolors (Anonymous 1946:117). Irwin-Williams (1990: 12–13) notes that, although Morris did collaborate with her husband on all his work and is believed to have written major portions of the technical reports, her best known credited publications were two nontechnical popular volumes.

After a long and crippling illness, Ann Axtell Morris died in 1945 (Kidder 1957:394). At the time of her death, her popular volumes, *Digging in the Yucatan* (Morris 1931) and *Digging in the Southwest* (Morris 1933), had sold widely. Both volumes did much to introduce the layperson to the methods and aims of archaeology (Anonymous 1946:117). Despite her fieldwork, research, and publications in archaeology, she described her career as being an archaeologist's wife (Morris 1933:16). Aside from this comment, her popular and highly personalized accounts of archaeology do not display gender consciousness of any sort. It is difficult to determine how she viewed her contributions to archaeology and her role as a woman, wife, mother, and member of a professional career couple during the inter-war years.

Anna Osler Shepard (1903–1973)

Anna O. Shepard was born in Merchantville, New Jersey in 1903. She became interested in anthropology as an undergraduate at California State College at San Diego and the University of Nebraska. In 1926, she earned an A.B. degree with a major in sociology-anthropology and a minor in philosophy (Morris 1974:448). Prior to earning her diploma she had already attended the School of American Research Archaeological Field School at Gran Quivera, New Mexico and become a Fellow in Archaeology at that institution (Morris 1974:448). She briefly attended the University of New Mexico for graduate study, but withdrew when Edgar Lee Hewett would not approve her thesis topic (Thompson 1991:14). Although Shepard never obtained graduate level degrees, she studied chemistry, physics, math, optical crystallography, Spanish, geology, mineralogy, and microchemical spectroscopy at the Massachusetts Institute of Technology, University of Kansas, University of Colorado, Claremont College, and New York University (Morris 1974:448). The range of her academic training is rivaled only by the variety of professional appointments she held throughout her career as a specialist in ceramics as well as Mesoamerican and Southwestern archaeology.

Shepard was first employed as Curator of Ethnography at the San Diego Museum of Man. Between 1926 and 1929 she prepared exhibits on pottery and basket weaving, assisted a colleague with a study of Mimbres pottery, and participated in the University of New Mexico's Archaeological Field School at Chaco Canyon (Morris 1974:448). From 1931 to 1936 she served as an unpaid research associate for the Laboratory of Anthropology in Santa Fe, New Mexico (Thompson 1991:24). During this time she focused specifically on petrographic analyses of Pecos ceramics, became acquainted with A. V. Kidder, and published for the first time (Morris 1974:448). Along with Frederick Matson, Shepard initiated the modern application of optical petrography to the study of archaeological pottery (Thompson 1991:18). Two of her earliest publications were responses to articles printed in the first volume of *American Antiquity*, calling attention to some weakly presented assertions put forth about analytical techniques used to study copper artifacts (Shepard 1936b) and pottery (Shepard 1936a).

The Carnegie Institution figured prominently in Shepard's professional career, a situation not unlike that described for Ann Axtell Morris and Tatiana Proskouriakoff. After working as a museum curator and laboratory research associate, Shepard worked as a Ceramicist for the Carnegie for the two decades spanning from 1936 to 1957. Her association with the Carnegie began under the direction of A. V. Kidder who encouraged her to undertake petrographic analyses of potsherd paste, paint, and temper (Morris 1974:449). During this time, she worked at Mesa Verde and participated on J. O. Brew's Awatovi project (Babcock and Parezo 1988:139). Shepard continued to publish extensively on the technology of Southwestern and Mesoamerican pottery and produced *Ceramics for the Archaeologist* (Shepard 1956), a volume that is generally regarded as an outstanding original contribution to the discipline.

Although this volume is now in its twelfth printing and is regularly cited, much of Shepard's work and the implications of her research were "largely ignored in her lifetime" (Cordell 1991a:132). In addition, Morris (1974:448) notes that Shepard's conclusions were oftentimes at odds with the results obtained by others and her hypotheses so innovative or unusual that they were essentially disregarded. Shepard was bothered and disappointed by this lack of recognition as well as the frequent publication of her work as appendices to other researchers' monographs rather than as independent pieces of scholarship (Morris 1974:448). For example, "Technological Notes in the Pottery of San Jose" (Shepard 1939a) appeared as an appendix to J. Eric Thompson's volume entitled *Excavations at San Jose, British Honduras* and "Technology of La Plata Pottery" (Shepard 1939b) appeared as an appendix to Earl Morris's volume entitled *Archaeological Studies in the La Plata District: Southwestern Colorado and Northwestern New Mexico.* Interspersed with such contributions, she did author many monographs such as *Plumbate: A Mesoamerican Tradeware* (Shepard 1948). Her sizeable publication record is available in Morris (1974:450–451).

After the dissolution of the Carnegie's Division of Historical Research in 1958, Shepard was employed part-time by the U. S. Geological Survey in Denver (Thompson 1991:32). Although this government post was technically outside of archaeology, she continued to engage in anthropologically oriented geochemical and petrographic research until her retirement in 1970. During this time she reported on the Maya Blue pigment used by Mexican and Central American native populations, ceramic industrialization in four villages in Oaxaca, and the identification of materials used in the imitation of jade artifacts (Morris 1974:449).

It is important to note that in 1936, Shepard moved her base of research to Boulder, Colorado (Bishop 1991:58). From that time onward, she carried out most of her work in a laboratory in the home that she shared with her father (Thompson 1991:36). Because her father was ill, she attended conferences infrequently and rarely went into the field (Bishop 1991:82). From her private laboratory she worked in relative isolation. Although this situation may have limited her interaction with the archaeological community, Thompson (1991:38) does argue that her private laboratory allowed her to escape the pressures experienced by women in male dominated labs. Shepard controlled her own working conditions. She insulated herself from challenging male colleagues in the work place and the privacy of her lab allowed her to voice all her concerns in print, avoiding potentially risky face-to-face confrontations (Thompson 1991:38).

Thompson (1991:38) notes that Shepard "identified a neglected field of science and made it her own, choosing the analytical laboratory as the site of her work." Crown (1991:385) further suggests that Shepard "was among the vanguard of women in archaeology who created a niche for herself in order to participate in the profession." Cordell (1991a:148) argues that Shepard's decision to specialize in petrography may be comparable to Florence Hawley Ellis's desire to ensure a place for herself in science by specializing in tree-ring dating. Shepard herself wrote the following: "I am well aware that most people consider that a girl is not fitted for field work. As far as 'discomforts' and 'hardships' of camp life are concerned I think the idea is a joke. . . . Nevertheless because of this general belief a girl must show some special qualification to get any chance in archaeology. And the opportunity to work into field work through laboratory work has seemed the most practical. Mr. Bradfield was very strongly opposed to girls in the field but I got a chance in the field with him by satisfying him in the laboratory" (quoted in Bishop 1991:51). In attempts to meet the heavy demand for perfection that Shepard placed on herself (Thompson 1991:31), she frequently suffered from anemia, a condition resulting from overwork. According to her father, Shepard had a "tendency to work until exhaustion overtook her" (quoted in Bishop 1991:52).

Shepard, described by Morris (1974:449) as an essentially shy, solitary, research scientist, occasionally taught university courses while still affiliated with the USGS. She gave numerous lectures at the University of Colorado, taught a seminar on ceramic technology in 1969 at the University of Missouri, and spent 6 months as a Visiting Scholar at Hebrew University in 1966 (Babcock and Parezo 1988:139). In spite of these temporary positions, she remained relatively isolated from students (Thompson 1991:37). Cordell (1991a:149) notes that since Shepard's career was not anchored in a university setting, she did not have the opportunity to train students in her methods to carry on her work. Cordell (1991a:149) further suspects that this situation may have contributed to a lack of support for her approach which now, following re-examination, is praised and cited.

After an increasingly debilitating illness, Anna Shepard died in 1973 (Morris 1974:448). In her last article she utilized Maya blue to illustrate the interdependence between chemical and mineralogical methods (Shepard 1971). She also discussed the need for collaboration in the field between ceramic specialists and archaeologists. To illustrate her point she drew upon her experiences at Awatovi in 1940 and in the Near and Middle East in 1966. The issue of active collaboration is as much concern today as it was over twenty years ago when Shepard first called attention to it.

Isabel Truesdell Kelly (1906–1984)

Isabel T. Kelly was born in Santa Cruz, California, in 1906. Although she had originally planned to major in physical education at the University of California at Berkeley, by the end of the first semester she decided to pursue a career in anthropology. Berkeley's faculty then consisted of Robert Lowie and Alfred Kroeber in anthropology and Carl Sauer in geography. It was Sauer who discovered and nurtured her talent, intelligence, and energy (Knobloch 1988:175). In 1925 she received her B.A., in 1927 she received her M.A., and in 1932 she was awarded the Anthropology Department's twelfth Ph.D. (Knobloch 1988:175). Following the completion of her degree, she pursued a unique set of interests including Mexican prehistory and social anthropology, Southwestern archaeology, Plains Indian ethnography, and international public health (Knobloch 1988:175). The number of areas she specialized in is challenged only by the uncommonly diverse nature of the professional posts she held.

As a National Research Council (NRC) Fellow for 1931–32, Kelly carried out postdoctoral research among the Southern Paiute (Babcock and Parezo 1988:147). More information on NRC fellowships and women is available in Rossiter (1982:269–272). In 1935 she traveled to Mexico as a research associate to direct an archaeological project at Culiacan, Sinaloa (Knobloch 1988:176). The project was supervised by Carl Sauer and Alfred Kroeber for the Institute of Social Sciences at Berkeley. In 1936, she returned to her alma mater to be a teaching assistant for Sauer (Knobloch 1988:176).

Kelly went back into the field to excavate the Hodges site for the Gila Pueblo Archaeological Project in 1937 and 1938. Babcock and Parezo (1988:147) argue that "these excavations were essential to understanding Hohokam culture in southern Arizona. All subsequent publications dealing with Tucson Basin archaeology are based on Kelly's work." After that project ended, Kelly went back to Mexico with only limited funding but plenty of encouragement from Sauer. She carried out field projects in numerous locations throughout western Mexico, focusing especially on Sinaloa and Jalisco. Many of the areas investigated by Kelly had not been previously explored by archaeologists (Babcock and Parezo 1988:147). Although university funds and associate researchships were scant during World War II, Kelly kept her research going with grants from the Guggenheim Foundation (1940–41, 1942–43), Carnegie Institute (1943–44), and the American Philosophical Society (1943–44) (Knobloch 1988:176).

In 1946 Kelly was appointed Ethnologist-in-Charge of the office of the Smithsonian's Institute of Social Anthropology (ISA) in Mexico City; in addition to teaching at the ISA she carried out research with students among the Totonac of Veracruz (Knobloch 1988:176). In 1951, when the ISA became more concerned with international health, she initiated health care studies in Mexico as well as El Salvador. After the ISA shut down in 1952 she began working for the Institute of Inter-American Affairs and continued with her health care research (Knobloch 1988:176). From 1961 to 1976, while still living in Mexico, Kelly acted as a research consultant in archaeology and ethnography for the Arizona State Museum (Babcock and Parezo 1988:147). During this time she continued her research with the support of grants from the Rockefeller Foundation, Wenner-Gren, and the National Geographic Society. Her research consultancy position was the last professional post she held before her death in 1984.

Although Kelly received impressive financial assistance from foundations, the Anthropology Department at Berkeley, chaired by Kroeber, extended minimal professional support. Kelly's letters to Sauer throughout the 1930s and 1940s reveal her low opinion and distrust of Kroeber. Evidently, Kroeber offered little encouragement to women. Despite this, Kelly never criticized archaeology as a male-dominated discipline. She did however comment that lack of support for female anthropologists was nearly universal. In contrast to Kroeber, Sauer did treat her as a colleague. Knobloch (1988:177) notes that Sauer as well as Kidder "expressed frustration that she never received the professional appointment she deserved." In a letter to Sauer, Kidder noted that Kelly should have received a permanent post and wrote that "she is one of the most effective workers I know and thoroughly sound."

Jean McWhirt Pinkley (1910–1969)

Jean McWhirt was born in 1910 in Arizona. Since her father was an Army doctor, she spent her formative years on many different Army posts throughout the United States (Thomas 1969:471) and returned to Arizona for training in anthropology and archaeology. At the University of Arizona, she received her field training from Emil Haury and earned her B.A. in 1933 and M.A. in 1936 (Thomas 1969:471). In contrast to the women mentioned in preceding sections, she worked for the National Park Service, devoting her life to the preservation and interpretation of the past.

Archaeological areas were among the first to be proclaimed national monuments and parks when the National Park Service was established in 1916 (Kelly 1940:275). I have not determined the extent to which female archaeologists participated in the Park Service from 1916 until

Jean McWhirt joined in 1939. She was employed from 1939 until her death in 1969 and first served as a Museum Assistant for the Mesa Verde National Park. She wed Addison Pinkley in 1942 and left the Park Service in 1943 to join her husband who was in the Navy. Her husband died in combat that year. Following her husband's death she "devoted her life to her job" (Thomas 1969:471).

Even though a number of qualified men applied for the position of Chief of the Interpretive Division at Mesa Verde, Jean Pinkley was selected for this post. Her many responsibilities included supervising research pertaining to the interpretation of the Park, overseeing excavation and stabilization projects, and planning for future interpretive programs. She also played a prominent role in the development of the museum at Mesa Verde from 1946 to 1959. She was instrumental in designing visitor tour routes that presented sites in chronological order. In addition, she participated in the planning of the Wetherill Mesa Archaeological Project as the Superintendent's advisor on interpretive and research matters. Under her guidance, new techniques were developed for preserving archaeological ruins. She persuaded the Texas Refinery Company to undertake a $100,000 research project to develop a product that would preserve adobe and sandstone walls without altering their character or color (Thomas 1969:471–472).

In 1966, Pinkley was selected to direct the Pecos Project. She supervised the excavation and preservation of the Pecos Mission and discovered the remains of a church dating to A.D. 1600 that historians believed existed only in myth (Thomas 1969:472). Her efforts shed new light on the history of Spanish missions in New Mexico.

Pinkley's professional publications were few. She coauthored an article on Mesa Verde in 1952 and published a paper that addressed the domestication of turkeys among prehistoric Native Americans (Pinkley 1965). Her dedication to interpreting and preserving the past earned her numerous awards and honors. For her outstanding career and success as a woman in the Federal Service, Ladybird Johnson invited her to a White House luncheon. In 1967, she received the Department of the Interior's Meritorious Award "in recognition of outstanding professional archaeological services and contributions to interpretive programs of the National Park Service" (Thomas 1969:472–473).

Mildred Mott Wedel (1912–)

Mildred Mott earned her A.B. in History from the State University of Iowa in 1934 and her M.A. in Anthropology from the University of Chicago in 1938. In a letter responding to my inquiries about her life as a female archaeologist, she wrote that she was possibly the first woman awarded a fellowship in anthropology at the University of Chicago (Mildred Mott Wedel, personal communication 1986). Her master's thesis, published in 1938 (Mott 1938), sought to determine the relationship between historic and prehistoric Indian populations in Iowa. She received her field training by participating in the University of New Mexico's Jemez Field School at Pueblo Unshagi in 1935, the University of Chicago's Kincaid Field School in 1937 and 1938, and in excavations in Iowa in 1939. She acquired further field experience with her husband on projects in South Dakota, Wyoming, Kansas, and Texas.

In 1939, she married Waldo Wedel, a Plains archaeologist. The couple had three children. Due to the responsibilities that came with childbearing and childrearing, Mildred Mott Wedel elected to interrupt her career for approximately twenty years. However, since 1959 she has published a score of articles on archaeology, history, and ethnohistory. She writes: "Although I started my career in anthropology specializing in archeology . . . I switched to ethnohistory after I raised my family" (Mildred Mott Wedel, personal communication 1986). She also wrote that "Male chauvinism has not been a problem for me. My husband has always been encouraging and helpful" (Mildred Mott Wedel, personal communication 1986). In 1974 she became a Research Associate at the Smithsonian Institution. Her current research focuses chiefly on ethnohistoric analyses of Plains Indian populations.

Discussion

A substantial number of women pursued alternative career styles in the years between the wars. Although Mary Butler and Isabel T. Kelly earned their Ph.D.s, the majority of women in this group did not receive that coveted degree. With institutions such as Harvard discouraging Doris Stone and other females from graduate study, women were clearly aware of their limited welcome in the profession and sought to carve out a place for themselves in spite of an environment that attempted to curb their participation.

Although the group of female museum research associates profiled earlier may not be unequivocally representative of the entire universe of women who worked in this capacity, it is instructive to point out that in contrast to women who worked as museum curators and directors, female research associates received training at prestigious institutions in the East. Mary Butler attended Vassar, Radcliffe, and the University of Pennsylvania; Tatiana Proskouriakoff attended the University of Pennsylvania and Pennsylvania State College; and Doris Stone attended Radcliffe. Furthermore, all three women worked out of Ivy

League institutions such as the University of Pennsylvania and Harvard. In contrast to those women in museum curatorship positions who were predominantly Southwestern archaeologists, Butler, Proskouriakoff, and Stone were all effectively Mesoamericanists. Female research associates were also skilled field archaeologists and well published.

Research associateships provided all three women with an institutional affiliation and the opportunity to "do archaeology." At the same time, research associates offered inadequate financial compensation and limited opportunities for promotion. All three women accepted these posts as a way to remain professionally active, and some may have gravitated toward them as a way to reconcile professional aspirations with domestic responsibilities. For example, for Mary Butler, family came first. Utilizing the strategy of "backyard archaeology," legitimized by her position as a research associate, enabled her to continue with her career and have children without completely restricting her participation in fieldwork.

At least five women followed career styles that led them far outside of the academy and museums. Ann Axtell Morris secured a place for herself in archaeology by writing for the public. She removed herself from any competition by creating a niche of her own to occupy. Being part of a dual archaeology career couple may have, to some extent, governed her decision to contribute to archaeology as a popular writer. By publishing nontechnical accounts, she may have sought to structure her career in such a way as to complement, rather than be at odds, with her husband's professional ambitions. Lamentably, there were few concrete professional rewards associated with this pathway. Like Ann Axtell Morris, Jean Pinkley pursued her interest in archaeology by colonizing an empty niche. For a variety of reasons, Anna Shepard effectively isolated herself from the worlds of academia and museums by conducting her research from a laboratory constructed inside her home. She designed her workplace and created her own working conditions. Shepard carved out an intellectual space for herself by developing an expertise in uncontested territory, petrography. For Shepard, independence and privacy were gained at the expense of recognition and student progeny.

During the inter-war years, some women including Isabel Kelly followed career trajectories defined by itinerancy. Isabel Kelly held numerous professional posts but never received a permanent position. Without permanent ties to an institutional research base, Kelly made do with a series of short-term grants and fellowships. This situation enabled her to remain professionally active but limited her influence in the discipline. This survival strategy was not uncommon for female anthropologists in the years between the wars. Rossiter (1982:272) states: "Anthropology presents an extreme case of this dependency on foundation and fellowships during the 1920s and 1930s. Since it was a small field and had few teaching positions available, most of its younger women did important work and built whole careers on little more than a series of temporary fellowships from NRC and SSRC. In fact, there seems to have been a tendency, in this field at least, to give the fellowships to the women to 'tide them over' while the few jobs available went to the men." In the 1920s and 1930s, some female archaeologists chose another strategy all together. Some women chose to interrupt and postpone their careers. Mildred Mott Wedel subordinated her career in the inter-war years to marriage and family. She did not abandon her professional aspirations, however, but resumed her career after raising her children.

Conclusions

Uncovering the history of the "people without history" is a challenging process involving detective work and patience. Collecting information on people who have occupied the margins of the professional mainstream, the first and second generation of female archaeologists, has been difficult, at times even painful. Information on women in archaeology has been considered insignificant, so much so that the Southwest Museum for example, evidently kept no readily accessible record of the birth and death dates of Elizabeth Crozer Campbell and Frances Watkins. With that in mind, there must be a considerable number of female archaeologists whose histories have yet to be uncovered.

Rossiter (1982:128) reports that by 1920, "many doors to the house of science had been unlocked and opened to them, but women were still on the first floor and still faced many obstacles to their further acceptance." At this time, the number of women who entered archaeology greatly increased yet women still constituted only a tiny fraction of the total population of archaeologists. Although women active in Americanist archaeology in the years between the two world wars encountered barriers to advancement and recognition, they achieved greater visibility in museum settings and entered the groves of academe for the first time. This improvement was not without consequence and women soon recognized that their infiltration into archaeology would require special strategies. I have argued here that exploring the career styles of women active in only these two settings conceals much of this strategizing. At least eight female pathfinders followed routes that lead them outside of museum curatorships and academia.

The development of archaeology, like any discipline, required an expansion of niches within it. In the years between the wars, the

academy offered little to women seeking careers in training and research. As resistance to such impediments, women created a variety of
niches for themselves that enabled them to contribute to archaeology
in new and significant ways. These eight women managed to find
places in the cracks that were open in research institutions, writing for
the public, grant-supported research, and the administration of public
trusts. These women defined roles that could complement and co-exist
with those of the dominant gender. Without the direct competition
that could have defeated them, these pathfinders carried on with their
work and made sizeable contributions to the discipline. During the
1960s and 1970s, the discipline experienced further niche expansion.
This diversification, defined by mandates for historical preservation,
offered the main pathway for a considerable increase in the number of
women in archaeology. In describing the post-1960 period, Irwin-
Williams (1990:38) states: "One effect of this restriction on employment in the traditional university framework has been for qualified
women archaeologists to lean strongly toward research or to seek
innovative jobs in the private and public sectors in the field of cultural
resources management." Because of their availability and qualifications, women colonized this unoccupied space rather rapidly.

Exploring the diverse routes to achievement that women followed in
the inter-war years, suggests that women were not passive victims of
prejudice. Despite attempts to marginalize women from the professional mainstream, some women were not paralyzed by these barriers.
That their participation in the discipline and their contributions to
knowledge are underrepresented in our standard disciplinary histories, is a failing that reveals the profound inadequacies of our written
histories to date.

Acknowledgments

In 1985, not long after becoming seriously interested in the history of
women in archaeology, the late Cynthia Irwin-Williams graciously for-
warded an unpublished version of her 1990 article "Women in the
Field," from which I have greatly benefited. I thank Jonathan Reyman
for including an earlier version of my paper in a 1989 SAA session,
"Women in Archaeology: The Second Annual Symposium on the History of American Archaeology." The comments I received at that session, particularly those from Tom Patterson and Alison Wylie, proved
valuable. I have also profited from the support offered by Alice Kehoe
and Nathalie and Richard Woodbury. My gratitude is further extended
to Frederica de Laguna, Doris Stone, and Mildred Mott Wedel for
responding to my letters. I would also like to acknowledge gratefully all

those, particularly James Delle, who read and commented upon earlier versions of this paper. My very special thanks are reserved for Martin Wobst who nurtured my initial interest in this project and especially for Dena Dincauze, a role model whose guidance, insight, and willingness to share personal experiences were invaluable. This article was prepared while I was a recipient of a 1992–1993 Social Sciences and Humanities Research Council of Canada Doctoral Fellowship.

Chapter 3
Ladies of the Expedition: Harriet Boyd Hawes and Edith Hall in Mediterranean Archaeology

Diane L. Bolger

Mules and Petticoats

Imagine the following photograph. The year is 1900, the place Crete. The women on muleback are Miss Harriet Ann Boyd and Miss Jean Patten, both from Boston. Jean Patten is a botanist and has come to study the island's flora. Harriet Boyd has come to survey the isthmus of Ierapetra in order to find a promising site to excavate. As the mules move forward, the women's long skirts rustle and their broad hats rock rhythmically. The hundred-year-old photograph still manages to convey the essential trait of its chief subject, Harriet Boyd: confident, with unassailable determination to persevere. Silently but firmly she announces her arrival to the sleepy villages that lie ahead. The rugged Mediterranean landscape beyond her appears dull and flat by comparison.

In a memoir published years later, Harriet Hawes recounted the strategy she adopted to locate the sites of her excavations. Her Epirote foreman Aristides Pappadhias was instrumental to this goal:

When nearing a village he would ride ahead, go to the inn and order coffee for himself and any peasants who received him kindly. By the time we arrived, an altogether exaggerated opinion of our importance had spread through the village, helped largely by the Greek national costume worn by our foreman, which Cretans had seen, if at all, only in patriotic plays on actors impersonating the heroes of the 1821 revolution. Ladies attended by a man in this garb must be great indeed! Soon seal stones, fragments of pottery and bronze would be brought to us quietly and men would offer to show the fields where these had been unearthed. (Hawes 1965a:98)

With characteristic modesty, Hawes cited three factors that had contributed to her success in the field: Cretan hospitality, villagers' hopes
of increased wealth, and Crete's recent independence from Turkish
rule (Hawes 1965a:98). Indeed, had Crete still been under Ottoman
rule, the political climate of the island would have been quite different,
and it is unlikely that she or any of the other foreign excavators on the
island (such as Arthur Evans at Knossos, Hogarth at Gortyn and Psy-
chro, or Halbherr at Phaistos and Ayia Triadha) would have met with
much success. Even Schliemann had been frustrated in his efforts to
secure a permit to excavate at Knossos several years earlier, and certainly the good will and self interest of local inhabitants contributed to
a foreign team's success as much then as today. Equally important,
however, and what Hawes failed to mention in her memoir, were her
own invaluable contributions—fluency in Greek, attained in part
through volunteer work with the Red Cross during the Greco-Turkish
war of 1897; success in attaining permission from the Cretan authorities and the American School of Classical Studies in Athens to undertake excavations; and considerable organizational and scholarly capabilities which enabled her to direct a major project and see it through
to publication in a timely manner. As a young woman in an era that did
not generally encourage women, even highly educated women, to act
independently, these were remarkable achievements.

Ten years after Harriet's initial journey to Crete, another young
woman, Edith Hall, traversed the same terrain by mule and began
excavations at several sites inland from the Gulf of Mirabello. She had
worked for a season with Harriet's team at Gournia and had written a
chapter on Early Minoan pottery from that site. She was also the recent
recipient of a Ph.D. from Bryn Mawr College with a dissertation on
Minoan pottery styles.

Like Harriet, Edith preferred to travel on muleback, as it was the
most economical and pleasant mode of travel (Hall 1912b:40). Accom-
modation was easily acquired by setting up a camp bed in a spare room
of a village or at a monastery. Living conditions at the site itself,
however, left much to be desired, as she describes in a brief memoir:

> It was in a wild and rugged district where our ponies could scarcely make
> their way over boulders and along dizzy ledges, and where it was difficult to
> find a level spot big enough to pitch my tent. . . . But in spite of our hardships
> and difficulties we accomplished our end, for we found deep deposits of earth
> crammed with pottery, the very best evidence possible. (Hall 1912b:40)

Hall's excavations were published by the Museum of the University
of Pennsylvania (Hall 1912a and 1914). At the same time, she was

appointed a curator of the Museum's Greco-Roman section, a post she held until her sudden death in 1943. In this paper I look more closely at the careers of Harriet and Edith, in order to illustrate their personal achievements and to assess the degree to which they were representative of the large group of women entering the scientific establishment of American academia for the first time.

Friends and Foes: The Women's Colleges at Home and the American School in Greece

In several important respects, Harriet Boyd Hawes and Edith Hall were typical of a new class of women that emerged in the latter part of the nineteenth century as the result of economic changes and social transformations within American society after the Civil War. The most significant of these social transformations for present purposes was the feminization of secondary and higher education in the United States during the 1870s and 1880s and the creation of an academic sphere in which women could participate, obtain higher degrees, and gain employment (Bates et al. 1983; Bernard 1964; Giele 1978; Lerner 1977; Ryan 1983). Like others of their peers, both women were born in New England in the 1870s; both grew up in middle class families who valued education for daughters as well as sons; both attended private secondary schools; and both received bachelor's degrees from Smith College, Hawes in 1892 and Hall in 1899. Both women majored in classics, a discipline that afforded them teaching experience and employment opportunities during their graduate and post-graduate careers. In this regard they were better off than many of their sisters in the social sciences, who as a rule had to overcome many more obstacles to obtain doctoral degrees and for whom the opportunity for postdoctoral employment in the academic world was severely limited (Lurie 1966, Gacs et al. 1989). Anthropology, for example, was not generally taught at the women's colleges until after World War II, Barnard College being the one important exception (Rossiter 1982:24).

Accordingly, Hall received a Ph.D. from Bryn Mawr College in 1908 with the completion of her dissertation, "The Decorative Art of Crete in the Bronze Age" (1907); and Hawes a master's degree and an honorary doctorate from Smith College, the latter in 1910 following the publication of the final report on Gournia (Hawes 1908). Hawes's was the first doctoral degree granted by Smith. In addition to granting advanced degrees, the women's colleges furnished regular employment. Hall was hired as an instructor in classics at Mt. Holyoke College directly after the receipt of her Ph.D. She remained there until 1912 when she assumed a curatorial position at the University Museum in Philadelphia. She also lectured frequently at Bryn Mawr College. Hawes meanwhile worked as an instructor at Smith from 1900–1906 and was later employed for sixteen years as a lecturer at Wellesley until her retirement (1920–36).

In addition to the backing they received from the women's colleges at home, Hawes and Hall received important research support from a traditionally male-dominated institution in Greece, the American School of Classical Studies at Athens. The first record of a woman in attendance at the School was during the 1885–86 academic year (Lord 1947:268). The School's director at the time, Professor Richardson, did not bar women from attending classes, but did not allow women to participate in field trips or excavations since, in his words, "women cannot travel well in the interior of Greece nor share in the active work of excavation" (Lord 1947:94). Richardson was soon put under pressure to alter this policy, however, for as soon as School fellowships were made competitive (1896) women began arriving in greater numbers. By the 1899–1900 academic year women numbered eight of the fifteen students in residence (Lord 1947:95). Tactfully but firmly, they pressured for a more active role in research. Harriet Boyd was one of the first women to hold a School fellowship (1898–99). Her intrepid service as a nurse in Thessaly during the Greco-Turkish was of 1897 put to rest any doubts concerning women's ability to travel and live in the hinterland. Declaring that she was bored with translating Eleusinian inscriptions and "not cut out for a library student" (Allsebrook 1992:85), she requested permission to join the School's excavations in Corinth. When Richardson refused, she remained undaunted and went on to challenge the School's policy more directly by proposing that she direct excavations in Crete by herself. She consulted two central figures in Cretan archaeology for advice, William Hogarth, director of the British School at Athens, and Arthur Evans, who was just beginning his excavations at Knossos. Both men offered advice and encouragement, and their affirmative responses helped in the end to gain Richardson's consent. Thus in April 1900 was launched the first expedition in the Mediterranean directed by a woman.

Harriet's pioneering efforts and early success helped open doors for other aspiring women archaeologists at the school, among them Edith Hall. Women's active participation in excavation and research activities has been bolstered further by the establishment in 1898 of the Agnes Hoppin Memorial Fellowship, awarded to women only because in the words of the founding committee, "the activity of the School for women students was limited to a certain degree" (Lord 1947:94).

Hawes was the second Hoppin scholar (1899–1900) and used a portion of her stipend to finance her first excavation in Crete. Edith Hall was the fifth and final Hoppin Fellow (1902–03). After that time the fellowship was discontinued on the opinion of the donors that there was no longer a need for this type of affirmative action (Lord 1947: 111).

Into the Field: Kavousi, Gournia, and Other Excavations

The muleback survey by Harriet Boyd and Jean Patten in the spring of 1900 had as its end station the small village of Kavousi in the hills above the Gulf of Mirabello. That site had been recommended to Harriet by Arthur Evans, who had recently been shown a tholos tomb there by local peasants. A detailed investigation by Jean and Harriet corroborated his view that the site was an important one, and soon Harriet obtained permission to excavate at three different localities. Nearly forty workmen were engaged in this operation, and although the excavations lasted for only three weeks, all three localities yielded important remains. Most spectacular was an unlooted tomb of the Iron Age that was found to contain four skeletons, iron weapons, and more than forty vases. The finds were brought to the Heraklion Museum where they were registered, studied and photographed. Harriet then published her results in the 1901 *American Journal of Archaeology* and publicized her excavations by lecturing at the annual meetings of the Archaeological Institute of America (December 1900). The lecture attracted the attention of members of the Philadelphia-based American Exploration Society (Allsebrook 1992:99). At the suggestion of Mrs. Cornelius Stevenson, a member of the board of AES and herself a student of Mediterranean archaeology, the society immediately voted to fund Harriet for further excavations on the island.

In March 1901 Harriet set out once again, this time with a former classmate from Smith, Blanche Wheeler. Her goal was to locate and excavate a site of the Bronze Age, and find it she did. After several weeks of survey, she was taken by a peasant and local schoolmaster to the site of Gournia, where the remains of ancient walls and Bronze Age pottery protruded in abundance. As soon as a permit was secured and approval granted from Philadelphia, she began supervising a hundred workmen at what would become the most important excavation of her career. Gournia was earlier than the great sites of Knossos and Phaistos, and quite unlike them, but it was the first Minoan town site ever uncovered, and it was extremely well preserved. Hogarth described it

Figure 1. Harriet Boyd Hawes sorting sherds at Herakleion, 1902. Photo reprinted from *Born to Rebel* (Allsebrook 1992) with permission of Mary Allsebrook and Oxbow Books.

as "the most perfect example of a small 'Mycenaean' town and . . . after the two great palaces the sight (sic) best worth visiting in Crete" (Allsebrook 1992:106).

After three seasons of work (there were further campaigns in 1903 and 1904) nearly three acres had been uncovered, along with the remains of more than sixty rectangular buildings and tens of thousands of sherds and other finds. The final report (Hawes 1908) was a masterful achievement that drained heavily on Harriet's time, energy and financial resources (she had chosen to illustrate the best finds in expensive color plates). The book is still widely consulted by Aegean archaeologists and is an early example of collaborative effort in archaeological publication, with chapters by Blanche Williams (formerly Wheeler), Richard Seager, Jean Patten, and Edith Hall. The *Times Weekly Edition* of London (6 August 1909) summed up the achievement as follows:

> In these days of woman's emancipation there should be nothing surprising in the successful conduct of a scientific excavation in the Near East by a lady, and least of all by an American lady; but, as a matter of fact, Mrs. Hawes comes before us as actually the first of her sex who has both directed in person a scientific excavation in classic soil and edited in chief the scientific statement of its results. . . . It is very much to Mrs. Hawes' credit that she lighted on the site at all, and, more, that she could explore it, when found, as thoroughly and intelligently as she did. (Allsebrook 1992:134)

Two years after the publication of Gournia, and while still an instructor at Mt. Holyoke, Edith Hall returned to Crete to assist Richard Seager in the direction of several sites for the University Museum in Philadelphia. Her purpose in undertaking the project was to elucidate the origins and development of Minoan civilization:

> It seemed in fact that we might learn from an extended excavation . . . especially if we could also find the tombs, the answers to some of the vexed questions as to when and how the Minoan power fell. . . . (Hall 1912b:40)

Under Seager's supervision Hall first excavated the site of Sphoungaras near Gournia. It had been identified by Hawes and Seager in 1904, but Edith's three-week excavation uncovered over 150 larnakes and masses of Late Minoan pottery. It was the first Minoan cemetery site to be excavated on the island. Shortly after finishing at Sphoungaras, she began work at Vrokastro, again following the advice of Seager, who had visited the site with Hawes in 1903 and had recognized Iron Age pottery. This time Edith experienced luck and success to rival Harriet's, for she managed to uncover a series of unlooted Iron Age tombs. One tomb alone yielded 40 vases and several Egyptian seal stones, which could be used to date the site. In all, six tombs were excavated and after a second season of work (1912) the results were published by the University Museum as two separate monographs (Hall 1912a, 1914). By this time Edith had assumed the post of Assistant Curator at the Museum and was engaged to Joseph Dohan, a Philadelphia lawyer. For Edith as well as Harriet, marriage and motherhood meant an end to fieldwork, although not an end to their professional careers.

Domestic Architecture: Maintaining the Balance

For Hawes, the first years after Gournia were spent raising a family (her first child, Alexander, had been born while she was preparing the final report). True to form, Harriet was no typical turn-of-the-century mother. As her daughter Mary relates:

Nomads even in modern guise hardly settle down in the proverbial cottage built for two. . . . she coped with family and interests in a remarkable way, although the consequences were at times startling. But she later freely acknowledged the great advantage of those times: then many could have help in the home, some protection from all the picayune domestic demands. (Allsebrook 1992:133)

Harriet was not a feminist, feeling strongly that a woman's chief concern should be the arts of living and homemaking and doubting "whether unlimited suffrage would be good for the nation" (Allsebrook 1992:153, 228–229). In her actions, though, she failed to live up to her own ideals of motherhood and continually involved herself in a variety of political issues: heading a Smith College relief unit in France during the First World War; reporting personally to Eleanor Roosevelt after travels to Europe during the Second World War; and organizing strike action at an East Cambridge shoe factory, which led to her pursuit by gunmen and a lengthy court case. She also corresponded frequently with Jane Addams, whom she had met during a brief stint at Hull House in Chicago in 1903 (Allsebrook 1992:114). Although she continued to pursue her interest in archaeology and taught at Wellesley from 1920–36, it was her commitment to political action and her zeal for social reform that most absorbed her energies and interests during those years. Once barred from fieldwork, she consciously sought active involvement in other, more accessible spheres and could never have been happy in the role of "armchair archaeologist."

Hall, meanwhile, having taken a five year leave from the University Museum to have two children, returned in 1920 as Associate Curator with renewed interest in academic pursuits. In addition to her curatorial duties at the Museum, she often lectured at Bryn Mawr (1923–24, 1926–27, 1929–30) and in 1932 became the book review editor of the *American Journal of Archaeology*, a position she held until her death. Unlike Harriet, she had no driving interest in politics, and instead devoted much of her attention to the maintenance, display and publication of the Museum's collections (Hall 1913). In her later years she became an Etruscan specialist through the careful study and publication of the Museum's collection of Italic tomb groups (Hall 1942). This book was widely considered to be her most important scholarly achievement (Jacobsthal 1943; Hanfmann 1944) and she was planning a companion volume on Etruscan bucchero ware from the Museum collections when she died (Richter and Swindler 1943; Thompson 1971). Although a less flamboyant and colorful figure than Harriet, Edith was able to continue her research interests into her later years in a way that Harriet could not. No doubt Harriet would have found Edith's work quite tedious, and the contrast is important, for it shows that two very different personalities managed to pursue life-long careers in archaeology and through it fulfill their peculiar goals and interests. Together they demonstrate the ability of women in the early decades of this century to enter and excel in a field that previously had been occupied exclusively by men.

Ladies of the Expedition: Then and Now

How typical were Harriet and Edith? Do their biographies reflect the standard positions and career paths of women in the U.S. academic establishment during the early part of the century? There is evidence to indicate that outside the women's colleges women did not fare as well. A report in the 1918 Journal of the Association of Collegiate Alumnae (later AAUW), for example, documents the almost total lack of advancement for women at coeducational schools, where promotional opportunities lagged far behind those at the women's colleges (Rossiter 1982:161–162). A similar report written in 1929 examining the advancement of 844 faculty women at 122 graduate institutions in the AAU summed up the situation as follows:

> Women with exceptional ability and proper influence testify . . . that they were able to rise to a position equal to that of male colleagues . . . but the rank and file of respondents . . . complained, waxed bitter and voiced resentment toward the conditions of which they were victims. (Rossiter 1982:164–165)

We must be careful, then, not to generalize on the experiences of Edith and Harriet, although they too might have achieved more had they been able to continue excavations after they were married. In Harriet's view, the women of her day had been liberated from the "trammels previously imposed by men" (Allsebrook 1992:228) and she remained confident throughout her life of continued progress for future generations of women scholars. Yet despite a doctorate and extensive field experience, she herself never advanced past the level of instructor at Wellesley. In this respect she was typical of many women academics of her day.

The title of this paper, "Ladies of the Expedition," was taken tongue-in-cheek from the dedication of the all-male Swedish Cyprus Expedition to their wives and assistants during the 1920s. Yet it stands as a sober reminder that despite the significant strides made by women like Harriet Boyd Hawes and Edith Hall Dohan, traditional gender roles in fieldwork still predominated throughout the first half of the century—and continue to predominate today. Few women have risen to directorial positions indicating that conditions have not improved. It is somehow ironic that the only archaeological project currently directed by a woman in Crete is the renewed excavation of Kavousi by Geraldine Gesell. The accounts of the efforts by Hawes and Hall thus serve as testaments to the great achievements by women earlier in the century, and as barometers for the struggles that have yet to be won by women in the U.S. scientific establishment.

Chapter 4
Dorothy Hughes Popenoe: Eve in an Archaeological Garden

Rosemary A. Joyce

Young Wife, Young Archaeologist

Down in Honduras, Dorothy Popenoe, young wife of a botanist, obtained important information about the forerunners of Middle-America's early civilizations. Choosing to dig at the Beach of the Dead, in a sodden, cracking shelf of land, overhanging the swift current of the Ulua River, Mrs. Popenoe tied a rope round her waist and set to work. Twice, without warning, the treacherous shelf cracked and dissolved beneath her feet. But the safety rope held, and she survived her adventure [Figure 1].

From that exploit, the young archaeologist brought away nothing very spectacular to capture a public's fancy. The objects she salvaged are chiefly pottery of plain brown color. The pieces lay buried in the Beach of the Dead with the bones of an ancient people, whose manner of living was simpler, and, it seems, earlier than the glories of Mayan, Aztec and other Middle American civilizations. Following her first struggle with the river, Mrs. Popenoe returned again when the capricious Ulua permitted. Then, December 30, 1932, she died of a sudden illness.

"The plain colored pottery that she dug from fifteen graves . . . [is] sufficiently numerous and prevalent to represent a distinct group of people with a culture of their own," according to Dr. George Vaillant, of the American Museum of Natural History, who places the clay wares as "affiliated to other pre-Mayan culture groups in Central America, though probably not the product of the same tribe or people." (*El Palacio* 1935:124)

How can we tell the story of a woman's life? Carolyn Heilbrun (1988) has explored the dilemma that this task poses. Women's lives are always refracted through the "marriage plot," their independent action ending when they marry, or else their failure to marry viewed as the central enigma to be unraveled. Any enactment of the "quest plot," the search

Figure 1. Dorothy Popenoe examines an exposed skeleton and burial goods in her excavation 5 at Playa de los Muertos, on the Ulua River, Honduras. Courtesy Peabody Museum of Archaeology and Ethnology, Photo #N11543.

for expression and achievement, is shattered into the pieces of a puzzle, re-arranged along the chronological narrative of marriage/not-marriage.

How much more problematic does it seem, then, to tell the story of a woman's life as a scientist, an explorer and archaeologist? Such a life must be recovered by sifting the broken fragments that remain for the clues they give about the decisions made, theories adopted and abandoned, understanding arrived at and embodied, finally, in written texts. A scientist writes her life in her papers, and they give her voice. What could be more tragic than the loss of that voice, the slippage from the quest plot to the marriage plot?

My first encounter with Dorothy Hughes Popenoe was a folktale, part of the lore of Honduran archaeology, an allegory with mythic overtones. Much of what I was told was false, and its central image may be questionable. This work is my attempt to recover the myriad threads of her life.[1]

A Chorus of Voices

To tell this story, a murmuring of voices must be admitted, the nuances of their speech considered. For Dorothy Popenoe, there is only her own writing to speak. And this writing has been layered over by other, more authoritative tones: George C. Vaillant, promulgating the true significance of her work at Playa de los Muertos (the only voice in the chorus heard in *A History of American Archaeology*); A. M. Tozzer, guiding Dorothy's decisions in research, and placing his own interpretation on her life; Doris Stone, retelling her work at Playa, Cerro Palenque, and Tenampua, writing out Dorothy Popenoe's own conclusions based on her pursuit of stratigraphic control; and my own encounters with her photographs, objects, unpublished reports, and ignored interpretations of her own work.[2]

---

1. The present paper is a version derived from a computer-based hypertext document I have been developing. Hypertext, which links information in nonlinear fashion and allows for multiple ways of reading, allows an experience that cannot be translated to the page. I use the hypertextual conventions of the printed text (footnotes, indented quotes, and varied typefaces) to give some impression of the quality of hypertext, but nonetheless this is a single fixed reading. To recapture some of the nonlinear effects, readers should consider following Dorothy Popenoe's own words (italicized throughout), or the quotations form primary texts (set apart from my own commentary by typeface). Letters from other people are indented.

The source hypertext was developed using Storyspace™, a writing environment developed for the Macintosh computer published by Eastgate Software in Cambridge, Massachusetts.

2. My own engagement with Popenoe began when, as a novice in Honduras, I first was

First Voice

The first voice must surely be that of History, the chronicle of a life stitched together from contradictory sources. What stands out here is the pace of this life, the uncompromising commitment to research which makes the presence of five children an almost irreconcilable contradiction.

CHRONOLOGY

1899	Born June 19 or June 16
1914	Left school at start of World War I
1918	Began work at Kew Gardens
1923	Invited to join staff of US National Herbarium, July
	Married Wilson Popenoe, November
1924	Birth of son (Peter)
1925	Move to Tela, Honduras with Wilson, December
1926	Birth of daughter (Nancy)
1927	Exploration of Tenampua
	Exploration of Cerro Palenque
	First writing: typescript on bells in Tozzer library
1928	Initial work at Playa de los Muertos, November 5
	Publication in Spanish of report on Tenampua
1929	Renewed work at Playa de los Muertos, February
	Birth of son (Hugh)
1930	Move to Guatemala with Wilson
	Birth of daughter (Marion)
1931	First English publication, with Wilson, in *Unifruitco Magazine*
1932	Birth of daughter (Pauline)
	Return to Tela with Wilson, December
	Operation and death, December 30

---

told a slightly inaccurate version of her death, describing her as childless at the time. She preceded me at my dissertation site:

> Cerro Palenque first entered the archaeological record in Doris Stone's brief commentaries, based in part on the unpublished work of Dorothy Popenoe. Popenoe referred to her work at Cerro Palenque in 1927 in her discussion of Playa de los Muertos. Unpublished photographs by Popenoe in the Peabody Museum pinpoint the areas where she worked . . . Popenoe's photographs show massive cut stone balustrades, steps, and U-shaped drain stones, features still in place at the hilltop site today. The building associated with these features is part of a group which shows signs of major excavations, perhaps to be attributed to Popenoe. (Joyce 1991:35–36)

It was only in researching the Peabody's Honduran collections that I began to realize how much of her legacy had been lost.

1934   Publication of study of Playa de los Muertos
1936   English publication of study of Tenampua by Smithsonian
        Institution

Second Voice

The second voice must be her own, writing for scientific guidance to
A. M. Tozzer, to Harvard's Peabody Museum. Her own vision of her
task was brilliantly clear. By seeking stratified deposits—years before
the authoritative history states that this became accepted practice in
Central America—she would place the abundant material remains of
the Ulua Valley in their proper order.

Dear Dr. Tozzer,
    I have just returned from making your Ulua River Expedition to Playa de los
Muertos. As soon as the report is complete I will mail it to you and seek some
way to send you all the artifacts and skeletal material . . . .
    I am daring to hope that you will consider the work satisfactory. My
greatest desire is to win your approval and confirm the confidence you so
generously placed in me. This was the thought that overshadowed all others
throughout the trip. And now I must await your frank criticism of the report
before knowing if I have succeeded. . . .
    "Hoping, more earnestly than I can say, that you will consider your
expedition to have been worth while; with warm personal regards to your-
self and Mrs. Tozzer. (Dorothy Popenoe 1929)

Dear Dr. Tozzer,
    You may have heard by now that the Popenoes have been transferred
back to Tela. This gives me a good opportunity to resume my studies of the
Ulua Valley. I am now writing up my report on the expeditions of 1930 and
1931. It should be ready for you in a few weeks. . . .
    As always I shall be more than grateful for any advice or guidance you can
give me. I am paying particular attention to stratification and types of deposits. Are there any other points I might be able to help clarify? (Dorothy
Popenoe 1932)

Third Voice

George Vaillant, placing a value on her work:

    In 1896 George Byron Gordon . . . distinguished several types of decoration,
which he was unable to reduce to chronological sequence. The freakish

changes of course made by the Uloa River and its tributaries during the flood seasons redistributed the refuse lenses, so that Gordon found none fit for stratigraphical dissection.[3] . . .

The preceding report by Dorothy H. Popenoe . . . lays a firm basis for an orderly historical and ethnographical arrangement of Uloa Valley archaeology. It is a tragedy for all her co-workers in the Central American field that Mrs. Popenoe could not have been spared to complete a work with so promising an inception. Nonetheless her finds have great value, since they reduce to specific problems some of the outstanding general questions relating to Central American ceramics.

The outstanding results of Mrs. Popenoe's excavations are the separation of the monochrome from the polychrome wares. . . . Mrs. Popenoe's work at Playa de los Muertos should take its place among the definitive descriptions of culture groups upon which rest the foundations of Central American archaeology. (Vaillant 1934:87, 96–97)

Faint Voices

And now Dorothy Popenoe is lost. A murmur comes from her successors, each taking as guide Vaillant's work:

Gordon excavated . . . on the Ulua River, and indicated a difference in depth of deposit between the monochrome and polychrome wares. . . . Late, Dorothy Popenoe (1934) isolated at Playa de los Muertos a series of burials which were quickly recognized as a phase of the Mesoamerican Formative or Preclassic (Vaillant 1934). Further excavation at the site by Strong, Kidder, and Paul confirmed the stratigraphic position of the Playa de los Muertos phase. (Glass 1966:162)

No study of the north coast of Honduras . . . can be complete without at least a brief examination of Playa de los Muertos culture.

The earliest report . . . is that by Gordon who conducted the Peabody Museum expedition in 1896–1897. It was Mrs. Dorothy Popenoe, however, whose excavations . . . and subsequent report led to the naming of this type of ware. Dr. George Vaillant has pointed out the presence in the Playa de los Muertos culture of many of the traits prevalent in the Q culture.

Strong, Kidder and Paul have enlarged the scope of Playa de los Muertos ware. . . .

They have called attention to the relationship between the Playa de los Muertos culture and that of the early Guatemalan highlands. . . .

If we accept the excavations of Strong, Kidder, and Paul at face value, then we are forced to admit that objects of Playa de los Muertos culture are indeed the most ancient recorded from the Sula-Ulua. According to Mrs. Popenoe the only hint at stratification was the absence of jadeite in the upper stratum. . . .

---

3. In fact, Gordon's notes indicate that he dug in a primitive attempt at stratigraphy, with levels of 1–2 feet recorded. The materials he found were clearly stratified, not mixed as seems to be implied in this passage. They confirm the sequence Popenoe hoped to demonstrate, although absolute depths of similar materials vary markedly.

Mrs. Popenoe stresses the lack of uniformity encountered among the burials, and goes so far as to say "that whatever code of burial rules the people possessed, it must have been a lax one." This comment suggests that here in the Sula-Ulua were divers groups living simultaneously. . . .

With regard to the age of the Playa de los Muertos culture, the writer . . . believes the presence of this ware does not necessarily suggest that each piece is of great age . . . the writer accept[s] the possibility that people made Playa de los Muertos articles. . . until quite late during the Indian occupation.[4] (Stone 1941:56–57)

Yarumela and Los Naranjos contrast in basic ceramic inventory at this time period. This regionalization of Period IV Honduran ceramic complexes extends also to Copan and to the Playa de los Muertos culture of the Ulua Valley, although all of these sites share an emphasis on monochrome pottery and decoration by plastic techniques, including incision, zoned burnishing, applique, and modeling. Only the rare burial ceramics seem comparable across the area. . . . Playa de los Muertos lacks the elaborate incised decoration noted in early Middle Formative burials elsewhere in Honduras, and instead shares the Mesoamerica-wide adoption of the "double-line-break" motif on bowl rims. (Joyce 1991a:23–24)

Ventriloquism

Only through the lens of George Vaillant's interpretation is Dorothy Popenoe's work inscribed in *A History of American Archaeology*, entwined in the early stage of classification, establishing chronology and defining cultures. Popenoe herself transgresses the categories of this history. Like significant figures from before World War I, she had no formal affiliation with an institution and worked as a lone explorer. But her reports, published and unpublished, are concerned with more than mere chronology. Her lack of formal training in archaeology led her to develop her own structures of meaning, and these fit poorly into the main strands that authoritatively account for the development of Americanist archaeology.

According to Willey and Sabloff (1974:83), the great developments of the period to 1914 were "a steadily growing professionalization of the discipline in an academic alliance with anthropology as a whole." People like Dorothy Popenoe, access to the emerging centers of research denied them, could only work on the margins. Popenoe turned to A. M. Tozzer of the Peabody Museum for guidance and legitimation.

During the period of classification and culture history (1914–1960), Willey and Sabloff recognize several important methodological de-

4. Radiocarbon dates for Playa de los Muertos range from ca. 240 BC +/− 150 to 430 BC +/− 180 (Kennedy 1981:110–111).

velopments and common goals. The "stratigraphic revolution" resulted in the recognition of a means to place deposits in sequence. George Vaillant, Dorothy Popenoe's alter-ego, appears again and again in this account of the unified mission of archaeology:

> Outside of the Southwest, G. C. Vaillant, who had been a student assistant of Kidder's at Pecos, published his first detailed stratigraphic work on the Valley of Mexico in 1930 . . . Kidder appears to have been one of the few, or perhaps the only, American stratigrapher of the 1920s and 1930s who favored the natural as opposed to the metrical method . . . The reasons for this difference between the American stratigraphic digging methods and the more frequent use of the natural or physical soil zone unit of digging in the Old World are, like the reasons for the delay in the acceptance of the method as a whole in the Americas, uncertain and open to speculation . . . Vaillant argues that the physical complexities of the Zacatenco site, in which refuse and semi-destroyed architectural features were found over a hill slope, made physical strata digging impossible or inadvisable. . . . (1974:96–98)

> Both Vaillant and Bennett tended to look upon the pottery complex or the "pottery period" as a whole. That is, certain forms and features characterized a period, in contrast to another period. (1974:109)

> In fact, even as early as the late 1920s, G. C. Vaillant was beginning to question Spinden's chronological ordering . . . Vaillant had actually begun such a synthesis in 1927 in an unpublished Ph.D. dissertation . . . in 1941, he gave his ideas detailed expression. . . .
> Spinden's "Archaic Hypothesis" . . . had both chronological and developmental implications. . . . In other words, this "Archaic" was a kind of American Neolithic. Having its origins in the Valley of Mexico, it had spread outward to other parts of the hemisphere from this center. . . . Vaillant, among others, took issue with Spinden. (1974: 120, 124–125)[5]

Dorothy Popenoe

Dorothy Hughes Popenoe was born on June 19, 1899 and died on December 30, 1932. At the center of the life written for her is an allegory. Twisting through the allegory is another reading of her life. Carolyn Heilbrun, in *Writing a Woman's Life* (1988), suggests that each woman's life has four narratives: the one she may envision before she lives it; the one she may write as fiction; the one she may write as "autobiography"; and the one that may be written for her as "biography." This is my reading of Dorothy Popenoe's life, intent on seeing an alternative to the tragic allegory in which she has been cast.

---

5. A footnote on Vaillant's arguments against the Valley of Mexico origin of the "Archaic" cites his interpretation of Popenoe's excavations at Playa de los Muertos in Honduras, the only echo of her voice in this history.

The Marriage Plot

In July 1923, Dorothy K. Hughes, an attractive, intelligent young British woman, was hired by the Bureau of Plant Industry. Born at Ashford, Middlesex, England, in June 1899, Dorothy had studied at the University of London and worked for several years on African grasses in the herbarium at Kew. She had become a capable botanist and botanical illustrator. . . .
It was love at first sight. A few days later she called him and asked *if he had any work for her.*[6] Wilson thought to himself, "Yes, I have a lifetime of work for you." He soon proposed to Dorothy and they were married in November 1923. (Rosengarten 1991:91–92)

In 1925 Wilson Popenoe resigned from the USDA and accepted a job with the United Fruit Company in Honduras. "His wife, Dorothy, *was very much in favor of this move"* [7] (Rosengarten 1991:97).

Eve

When she first came to Honduras, Dorothy had a pink and white complexion and a youthful appearance. By 1932, however, having given birth to five children in just a few years while continuing to work on archaeology in Honduras and the reconstruction of a seventeenth-century house in Antigua, Guatemala, she seemed tired. In December of that year, a very tragic event took place in Lancetilla. Dorothy Popenoe ate an unripe, uncooked akee fruit which is said to have poisoned her. (Rosengarten 1991:108–109)

A Sermon

If this were only to be a little sermon I should choose for its text a single word. That word would be gallantry, and why this word was chosen will be evident to the reader of this short life history, for it tells of the most gallant soul I have ever known. I chose the word to indicate dynamic, not static, qualities and for want of a better. Steadfast she was, but one might be steadfast and lack the verve, the vision, and the personal valor of Dorothy Popenoe.
Dorothy Hughes Popenoe was born 19 June, 1899, at Ashford, Middlesex, England. She attended the Welsh Girls' School at Ashford until the beginning of the Great War. Then she went into "land work" until she suffered an injury in Anglesea which made necessary an operation and which forced her to remain inactive until 1918. During this year she entered the Royal Botanical Gardens at Kew as student-assistant to Dr. Otto Stapf. Here at Kew she remained five years, but studied during all her spare hours at the University of London. Dorothy had a brilliant, acquisitive mind, and she soon became an authority on several genera of African grasses and described a number of new species in the Kew Bulletin.

6. Whispers of Dorothy's voice?
7. More whispers?

In July, 1923, by invitation of Mrs. Agnes Chase of the United States National Herbarium, she came to Washington and entered the Office of Foreign Plant Introduction, of which her husband-to-be's old friend Dr. David Fairchild was the distinguished head. Here she carried on taxonomic studies of the cultivated bamboos, and so in Washington she met Dr. Wilson Popenoe, himself a distinguished botanical explorer. They were married on 17th November, 1923. . . .

It is hard for a woman to go to live in the American tropics, especially in the hot wet coastal zone of the more backward Central American states. Life in India, Ceylon, or Malaya presents a very different aspect. In the East there is in many places a considerable European society, and the amenities of life have developed naturally with the long occupation of the land by cultivated folk. To be sure there were congenial Americans at Tela who soon became warm friends, but Dorothy was much more than usually fearful of stagnation of mind and indolence of body.

In 1927, with only Jorge Benitez, her Ecuadorian assistant and friend, she travelled for days on muleback and finally reached and described and mapped the prehistoric mountain-top fortress city of Tenampua, abandoned centuries ago and a site which few explorers have ever seen. . . .

At odd moments for a long time Dorothy had been reading avidly on Maya art and archaeology, and from 1928 to 1932 she spent weeks at a time, when the waters were low, excavating a rich pre-Colombian [sic] cemetery at La Playa de los Muertos on the Ulua River. She unearthed several splendid collections of pottery and many skeletons, and prepared a scholarly report. . . . She never hesitated to camp alone at this wild and lonely spot among the most notoriously unreliable people in Central America. . . .

From time to time five children came, but these events never held up Dorothy's explorations for long. . . .

On 23rd December, 1932, she wrote me: "*We have been transferred back again to Tela and I have written Professor Tozzer that I am ready again to struggle with the problems of the Ulua Valley pottery.*". . . .

Three days after her last letter to me she died suddenly at Tela, after an emergency operation. So passed another young Valiant-for-Truth, and who can doubt but all the angels' trumpets sounded on the other side? (Thomas Barbour 1933:vii–x)

Death Retold

Dear Doctor Barbour:

Thank you for your letter of January 5th. I knew how terribly you would feel about Dorothy Popenoe's death. It is unutterably sad. On December 30th she suddenly felt very badly and telephoned the Tela hospital. The doctor came for her in a car and on examination deemed an immediate operation necessary. . . . The operation was performed at once and the surgeon was entirely satisfied with her condition. He stepped out of the hospital to telegraph as much to Dr. Popenoe, and when he returned to the hospital, Dorothy had died. . . . It now appears possible that eating overripe akees, the fruit of *Blighia sapida*, may have contributed to her sudden illness.

The last time I saw her we spent the day together at her house in Antigua, which you know. After an absence in Tela she was like a freed bird in her joy at being in the place she loved. . . . What a companion she was, with her youthful gaiety and her mature and cultivated mind. There were times when she looked like a little girl with her smallness, her pink and white complexion and her bright happy expression. Behind this she possessed the mind of a born scholar, accurate, penetrating and untiring. With her keen intellect, went a feeling for beauty and romance and a sound common sense. I have known no woman so gifted and none so modest. . . .

Dorothy was my nearest neighbor, and often when I dropped in to see her she was in bed resting before or after the birth of one of the babies. . . . Her husband often came in with an old painting or a frame for their collection, which he had just bought. If it was a portrait, every clue would be followed up to identify the subject—costumes, coat of arms, etc.—all were carefully studied. . . .

Dorothy radiated cheerfulness and strength even when far from well herself. For her strength was that of the Spirit and she was completely selfless. Her death touches all who knew her deeply. This gay and fascinating girl in her early thirties has been taken from her devoted husband and her large family of children, and her life, full of accomplishment and promise, is over. (Mary Alexander Whitehouse, in Barbour 1933:xi)

Allegory

It now appears possible that eating overripe akees, the fruit of *Blighia sapida*, may have contributed to her sudden illness.(Mary Alexander Whitehouse, in Barbour 1933:xi)

Dorothy Popenoe ate an unripe, uncooked akee fruit which is said to have poisoned her. (Rosengarten 1991:109)

The significance of akee in Dorothy Popenoe's death seems more as symbol, less as fact; unconfirmed in all sources and varying in its poisonous stage, unripe or overripe. It is one of the accepted stories for women: warned by her husband not to eat the fruit of one particular tree in his garden, yet she does: Eve in an archaeological garden.

Second Voice Returns

What is the intellectual course of Dorothy Popenoe's work and thoughts? The motives for her first trip to Tenampua are lost and only speculation can provide some idea of the forces that drove this woman to ride, accompanied only by a Spanish-speaking colleague, leaving her husband and children behind, far from their coastal garden home.

Lancetilla/Eden

The Tela Railroad Company, the Honduran guise of the United Fruit Company, established an experimental botanical station at Lancetilla in 1925 under the direction of Wilson Popenoe. The Popenoes published a study of the archaeological material encountered here (W. and D. Popenoe 1931). At times they seem to treat it as products of the contact period; at others, they apply developmental frameworks implying earlier dates. Lancetilla is presented as a unified culture, not an archaeological component in stratigraphic context, a striking contrast with Dorothy Popenoe's later work:

> The greater part of the collection from Lancetilla is made up of stonework. Pottery is generally of coarse sandy clay, poorly baked. . . . The knowledge of chipping stone was followed by another discovery, that of the effect produced by grinding and polishing the chipped articles. . . .
>
> All of the objects so far described seem more suitable for the use of men than for that of women. But the one illustrated at the bottom of Figure 3 was most likely employed by the latter. It is a bark-beater, and provides a clue as to the type of clothing worn by these people. (W. and D. Popenoe 1931:6–8)

A tension was maintained in this early work between classification, always developmental, and interpretation in human terms.

Playa de los Muertos/The Beach of the Dead

It is at this juncture that Dorothy Popenoe's contact with the Peabody Museum began. In the wide reading she had done, she encountered G. B. Gordon's work (1898). Here he set the problem of monochrome and polychrome ceramics in its place, and it was this problem Popenoe set out to solve.

> Thirty-five years ago, when the Ulua Valley was still clothed in a tangle of dense jungle, an incident occurred which served to arouse the suspicion that beneath its tropical forests and within its stratified banks there lay hidden the story of a vanished race. . . .
>
> In February 1928, while I was engaged in an investigation of some ruins on a hill near Pimienta, one of my workmen mentioned Playa de los Muertos. . . . I had long wanted to visit this site where Byron Gordon had worked, but had hitherto been uncertain as to its exact location. Upon ascertaining that my informant knew the place well, I secured him as a guide, and with two others of my men, rode across the country from Pimienta. . . .
>
> Perhaps one of the most striking problems is the riddle of the different types of pottery. At certain points in the river—for example, Playa de los Muertos, described in this report—all the pottery found in both upper and lower strata is of the simple monochrome type (Figure 2), while at Rancheria, about eight kilometers upstream on the same side, a rich dump of polychrome ware yielded fragments as beautiful as some of the finest Central

American examples. . . . It seems inconceivable that these two distinct types of ware could have been manufactured by the same people, and equally strange, that tribes differing widely in cultural traits could have been found living synchronously in such close proximity. (Popenoe 1934:61–62, 79–80)

With Tozzer's encouragement, she extended her stratigraphic studies to other sites, seeking to clarify the relationship of monochrome and polychrome pottery complexes in the valley:

In 1930 we wished to direct our attention to the problem of the Ulua Polychrome pottery. . . . The uncovering of the burial ground at Playa de los Muertos in 1929 and the finding of much entire plain pottery together with the complete absence of polychrome fragments led us to suspect that the latter might lie in a different type of deposit. . . . The horizontal or "onion-peel" method of digging disclosed in a number of cases that the pieces of a single vessel would be scattered over a large area. (Popenoe 1930)

In her earliest work at Lancetilla, Popenoe classified material remains as passive reflections of cultures. In her study of Tenampua she demonstrated an emerging concern with process. Tenampua, she argued, was a hilltop fortress, like others known archaeologically and described ethnographically. Its strategic location, water sources, and walls were her evidence, and direct historic analogy her confirmation. Her unpublished work at Cerro Palenque must have been a comparative investigation of another presumed hilltop redoubt. Rapidly thereafter, her emphasis shifted, and she sought to demonstrate stratigraphic relationships. Her final manuscript on Playa de los Muertos describes a series of burials exposed in a fresh river cut. She examined environmental data to explain the sedimentation and recutting of these sites, an early essay in site-formation processes. She left unfinished her report on the work she hoped would win her A. M. Tozzer's approval:

On going through her notes and files, I failed to find much regarding the polychrome pottery work. She had taken it up a few weeks before her death, on completing the little book on Antigua, and I know that she was about ready to write up the whole subject. But I am afraid she had put very little in writing at the time her work came to an end. (Wilson Popenoe 1933b)

Erasure

How did Dorothy Popenoe's death come to mean more than the work she wrote? I return here to Heilbrun's (1988) observations about the limited nature of stories available for women's lives. How can the quest plot be combined with the marriage plot? Not since Eve has this combination been easily accepted. Dying a young mother and wife, with most of her work unfinished, Dorothy Popenoe's life was subject to evaluation by others in control of her essential meaning.

Her Mentor's Voice

Although she had no formal affiliation with the Peabody Museum, A. M. Tozzer was the scholar to whom she turned for guidance and approval. He acted as the filter for her ideas both during her life and after her death.

To Dorothy:

It has been a long time since I have heard from you, and along with your letter comes a fine collection of polychromes. . . . As I have already told you, this polychrome with its background is most important. Your report will furnish the background and fit it into the complex where it belongs in relation to the unpainted wares which you have already sent us. (Tozzer 1932a)

To the archaeological community:

Dorothy Hughes Popenoe was born on June 16, 1899 at Ashford, Middlesex, England. As a student assistant at the Royal Botanical Gardens at Kent and at the University of London, she acquired that knowledge of botany which led to a position in 1923 at the United States National Herbarium. Here she met and married Dr. Wilson Popenoe, the distinguished botanist. In 1925 they moved to Tela, Honduras, to organize a plant introduction station and undertake agronomic research for the United Fruit Company. In 1927 after great hardships she described and mapped the fortress city of Tenampua. This report was published by the Government of Honduras. From this time onward to her death she was intensely interested in the Maya ruins. She devoured the old and the modern authorities and made many most arduous trips which yielded important results. Her special field was the Playa de los Muertos on the Ulua River. Most of her work was undertaken under her own initiative and with no outside aid. From time to time the Peabody Museum gladly gave her small grants for her expenses. The present paper, printed exactly as she left it, is the account of a series of burials of unpainted pottery on the Ulua. She was about to search for a burial yielding polychrome pottery, at the time of her death on December 30, 1932. . . . Archaeology has lost one of its most inspired students and her friends one whose life was marvellous and full of beauty. (Tozzer 1934b:86)

To Wilson:

I am looking forward to Mrs. Wilson writing up in detail this collection from the Playa de los Muertos. She has with her investigations a good background for fitting in the other material. As I wrote her, I wish some time that a grave with polychrome pottery could be found and investigated as this would place this type of ceramics into the context. (Tozzer 1932b)

Figure 2. Photograph by Dorothy Popenoe of objects from burials at Playa de los Muertos, presented against a background of modern Maya textiles. Courtesy Peabody Museum of Archaeology and Ethnology, Photo #N11516.

Tom and I are very anxious to publish a paper by her on the Ulloa Valley. I have in my hands her finished report on the excavations at Playa de los Muertos, which could be printed almost as is. If, in the near future, you could send me the material on which she was working, the reports for the seasons 1930 and 1931, I think we could get together an excellent paper. (Tozzer 1933)

With your permission, I am going to publish Dorothy's paper on the Ulua. I am writing a short note on her life and Dr. Vaillant is going to write on the place of Ulua ceramics in the Maya pottery complex. (Tozzer 1934a)

The Final Voice

I cannot tell you how much I appreciated your letter about Dorothy. Both she and I always felt extremely grateful to you and Mrs. Tozzer for the deep interest you took in her. As I think you know, you were her inspiration and her mentor, and she always looked forward to the day,—now never to arrive,—when she might do more serious work under your sympathetic guidance. (Wilson Popenoe 1933a)

Chapter 5
Blue Corn Girls: A Herstory of Three Early Women Archaeologists at Tecolote, New Mexico

Robert W. Preucel and Meredith S. Chesson

The main contention of them all [the male anthropological establishment] is that girls are all right, entertaining, etc. but no good in science because you can't do anything with them. Kroeber ends all remarks with "Boas will place her." It never seems to occur to any of them that if he can others might be able to were they sufficiently interested. (Reichard 1929)

Ours, I think, was the first [expedition conducted by women] ever officially attempted, and we three were determined that it should prove successful. And we did take it so seriously! We dug into those unpromising mounds as if we expected to find a combination of Pharoah's tomb, Solomon's temple and *Homo Heidelbergensis* in the flesh. (Watkins n.d. p. 6)

Women played pivotal roles in the development of southwestern archaeology from its very inception (see Babcock and Parezo 1988). Most visible are those archaeologists sponsored by Edgar Lee Hewett, Byron Cummings, and E. B. Renaud, who received advanced degrees in anthropology. These include Bertha Dutton, Katharine Bartlett, Marjorie Ferguson (Lambert), Florence Hawley (Ellis), Isabel Kelly, Dorothy Keur, Clara Lee Tanner, and H. Marie Wormington, several of whom obtained teaching positions and trained a new generation of students. Other prominent women working in the field include Ann Axtell Morris, Mary Russell Colton, Nora Gladwin, Madeline Kidder, and Harriet Cosgrove, who took leading roles in founding museums, collaborating on archaeological fieldwork, writing books, and fostering Native American craftspeople.

These women, however, represent only a small minority of women actively engaged in southwestern archaeology. A closer reading of the historical record reveals that women contributed on many different fronts. Women commonly served as patrons and benefactors; they served as staff assistants, curatorial assistants, and board members at major museums; they conducted state-of-the art scientific analyses as laboratory scientists; they filled university classes in anthropology and archaeology; and they participated in archaeological field schools. Yet, it is a fact that these women are not recognized by the profession; in many ways their voices are silenced and their works go unmentioned. This "invisibility" suggests that Southwestern archaeology, like other academic professions and early twentieth-century society in general (Brown 1987), embraced a patriarchal framework, marginalizing the roles of women (e.g., Kroeber's behavior toward Kelly [Knobloch 1989:12]).

Several studies have now begun to celebrate the nature of individual women's contributions within archaeology (e.g., Bishop and Lange 1991). While valuable projects in their own right, these studies often fail to consider the extent to which women were able to confront biases of sexism, and to negotiate their places in a male-dominated profession. For us, the identification of women and their work is only a first step in this process, and must be complemented by an analysis of the social context within which they worked and lived. In addressing this question, we need to ask what it was like for women to conduct fieldwork. Did society at large impose social constraints on them as women archaeologists? How did they interact with their male colleagues? In what ways did ethnicity, class, and gender affect their experiences?

Our chapter addresses some of these questions by using a feminist perspective to investigate the daily life of Isabel Kelly, Frances Watkins, and Eva Horner during their archaeological fieldwork at the site of Tecolote, near Las Vegas, New Mexico in 1929. In the process of researching this project, we have found it helpful to think how the women's roles and interactions changed within different communities. Toward this end, we outline a theoretical framework that recognizes the intense and dynamic interrelationships of gender, class, and race. We readily acknowledge that this approach represents a break with how we have traditionally thought about issues of difference in the context of an archaeological research project, and that, as such, must be critiqued and revised. We do not claim that this chapter provides a comprehensive analysis of issues of race, class and gender relations in Southwestern archaeology. Rather we present only one specific case in which these issues inform our analysis significantly.

Feminist Theory, Gender, and Archaeology

Feminist theory represents a political commitment to a specific vision of society. For us, the (re)presentation of the archaeological past illustrates the link between our personal lives and work. How we communicate the past to people, especially in terms of our inclusions and exclusions, reflects our personal and political identities, interests and agendas, intentionally or not. The subjects we choose to write and talk about, and the rhetoric that we employ, all send messages to audiences, giving clues as to what our political vision of the future entails, as well as our conceptualization of the past (Leone and Preucel 1992; Nussbaum 1990).

The label "feminist theory" does not adequately capture the enormous diversity of approaches, epistemologies, and theoretical frameworks which are currently being explored in the natural and social sciences. Three major trends, or "schools of thought," within feminist research can be identified—feminist empiricism, feminist standpoint theory, and postmodern feminist theory. A comprehensive discussion of these frameworks lies outside the scope of this chapter, and several historians of science and philosophers have already addressed them in print (Alarcon 1990; Harding 1991; Wylie 1991b). We mention them here, however, because we want to call attention to the dangers of assuming that all feminist approaches are the same.

Likewise, we caution the reader against equating feminist research solely with gender studies (cf. Gilchrist 1991). It is certainly the case that feminist research often problematizes gender as a key theoretical category, and in fact this represents one of the major contributions of feminist theory. Although feminist scholars bring to their work a particular political vision of society that informs their conceptualization of their work, they address many of the same questions upon which non-feminist researchers work.

Finally, we reject the popular critique of feminist theory that claims it does not produce "good science" because of its political associations. This critique is based upon the myth of scientific objectivity, which several philosophers of science have now shown to be a sociocultural construct. Harding (1991) has specifically addressed this issue in terms of feminist research agendas, and both Conkey (1991) and Wylie (1991b) have confronted it in archaeology.

It is vital for us to acknowledge the connections of our own past, both our herstories and histories, with the present and future work that we and our colleagues produce. As teachers and students, we must be concerned with the lacunae in the archaeological and historical record that perpetuate pernicious ideologies of oppression, of which sexism is only one. We feel that working to recover women's voices and work from the dusty, back shelves of libraries, archives, and museums is crucial to the future transformation of archaeology, constituting a potent response to the non-inclusive presentation of the past.

Feminist Theories in Archaeology

Feminist theory encompasses a rich and diverse literature that has only recently been implemented in archaeology (e.g., Conkey and Spector 1984; Claassen 1992; Gero and Conkey 1991b; Seifert 1991; Walde and Willows 1991). In a series of articles, Alison Wylie (1991b, 1992) has posed the question of why it is only now that feminist theory should be embraced by archaeology, given the over twenty years of explicitly feminist research in the arts, humanities and social sciences. In posing this question, she calls attention to archaeology as a distinct social practice with a specific ideology supporting a patriarchal structure, an ideology and structure that permeate the natural and social sciences.

An analysis of the history of archaeology cannot fail to show that it has been dominated by male practitioners and their research interests. This pattern of exclusion is, of course, closely linked to the historical status of women in academia, and archaeology appears to have been one of the more restrictive disciplines. What is less often recognized is that these androcentric interests and procedures were typically justified on the grounds that they were inherently more "natural" and "scientific" than other (non-male, non-Western) forms of knowledge acquisition. Women, by contrast, appear at the margins of the discipline, pursuing non-traditional career paths (see Bender and Parezo 1993; Levine, this volume). Their active efforts and acknowledged successes in defining alternative research interests and developing new methodologies undermine claims that archaeology is somehow an objective pursuit, divorced from its social context (Gero 1991a).

The socially constructed nature of archaeology is a theme that resonates strongly with certain elements of postprocessual archaeology. Hodder (1986), Leone (1991) and Shanks and Tilley (1987) have all presented persuasive critiques of processual archaeology that expose its unacknowledged social and political agenda intimately bound up with its origins in Western capitalism. But it is a curious and disturbing fact that very few postprocessualists have seriously engaged feminist theory, which challenges the status-quo of patriarchal "science-as-usual." Engelstad (1991), for example, has recently argued that postprocessual archaeology, despite its overt acceptance of pluralism, simply represents yet another new orthodoxy dominated by white male intellectuals.

One underdeveloped area of feminist research involves examining the complex interconnections between issues of race, class, ethnicity, sex, and sexual orientation (see Dill 1983; Sacks 1989; and Zinn et al. 1990). A small community of scholars, however, has focused on the dynamic relationship of race, class, and gender for at least a decade in history, women's studies, literature, and literary criticism (Jones 1985; Davis 1981; Smith-Rosenberg 1986). In addition, some of the most eloquent studies of these issues have appeared in novels by authors like Toni Morrison, Alice Walker, Gloria Naylor, Audre Lorde, Leslie Marmon Silko, and Maxine Hong Kingston.

In archaeology, however, scholars have only recently begun to consider these issues. For example, Wylie (1991:21) has argued for developing the "analytical tools" for examining the inter-relationships of gender, race, and class ideologies:

The struggle now is to find ways of theorizing gender which recognizes that it is fundamental (in Harding's sense, as non-reducible) but incorporates an appreciation of the ways in which it is cross-cut by, or refracted through, myriad other structuring forces (class, race, age, sexual orientation, for example).

Wylie is one of the few scholars in the field advocating this multi-dimensional vision of social identity.

The ways in which a specific culture marks social similarities and differences are historically situated and embedded in ideologies of ethnicity, class, and gender. These ideologies, by definition, provide only a partial picture of society by representing existing power relations as the only possible ones. For example, Moore (1986:168) has shown how gender relations among the Endo work in favor of men by trivializing the work of women in the relations of production. The linkage between gender distinctions and power seems to be universal, as there is no culture that we know of which does not in some way create social categories from the observable differences between males and females (Ortner and Whitehead 1981).

Zinn et al. (1990) have analyzed the current trends in feminist theory attempting to include issues of race and class in investigations of gender inequalities. They have found that, in general, researchers have utilized one, or some combination of three main approaches: (1) "The first treats class and race as secondary features in social organization with a primacy given to universal female subordination." (2) "A second approach acknowledges that inequalities of race, class, and gender generate different experiences and that women have a race-specific and class-specific relation to the sex-gender system. However, it then sets race and class inequalities aside on the grounds that, while they are important, we lack information that would allow us to incorporate them into the analysis." (3) "The third approach, often found in conjunction with the first two, focuses on descriptive aspects of the ways of life, values, customs, and problems of women in subordinate race and class categories" (Zinn et al. 1990:34).

Zinn et al. (1990) argue that each of these approaches can be seen to be limiting. The first amounts to a ranking of oppression, giving more weight and importance to gender inequalities and devaluing the concerns of women experiencing racial and class oppression. The second acknowledges the importance of race, class, and gender inequalities but refuses to include them in an analytic framework for methodological reasons, particularly difficulties in their implementation. The third approach is a purely descriptive one that seeks to merge experience with oppressed groups, but neglects to consider broader cultural or symbolic meanings and forces.

Zinn et al. (1990:34) suggest that a more cohesive approach entails an analysis of social organization, allowing the researcher to investigate the complexity of these structuring forces in shaping women's and men's lives within specific communities. We have utilized this framework in our analysis of the Tecolote field school because we believe that it is only through the recognition of these structures and their contextually-specific nature that we can begin to appreciate the challenges that Isabel Kelly, Frances Watkins, and Eva Horner faced and the pathways that they chose to pursue.

The Tecolote Project

The excavations conducted in the summer of 1929 by Isabel Kelly, Frances Watkins, and Eva Horner at Tecolote, New Mexico, stand out as one of the first archaeological field projects in which women held positions of authority. In the course of this project, they interacted with the workers and visitors at the site and in the Hispanic village of Tecolote, with the local ranchers and townspeople of Las Vegas, and with members of and visitors to Kidder's excavations at Pecos. In reviewing the materials, we have been especially concerned with the social context of the work and with how the dynamically interrelated issues of race, class, and gender affected these women's lives.

The prehistoric site of Tecolote (LA 296) is a large pueblo village located ten miles south of Las Vegas, New Mexico. One of the easternmost of all pueblo villages, the site was situated on a trade route linking the pueblo and plains regions. Apparently, the site originally extended on both sides of the Tecolote River, but the eastern half was washed away during a flood in 1872 (Kelly et al. 1929a:9). The ceramic types and tree ring dates indicate that the site was inhabited during the Coalition period (AD 1150–1325) with the most intensive occupation in the late phase (Smiley et al. 1953:29). Subsequent work at the site has been conducted. No final report, however, exists for any of this research.

The Tecolote project was part of a field school, jointly sponsored by the Laboratory of Anthropology in Santa Fe, the Department of Archaeology at Phillips Academy, and the Southwest Museum in Los Angeles (Kidder 1930). A. V. Kidder of Phillips Academy and the Peabody Museum served as the director of the field school and provided preliminary field instruction in the context of his final season at Pecos Pueblo. Charles Amsden, of the Southwest Museum, administered the project, and the newly founded Laboratory of Anthropology supplied financial support by awarding six student fellowships. The students receiving fellowships were Isabel Kelly (University of California at Berkeley), Frances Watkins (University of Denver), Eva Horner (University of Chicago), Tsu Yung Liang (Harvard University), Robert Greenlee (?), and a Mr. Bowers.

Kidder designed a rather intensive two-month field program for the fellowship recipients. From June 24 to July 17, he instructed them in field methods and interpretation at Pecos, reporting that they excavated a trench into the midden lying between the north and south buildings and exposed a number of burials (Kidder 1930:148). For the remainder of the season, he divided the students into two groups, sending the men to Tsama ruin in the Chama Valley and the women to Tecolote ruin. Both teams were given instructions to date the sites, to reconstruct daily life, to make architectural interpretations, and to perform site surveys of the respective regions (Greenlee 1933; Kelly et al. 1929a).

Historical Documentation

The relatively poor documentation of women archaeologists in the Southwest greatly complicates the task of writing a social history in which women are the focus of research (Parezo, personal communication). Fortunately the materials from Tecolote are unusually rich in this regard and consist of a field diary, notes, photographs made by the participants, miscellaneous letters, newspaper accounts in both local and hometown media, and brief progress reports by Watkins and Kidder.

Watkins has summarized her experiences at the site in two articles published in *The Masterkey*. The first of these, entitled "My Experiences as a Field Archeologist" (Watkins 1930), addresses the field and living conditions as well as the archaeological research at Tecolote. In "Archeology as a Profession for Women" (Watkins 1931), she discusses archaeology as a viable profession for women, using Tecolote as a case study. These two articles complement the field diary, as they flesh out some entries in the field journal and provide an idea of Watkins' perception of their work.

Of all these sources, however, it is the diary, written in the hand of each of the three women, that presents the most valuable information on the interactions within the various communities. The diary contains descriptions of excavation loci, field sketches, and anecdotal accounts. Unlike so many other sources of information, this document provides hints of the characters of the individual women, their attitudes toward the fieldwork, and the social context within which they lived and worked. One must recall, however, that these materials were written for Kidder as the ultimate audience, and that his eventual "ownership" of the documents undoubtedly affected the nature and extent of what the women recorded.

Three Patriarchal Communities

Through the sources mentioned above, we have started to explore how Isabel Kelly, Frances Watkins, and Eva Horner negotiated their positions within three coexisting, traditionally male-dominated communities over the single summer of 1929. We have defined these social realms as (1) the scientific community, consisting of representatives from the institutions sponsoring the field school; (2) the Hispanic community of Tecolote; and (3) the community of Las Vegas, including Anglo and Hispanic ranchers and townspeople. We focus on race, class, and gender ideologies, paying close attention to the structures of the different communities, the nature of the women's interactions within these spheres, and the frequencies of their contact.

The women's daily routine entailed an early morning breakfast and a quick drive to the site, where they met their hired Hispanic workmen from the town of Tecolote. They excavated throughout the entire day, stopping for lunch around noon. At night after supper, which was provided by their landlords, they entertained guests and worked on their portions of the site report. From Monday through Saturday this schedule prevailed, and the women spent Sunday driving into Las Vegas for supplies, surveying the surrounding area for sites, and working on their reports. Approximately once a week Kidder visited the women, checking on their progress. Members of the Tecolote and Las

Vegas communities, however, were the most frequent visitors, and it was uncommon for the women not to mention visits to the site on a daily basis in the diary and field notebook. In addition, the women occasionally drove to Pecos to dine and discuss the project with Kidder, Amsden, and H. P. Mera of the Laboratory of Anthropology.

The Scientific Community

The women's ability to participate in the scientific community was largely contoured by their status as students on Kidder's project. Apparently Kidder was initially ambivalent about taking women into the field; in a letter to Elsie Clews Parsons, he remarks that their tendency to get married was a distinct liability (Kidder 1929). His eventual acceptance of the three women reflects pressure from Parsons, who served as a financial benefactress to his project (Nancy Parezo, personal communication, 1992). Additionally, we believe it significant that he sent his male students to Tsama and his female students to Tecolote, the latter, smaller site being located within relatively easy access of Pecos, enabling regular contact with the women.

Kidder also arranged opportunities for the women to meet other archaeologists and dignitaries. At various times, he brought Charles Amsden and H. P. Mera to the site to assist in ceramic identification and mapping, and on one occasion, he invited the women to join him and his wife for dinner with Mr. and Mrs. Charles Lindbergh. We do not know if the men from Chama visited Pecos and received other archaeologists at their site.

To his credit, Kidder does appear to have treated the women as competent and independent professionals. He delegated to the women full responsibility for all daily field decisions and report writing; Kelly was to write the introduction, Watkins the ceramics, and Horner the outlying site survey. Kidder seems to have regarded their work highly, if somewhat on the slow side (Figure 1). In fact, he told Gladys Reichard that "the girls did a fine piece of work" and because their findings were mixed and extremely difficult to interpret, "anyone without a conscience would have ruined them" (Reichard 1929).

The field diary offers limited insight into the women's feelings toward Kidder and his colleagues. As might be expected, there are no recorded instances of disagreements over goals or methods, and the women simply noted his weekly visits and his advice for expanding their excavations. They appear to appreciate Kidder's frankness in acknowledging difficulties in interpretation. On one occasion, Frances Watkins writes that "he confessed himself as puzzled as we over the situation on Kiva I, even going so far as to suggest that it may not be a

Figure 1. Frances Watkins with A. V. Kidder (right) and an unidentified male (possibly Charles Amsden) at Tecolote ruin. Courtesy of the Southwest Museum, L572.

kiva at all, but a room" (Kelly et al. 1929a:93–94). The women were quite conscious of their status as students, and when asked to give a talk at the local Rotary Club they politely deferred, suggesting Kidder as the appropriate alternative.

In her 1931 article, "Archeology as a Profession for Women," Frances Watkins contrasts the work of the male and female excavation projects, explaining that

> The boys worked on a larger ruin [in the Chama Valley], and did about three times as much actual excavation, with excellent mapping, while ours was smaller, but with every bit of material and information worked out to the farthest degree. Dr. Kidder said that it was the tidiest little excavation he had ever seen—*and we are still puzzling over his exact meaning.* (Watkins 1931:176, emphasis ours)

The women's puzzlement over Kidder's condescending comment is well justified, and we feel that this statement mirrors other less than supportive statements about women as archaeologists (for example, his letter to Elsie Clews Parsons, April 8, 1929).

Within the same document, Watkins discusses the possibilities of archaeology as a career for women. She seems well aware of the tensions within the discipline, but believed that their work at Tecolote demonstrated the comparable nature of women's and men's abilities to conduct fieldwork and interpret the data.

We proved that women with a good background of laboratory and theoretical education, plus a few weeks of practical intensive field training under expert direction, could lead and manage an expedition and do reconnaissance quite as well as any young man with similar experience. Although our ruin was smaller, I think we did as good a piece of work as the three young men, members of the Laboratory, who were given the training course with us, and sent out to a different ruin at the same time. Ours will not be, I am sure, the last expedition of the sort; I hope it is the forerunner of a long series of women-directed expeditions.

The competition will be keen, for there is no sex in archeology, anymore than there is in business. There is exactly the same chance for advancement, and certainly the same opportunity for work as is given the men. We learned to wield a pick and a shovel, to carry and set up equipment, to climb in and out of the trenches, to survey with the same facility as the boys. The same holds true in the laboratory, the class-room, or the museum. If their vision is broader than ours, if they can see the bold outlines, at least we can handle the detail and see the relationships of the past to the present with more sympathy and interest. (Watkins 1931:176)

Significantly, Watkins points out that the physical labor did not overwhelm the women, and that if any differences existed between men and women, they concerned the attitudes in conceptualizing the past.

Watkins used her field experience to legitimize her status as a professional archaeologist. In her presentation "Archeology as a Profession for Women," she states that she, Kelly, and Horner conducted the project without male supervision, playing down the role of Kidder. Watkins (1931:175–176) explains that

I had the great good fortune to be one of the three feminine directors [at Tecolote], and I think that I can safely say that the experiment (for it was in the nature of an experiment) was a success. We selected our own equipment, chose our own ruin, hired our own laborers and excavated for four weeks without masculine supervision.

The context of this article, which was also presented in a series of public lectures, suggests that these discrepancies are intentional and reflect her actively negotiating her position in the field of archaeology in general, and at the Southwest Museum specifically.

The Hispanic Community of Tecolote

From the moment of their arrival at Tecolote, the women entered into a series of social relationships with the local Hispanic community. Tecolote, like most Hispanic villages in northern New Mexico, was organized according to an informal political structure dominated by the *tatas* (patriarchs) of the most prominent extended families. These extended families were bound together through the institution of *compadrazgo* (ritual parenthood) by which godparents were selected for the major life transitions of baptism, confirmation, and marriage (Figure 2). Intertwined with these networks was a quasi-religious organization called *La Cofradía de Nuestro Padre Jesús Nazareno* (also known as *Los Hermanos Penitentes*), that enforced community standards and mediated disputes. Women were not permitted membership in this organization, although they did organize chapter auxiliaries.

From our sources, it seems that the community did not impose upon the three women the same social standards that governed the lives of the community women. The villagers incorporated these women into their lives by categorizing them as outsiders or tourists.

At first we were treated with careful formality, tinged with wonder. The former wore off in time, the latter never. The first question our callers asked was "Where you papa?" then, "Where you husban'?" We explained that we were still in school, and so had no husbands, and that our fathers were at home. This proved a sensation in a community where an unmarried girl of seventeen was an old maid. (Watson n.d. p. 4)

In such a role, Kelly, Watkins, and Horner possessed freedom to interact with the family patriarchs, young families, older members of the community, and unmarried men and women.

Although they admit to a deficiency in Spanish, the women appear to have drawn on a fairly extensive kin-based network linked to the influential Romero family, which facilitated their work. Watkins relates that they boarded with a "young married couple, who entertained us at dinner with duets, accompanied on the guitar by the husband" (Watkins 1930:16) (Figure 3). For their part, the villagers seem to have been quite interested in the excavation and knowledgeable about local archaeological sites. Kelly notes that on the first day "We had a large audience at the works and discussion was very animated. There seems to be general admiration for the walls of 'los indios'" (Kelly et al. 1929a:8).

The nature of these interactions varied according to context, and on site a formal employer/employee relationship prevailed. The women hired three Tecolote men to assist in the excavations. Their names

Figure 2. The church at Tecolote Village. Courtesy of the Southwest Museum, L569.

were Ambrosio, Rafael Cedillo, and Pablo Gonzalez. On the first day, Kelly was concerned that "Our laborers were rather inclined to harangue than shovel and this may prove to be a problem" (Kelly et al. 1929a, July 18). Likewise, Watkins (1930:18) comments that "All the neighborhood came to gaze at us, and we were equivalent to a circus." Kelly's worries, however, appear to have been unfounded, as there is no further mention of problems with the workers (Figure 4).

In the village of Tecolote, the women interacted with the workers, their families, and community members in a decidedly more relaxed atmosphere. Each evening they received visits from their neighbors, and Isabel Kelly writes that "There is not much time to study at night. We have had a delegation on deck each evening. Fortunately the chair supply is adequate" (Kelly et al. 1929a:10). Considerable archaeological information was exchanged on these occasions, as locals often described nearby sites and offered to take the women to see them. Watkins (1930:17) writes that "Sunday we gave to reconnaissance, searching far and wide, afoot and horseback, for ruins—and sometimes finding them. The children loved to act as guides, and we en-

Figure 3. The women's living quarters in Tecolote village. Left to right: Charles Amsden, Pablito and Gructosa Romero and their two younger children (in doorway), Isabel Kelly, Frances Watkins (seated), Eva Horner. Photo by A. V. Kidder, August 1, 1929. Courtesy of the Southwest Museum, L568.

joyed having them." In addition, gift exchange cemented these new social ties; on one occasion, the two Romero children, Christobal and Paulito, visited Isabel Kelly at the house, giving her tin aspirin boxes containing *flechitas* (projectile points) (Kelly et al. 1929a :100). Likewise, various men and women brought artifacts that they and their children had found in the area. Kelly, Watkins, and Horner often reciprocated this generosity by calling on their neighbors.

However, despite these generally cordial relations, there existed overtones of ethnic and class tensions that distanced the women from the villagers. In her discussion of the significance of the Tecolote project, Watkins (1930: 13) states that it represented the first time in the history of Southwestern archaeology that an expedition was led and directed by women "with no men in the party." Here she is clearly ignoring the contributions of the Tecolote crew, whom she later describes as interested and willing workmen.

In one revealing encounter, the women chase after a Hispanic family that they pass on the road in order to buy a Navaho blanket literally out

Figure 4. Eva Horner and an unidentified workman excavating the 300 series mound. Courtesy of the Southwest Museum, L570.

from under them. This image recalls the pattern of privileged, Anglo collectors aggressively buying objects of daily life from Hispanic and Native peoples. Their distanced, outsider status is further reflected by the fact that they were not invited by the community to participate in its ritual life. Isabel Kelly's lack of knowledge about and participation in Santa Ana Day is recorded. On July 26, 1929 she wrote

> This is Santa Ana's Day and the girls of the village are to spend the afternoon riding horseback. Miss Horner who witnessed the performance reports it to be a very aimless proposition. (Kelly et al. 1929a:38)

The Anglo/Hispanic Community of Las Vegas

The women depended upon the town of Las Vegas for goods and services. Las Vegas was founded in 1836 by a group of colonists from the town of San Miguel del Bado in Mexico (Perrigo 1982). By the late nineteenth/early twentieth century it had grown into a mixed Hispanic/Anglo community and one of the leading commercial centers in New Mexico. During this period, town politics were strongly contoured along gender, race, and class lines. When Congress passed an act in 1910 to allow New Mexico to be admitted as a state, nine Republican delegates were elected to represent San Miguel County (Perrigo 1982: 90). Although Hispanos enjoyed greater representation on the committee with five positions, the chairperson was the local Anglo lawyer Charles Spiess. The Chamber of Commerce, formally established in 1923, served as a political vehicle for Anglo merchants to lobby the legislature to attract business and industry. Political alliances between upper class Hispanos and Anglos reflecting common economic interests were continually forged and renegotiated.

Each week the women went into town for supplies from the Gross Kelly Co. store. They routinely chatted with the clerk, who was a member of the Chamber of Commerce committee that monitored the site. Less frequently, townspeople and local ranchers visited the excavations. On one occasion, the postal clerk arrived on site seeking to arrange an exchange of artifacts, but refused to deal with anyone other than Kidder. Frequently, the women used these opportunities to negotiate trips to visit sites on the ranchers' lands.

In general, the local ranchers and townspeople appear to have been exceedingly curious about the Tecolote field school. Some suspected that the women were searching for gold.

About 9 AM we were honored by a visit from two Americans—one a sheep rancher in the vicinity, the other a state sheep inspector from Las Vegas. The latter had been at the Herrera ranch across the arroyo and said Mr. H. was convinced we were searching for gold. E. Horner convinced him otherwise and learned that Mr. Herrera had mentioned many circular pit formations on top of the mesa. (Kelly et al. 1929a:28)

Others were intrigued by the picture of women conducting archaeological research. This is best seen by the media attention surrounding the "snakebite incident." On July 25 a sheepherder suffering from a rattlesnake bite showed up at the Tecolote field camp and was rushed by the women to the hospital in Las Vegas. Charles W. G. Ward, a Las Vegas lawyer and part owner of the *Optic*, learned of this incident and paid a visit to the site. The women suspected that they were being interviewed "under the guise of friendship" and their fears proved correct when he returned two days later bearing copies of his article for each of them (Kelly et al. 1929a:99). The title of the article "Charming Young Archaeologists Rush Sheepherder to Las Vegas for Snakebite Treatment" (Ward 1929) simultaneously expresses wonder that archaeologists should be women and that they should be competent in providing emergency medical assistance.

Conclusion

Our reading of the careers of Isabel Kelly, Frances Watkins, and Eva Horner and other women reveals the presence of a status hierarchy in the profession vestiges of which still exist today. In this hierarchy, the upper echelon was restricted to college and university professors who conducted fieldwork, the middle echelon to museum curators and laboratory technicians, and the lowest to secondary school teachers and avocational archaeologists. This model may help explain some of the differences in the subsequent careers of the three women. Of them, only Isabel Kelly successfully negotiated her position at the highest level by becoming the leading expert in West Mexican archaeology until her death in 1982 (see Gonzáles Torres 1989). Frances Watkins secured a position as a curator and consultant for the Southwest Museum, while she published articles and completed her dissertation. We feel that her field experiences at Tecolote and on the Jemez plateau with Edgar Lee Hewett bolstered her opportunities to continue in the discipline. Eva Horner completed her Master's degree in Anthropology in 1931, and then, as was the case with many other women in the early years of North American archaeology, appears to have dropped out of the field.

The Tecolote case study sketches how issues of gender, class, and race affected the women's interactions within the academic community, the Hispanic village of Tecolote, and the multiethnic town of Las Vegas. In certain areas our knowledge and understanding of their interactions seems disjointed, reflecting in many ways the nature of the data base. What seems clear is that these women's status as "Other" shifted as they moved between these communities. Within the white, privileged, male-dominated scientific community, these women represented the dominated, marginalized sector. They deferred to Kidder and Amsden on all points, and leave no indication that they questioned Kidder's opinions and advice. On site, however, by virtue of their race and socioeconomic class, they moved from the dominated position to the dominator. Economically, they controlled employment, hiring and dismissing workers as they saw fit. As they entered Las Vegas, they once again returned to the dominated status. They relied on men in Las Vegas for any information about local sites and possible informants, and there are no mentions in the notes or diary of any interactions with women in town. Overwhelmingly, it seems that the men in Las Vegas were confused by these women's activities, and tended to treat them with a type of paternalistic license for eccentricity.

Women were and are a vital and influential force in the history of Southwestern archaeology. Yet only a minute percentage of women attained some respect and standing in the field; the vast majority of women remain invisible. This marginalization appears to be due to the patriarchal nature of the discipline, which resisted (and still resists) placing women in positions of authority and systematically neglected their contributions. Scholars concerned with rediscovering women's contributions in archaeology enable the creation of a more textured and colorful tapestry better reflecting the development of our field. And, perhaps more importantly, they introduce role models for women and men whose voices are and have been marginalized by the dominant scholars and departments in anthropology.

Acknowledgments

Many individuals have assisted us in researching the Tecolote field school and the careers of Isabel Kelly, Frances Watkins, and Eva Horner. We want to thank particularly Gloria Greis, Rosemary Talley, Willow Powers, Curtis Schaafsma, Laura Holt, Lucy Fowler Williams, Kim Walters, Robert Van Kemper, Bob Mishler, Margaret Vasquez-Geffroy, and Nancy Parezo for their assistance in this research. Marjorie Lambert and Robert Mishler provided information on their fieldwork at Tecolote. Rosemary Joyce, Joan Gero, Nancy Parezo, Mary Ann Levine, and Ian Kuijt commented on earlier drafts. Portions of this research were sponsored by a grant from the American Philosophical Society.

Chapter 6
Marian E. White:
Pioneer in New York Archaeology

Susan J. Bender

I have entitled this paper "Marian White: Pioneer in New York Archae-ology," and no doubt this titular assertion will raise the eyebrows of some readers. How can White be considered a pioneer when she was not, like William Beauchamp, the first to gather data about New York's past systematically? Nor was she among the first, like Ritchie and Parker, to excavate and interpret major sites yielding the broad culture historical framework of New York archaeology. In fact, several syn-theses of Northeastern prehistory have appeared without even refer-encing her work (e.g., Mason 1985; Ritchie 1985). In none of these respects does White emerge as a central, pioneering figure in New York archaeology. Let us, however, set aside such traditional perspec-tives for a moment, and consider the essential qualities of a pioneer. In this way we might determine if there are aspects of White's life work that could be considered pioneering.

A pioneer can be thought of as a person who breaks new ground or moves into areas that are at the margins or boundaries of normal activity patterns. Thus, for example, the American pioneers of west-ward settlement were the people who pushed at the boundaries of traditional settlement space and sought to establish their homesteads in areas where European derived populations did not ordinarily re-side. In this sense, our pioneer does not have to be a person who is "first" or "most prominent" in a particular area of endeavor (although these characteristics frequently accompany such pathbreaking ac-tivity), she or he must simply be a person who challenges the norm. It is through this perspective that we can identify the pioneering qualities of Marian White's career. First, White moved the boundary of profes-sional research in New York west and in doing so established a base of professional archaeological activity at the University at Buffalo where none had previously been. For many years she functioned as the only professional archaeologist in western New York (Milisauskas 1977: 192), and in this capacity became the locus for collection of an enormous, controlled data base about western New York's prehistory (Hunt 1986). Second, White's efforts to save the archaeological record from needless destruction and to work together with the Native Americans whose past she studied foreshadowed what has become a strong mandate for the profession in the nineties (Fowler 1986; Knudson 1986; Trigger 1986). Finally, White also challenged traditional gender roles throughout her career and in this sense, too, was a pioneer and a role model for those of us to follow. White was both the first woman to receive her Ph.D. from the University of Michigan by a wide margin (the next one followed some twelve years later), and she was the first woman to pursue an archaeological career within New York State. That it takes unusual dedication and spirit to meet the obstacles inevitably encountered by a pioneer on whatever path there can be no doubt. That White possessed these qualities is also certain. Let us here consider the pioneering qualities of White's career as they emerge and reconfigure in its various stages.

The Early Years (1921–1959)

Bill Fenton has remarked to me that he always understood Marian White to be part of a unique western New York tradition, the tradition that generated independent, strongly motivated, and professionally involved women. This region after all was home to Elizabeth Cady Stanton and is site of the Women's Rights National Historical Park. Certainly White (born 1921) was a western New Yorker through and through, and in her upbringing near Lockport, New York, she, in fact, developed the self-confidence and determination to pursue a professional career not normally entered by women in the 1950s. White's sister, Ethel, recalls that the family ethic included professional expectations for both her and Marian, and White's parents accordingly made sure that both their daughters received college educations. Marian received her B.A. degree from Cornell University in 1942, with a major in classics and minor in anthropology.

Apparently White also received her introduction and early training in western New York archaeology sometime during her undergraduate years. Here her mentor was Richard McCarthy, a prominent avocational archaeologist on the Niagara Frontier. Although I have not been able to pin down the exact dates of White's earliest association with McCarthy, I do know that by 1941 she was seeking professional field experience in American archaeology, as evidenced in her request for work with Mary Butler's 1942 lower Hudson Valley field crew (Butler 1939–1940). This request was not to be granted, however, because Butler's funding was eliminated due to the war effort, and professional field training for White was to be delayed.

For the next ten years, White's career in anthropology proceeded haltingly, disrupted by her military service during World War II and by the dissolution of the anthropology department at the University of Buffalo, where she was attempting to combine full-time employment at the Museum of Science with graduate study. Finally, in 1952 White began her graduate training in earnest at the University of Michigan, rapidly progressing through her MA in 1953 and on to a Ph.D. in 1956. Despite this rapid progress, it is clear that White's path toward professional certification was not all smooth sailing. Albert Spaulding recalls that when White entered Michigan there were no women in archaeology, as students, faculty, or administrators. Hence White made her way without role models. At the same time, Spaulding recalls, certain faculty actively discouraged women in archaeology. White's long time friend and associate Virginia Cummings (formerly of the Buffalo Museum of Science) acknowledges that such discouragement was simply a fact of graduate training for most women of that time. It was an experience that she, White, and many others shared during their graduate days. However, Spaulding goes on to relate that Marian White had all the qualities needed to overcome such obstacles. She arrived at Michigan with her program set. She already had a well developed interest and network in western New York archaeology, knew what she wanted to accomplish, and set about doing it with skill, determination, and exceptional maturity.

It should be noted, however, that White did not encounter only gender based discrimination during her years at Michigan. Support and encouragement were forthcoming from several sources. The University of Michigan granted her teaching (1953–54, 1955–56) and graduate research (1954–55) fellowships, and the New York State Science Service awarded her a small grant to sort and classify a set of Buffalo Historical Society artifacts. A good portion of this latter work subsequently became core to her dissertation research. Correspondence with Charles Gillette of the New York State museum spanning 1954–56, White's last years in graduate school, reveal a woman totally absorbed in dissertation work, archaeology, and career development concerns. In these respects her graduate career followed the normal trajectory of a committed and capable student.

While White's well known personal qualities of determination and commitment were clearly in evidence during the Michigan years ("single-minded" may well be the most often repeated adjective applied to White during interviews), it was also during this time that the intellectual agenda for her career was set. Under the influence of Griffin and MacNeish and the *in situ* hypothesis, White chose as her dissertation topic identification of a developmental sequence within a set of Niagara Frontier Iroquois village sites. No doubt her participation as Recorder in the 1955 SAA Seminar in Archaeology on "An Archaeological Approach to the Study of Cultural Stability" (Wauchope 1956) was also influential in the formulation of this work. In addition, White's association with Albert Spaulding while she was a graduate student contributed importantly to the intellectual framework of her work, particularly the use of statistical analyses in hypothesis testing. It is through her interactions with him that White developed, I believe, her insistence on rigorous analytical technique underlying interpretation. Spaulding describes, for example, her delight upon learning a new technique, based on a formula drawn from calculus, for calculating site area. Insistence on methodological and analytical rigor and a desire to explicate fully the cultural history and traditions of the Niagara Frontier Iroquois were the hallmarks of White's professional career. It is clear that the templates for both of these qualities were set during her Michigan years.

The years directly following Michigan, up to 1958, were again not easy ones. Employment was not immediately forthcoming, not only because of gender discrimination on the job market (cf. Bernard 1964), but also because White narrowly prescribed her job search to the western New York region. Her commitment to western New York archaeology necessitated employment in the area. In the interim between Michigan and full-time employment, White was briefly employed at the Rochester Museum of Science, and then in 1958 she gladly accepted a research associate's appointment at the University of Buffalo, a position which was jointly supported by the Buffalo Museum of Science. White wrote to Spaulding of this appointment in 1958, expressing hope that it might lead to a permanent faculty position. That her job search had been difficult is suggested by her hopes for the new job and her perception of her new colleagues:

They insist upon research, regard archaeologists as anthropologists, and are used to the idea of professional women. Without having to fight against all these things, one might have time to work for something.

In 1960 White's hope for stable employment was fulfilled, as she was appointed Assistant Professor at the university. With this appointment began the next phase of White's career, in which she became the hub of archaeological activity in western New York. In her early career years, however, she had already established the pioneering activities that would continue and reconfigure throughout the remainder of her career. As we have seen, she had met and overcome obstacles of gender bias in her pursuit of a degree and professional employment, and she initiated professional archaeological investigation in western New York. In doing the latter, she began the process of trying to record and control information contained in previously unanalyzed collections and she laid the ground work for her involvement with the Iroquois people.

The Middle Years (1960–1968)

The next stage in Marian White's career spans the period in which she moved remarkably rapidly through the academic ranks, achieving full professorship in nine years. In this period her career followed a rather standard academic pattern. White's activities were clearly centered on professional advancement and the establishment of a solid graduate program in archaeology at the University of Buffalo. However, even in following out the standard pattern, the pioneering qualities about her work remain. First, it is through her scholarly activity, including field-work, publication, and presentation of papers at local and national meetings, that she brought western New York prehistory into the professional arena. Moreover, she ensured continuation of this new tradition by training graduate students to augment and carry on her work. At the same time, we should note, White did not dismiss collaboration with avocational archaeologists but rather continued the cooperative pattern established with Richard McCarthy early in her career (Brennan 1976).

The second pioneering quality of White's middle career years seems to have emerged as a spin-off from her more traditional scholarly pursuits. I think of this quality as White's own brand of "action archaeology"; it included involvement with archaeological salvage and public education and with the Native American communities whose prehistory she sought to write. While it can be argued that salvage archaeology and public education have a long history in the United States (Fowler 1986), it is absolutely the case that White spearheaded these initiatives in western New York, if not the entire state. Finally, we must be always aware that White carried out all of this work as one of the very few women in archaeology and the only woman in New York archaeology. That she must have had to encounter systematic gender discrimination and forge new roles in these years is no more in doubt than her ability to sustain her career despite them (cf. Bender 1989; Bernard 1964; Gero 1985; Kramer and Stark 1988; Wylie 1991a). An examination of the individual elements contributing to this overall career pattern may aid our comprehension of why it is that Marian White came to be a pioneer.

The pace of fieldwork that Marian White maintained throughout her career is legendary in western New York. Dr. Margaret Nelson of SUNYAB estimates that approximately 75 percent of their present museum holdings derive from White's work, while Hunt (1986: 324) suggests that White is responsible for most of their compiled data on ca. 2500 sites. In the nine-year period under consideration here, White's curriculum vitae lists 19 different field projects, and much of this work was carried out on a shoestring budget. Tales of shared peanut butter meals and life in Spartan tent camps abound in Buffalo. One 1963 *Buffalo Evening News* article even notes that White's crew was almost evicted from a site because of "the lack of sanitary facilities." One might expect that the pace and conditions of work in White's field camps might have led to sloppy field technique, but such was most definitely not the case. Individuals who worked on her crews uniformly maintain that all of her work was held to the highest professional standards. Of his experiences with White, Donald Grayson says:

Nearly all of my fieldwork was done under her supervision; I learned field and lab methods from her, and I identify my undergraduate days with her. Although I would clearly have continued in archaeology had she not been at Buffalo, my approach to archaeology, and in particular to field and lab aspects of archaeology, would have been quite different and no doubt weaker. This was because her standards were . . . so incredibly high. (personal communication)

In short, Marian White created an exceptional database in her years at Buffalo, and this database was absolutely critical to her research agenda. White's research was classically inductivist (Grayson, personal communication), an intellectual stance set in her Michigan years. White required of herself and others full control of the data before allowing generalization. One sees this approach expressed again and again in her monographs and field reports (for example, White 1961, 1965, 1967). First she describes the data thoroughly. Then she integrates the data with comparable information, and finally moves to cautious and not infrequently insightful conclusion. It is clear that White also expected such inductivist caution of her colleagues. Bill Fenton mirrors this aspect of her collegial interactions by noting that, "Marian was good at telling you what wasn't!"

This inductivist approach does not, however, mean that White disregarded problem orientation in her research. Much of her fieldwork in these middle years was, in fact, problem driven. For example, she received funding for five seasons of fieldwork (1958–1963) from the National Science Foundation, and the award of such grants was based upon the clear articulation of a problem to be resolved by data collected in the field. Two problems which White addressed with these early grants were the reconstruction of Iroquois village movement patterns, following the model of Wray's (Wray and Schoff 1953) work in the Genesee Valley, and the impact of the introduction of agriculture on Niagara Frontier Iroquois settlement pattern. By 1968 White had "identified two village movement sequences, had evidence for two other sequences, identified some 46 archaeological sites, had completed surveys of Niagara Frontier Creeks, and had begun survey work in Cattaragus, Jefferson and Cayuga counties" (Hunt 1986: 318).

The maintenance of such a vigorous field program had of course both its rewards and debits. The rewards for White were clearly not only in the accumulation of a regionally invaluable database but also in the training ground that it provided for young archaeologists. Her correspondence reveals that one of her primary goals upon coming to Buffalo was to establish graduate research there, a goal she had accomplished by the mid-sixties. This is a remarkable accomplishment when one considers that in 1959 there was simply no archaeology at all represented in the department. White's festschrift, edited by Bill Engelbrecht and Donald Grayson (1978), provides clear testament to the many students that White influenced in the relatively few years (about 10) that she was involved with graduate education.

The debit of White's field schedule was simply the amount of professional time and energy that it absorbed. White's life was her work, and she is known to have worked long hours, seven days a week. Nonetheless, colleagues frequently remark that her publication record and thus her national reputation could not keep apace of her fieldwork program. While this may be true, it is nonetheless the case that in these middle years White placed western New York archaeology squarely in the pages of the professional literature. Her dissertation appeared in 1961 as a Museum of Anthropology, University of Michigan monograph and in 1958 in article form in *Pennsylvania Archaeologist*. This same journal was later the outlet for her settlement pattern studies. I, like many others, regret that she did not take the next step and move her very fine archaeology onto the pages of more nationally circulated outlets. But the results of her work are nonetheless in print, and they define an important segment of what is known about western New York prehistory.

Finally, these middle years were also the time in which White initiated two very important components of her later career years. The first is her work in salvage archaeology, something for which she is widely known to have had almost missionary zeal. The depth of her conviction for the necessity of this work clearly resides in her inductivist approach to knowing about the past (Grayson, personal communication). In White's view, simply put, any destruction of the data base would result in incomplete knowledge about the past. Each data point held significant information in itself and in relation to all other comparable data. The wanton destruction of the archaeological record due to construction or looting was intolerable because it would lead to a concomitant narrowing of our understanding of the past. Thus, on top of an already demanding problem-oriented field program, White accepted the challenge of salvage archaeology projects throughout the Niagara Frontier. From 1963 to 1968 she was engaged with no less than eleven salvage projects.

One of the salvage projects with which White was involved in this period was particularly noteworthy: the 1962 relocation of the Cornplanter Reserve cemetery. This project is important for understanding White primarily because it marks the beginning of the second important component of her later career, that of working together with Iroquois people on the reconstruction of their culture history. With the construction of the Kinzua Dam, the Cornplanter Reserve was to be flooded, including the cemetery area. Working together with the Seneca, White arranged to relocate the cemetery and to conduct skeletal analyses *only if* next of kin gave permission for study. With this project, White became directly involved with the people whose ancestral material remains she had studied throughout her career. She brought George Abrams, the first of her several Iroquois students, onto her field crew, and she became involved with the present concerns of the western New York Iroquois. An indication of this new involvement can be found in two articles about the Kinzua project that appeared in local newspapers. In one article, White gives a rather straightforward account of what can be learned from the archaeology of the project. In the second, however, she takes a more action and people oriented stance. In it, White airs her concerns that the Seneca reservation was to be flooded and no redress or aid was being offered to its native inhabitants by the State, quite apart from the archaeology that she was conducting. From this time on one notes that White consistently clipped and saved in her personal files local newspaper articles dealing with the concerns of Native American communities.

These newly emergent components in White's career may again be considered pioneering. They diverge from what was common practice for academic archaeologists in the mid-1960s (Trigger 1986; Knudson 1986: 395), and they foreshadow what archaeologists are just now telling themselves they should have been doing all along: working with native populations whose remains they study (cf. Trigger 1965) and working with public education and salvage programs to "Save the Past for the Future" (Taos Working Conference Report 1990). This work, in addition to establishing a professional program of research, data collection and publication for western New York archaeology, was clearly a pioneering effort by White in her middle years.

The Final Years (1969–1975)

It is disheartening to deal with White's final career years, since it entails having to accept the foreshortening of a career with so much promise. Nonetheless, even in these abbreviated final years White made contributions to the structure of New York archaeology that are with us today. It is my reading of White's career that the later years mark a time of reconfiguration of the elements seen earlier in her career. Her scholarly work certainly continued apace, but in these years the balance seems to have tipped and she became the model for action archaeology in New York State.

White's scholarly accomplishments in this period reflect much the same pattern seen in earlier years. Her field schedule included problem-oriented excavation on about ten different sites during this seven-year period. Once again, a portion of the work was funded by a National Science Foundation grant, this time to investigate the disruption of Iroquois village settlement pattern by warfare. With this problem White was exploring the link between historically documented cultural patterns and their extension into prehistory. Throughout this period White's intellectual focus was moving increasingly toward connecting the archaeological record with ethnohistoric accounts (e.g., White and Tooker 1968; White 1971), and her 1971 article on the ethnic identification of Iroquois groups is seen as a classic piece of Iroquoian scholarship (Fenton 1978). Moreover, White's correspondence with Fenton and Tooker from 1967 to 1975 reveals a growing interest in working together with ethnographers and linguists to create a complete historical understanding of the Iroquois. It is precisely the lack of this type of scholarship throughout the 1960s and 1970s that Bruce Trigger identifies as at the root of many of the conflicts between present day archaeologists and Native American communities (Trigger 1986: 206). How, asks Trigger, could we expect Native Americans to be interested and supportive of our work when what we sought to generate were generalizations about all cultures and when we perceived the archaeological remains of their ancestors as only laboratories for testing our hypotheses? American archaeologists' refusal during the 1960s and 1970s to see their database as the patrimony and culture history of extant Native communities has driven a solid wedge between what should be our mutual concerns. In this regard, we can once again consider White's work pioneering in that she was doing in the early 1970s precisely that kind of work called for by Trigger in the mid-1980s.

This later work of White's seems to reflect the intellectual pose of the Native American aspect of her action archaeology. White maintained good relations with the Indian communities of western New York, and taught her students to do so as well. During the summer of 1973, for example, White conducted excavations on the Cattaragus reservation and in a *Buffalo Courier Express* article about the work expressed her delight at having four Native American students on the crew. A friend and associate of White's, Shirley Stout, recalls that one of the recurrent themes of their conversations was White's interest in bringing together Native Americans with their past. Under White's direction a model of interaction, rather than isolation, between the archaeological and Native American communities was established in western New York.

As already noted, the second aspect of White's action archaeology included salvage excavation and public education. These concerns also dominated her activity in the last years, and are clearly articulated in her 1972 working paper on "The Crisis in Western New York Archaeology." Here she observes that the public and the professional archaeologist have a mutual interest in preserving archaeological records of past human activities. If a crisis has been precipitated due to the rapid and needless destruction of these resources, "then we have failed and the responsibility rests on both the archaeologist and the public" (White 1972:1). White, however, did her utmost to meet what she saw as her professional responsibility.

First, she established in 1969 the highway salvage program at the University at Buffalo which is still in operation today. This unit has been and continues to be an important institutional structure for the oversight and protection of archaeological resources in western New York. Second, she worked tirelessly on the organization of the New York Archaeological Council and served as its first president from 1972 to 1974. This organization's purpose was to function as an action group and watch dog to preserve standards and help maintain quality control over the blossoming contract activity within the State (White 1974). Third, White threw herself personally into the fray whenever the challenge arose. Perhaps the best example of this involvement can be found in the famous incident of the demonstrations she mounted against her own institution to protect an archaeological site which would have been destroyed by the construction of the new Amherst campus. Finally, White sought to educate the public and gave endlessly of her time to local civic groups. Her biographical clippings file at the

SUNY Buffalo archives reveals innumerable appearances at Zonta, women's clubs, local historical societies, and in educational enrichment programs in public schools—all in an attempt to enlighten the public about archaeology and the prehistory of western New York. One might add that these are precisely the kinds of activities that archaeologists are being asked to engage in now by our national professional organization (Taos Working Conference Report 1990).

Thus we see that in her final years Marian White shouldered yet another set of challenges and again forged new paths in New York State archaeology. Although her scholarly contributions continued in this period, much of her energy was devoted to an action archaeology which has left a strong imprint on the way that archaeology is conducted within the State today. In White's *American Antiquity* obituary, Milisauskas observed that the untimely death of Marian White "was an especially great loss to the archaeology of New York State." While this is certainly true, White left us with a pioneer's legacy including a model for action-oriented, community based archaeology in the broadest and best sense and a record of research that is, as Bill Engelbrecht would say, "the last word in Niagara Frontier archaeology."

Acknowledgments

A number of people have contributed importantly to the research represented in this paper. First and foremost, I would like to thank archivists Shonnie Finnegan and Chris Densmore for leading me through the White papers at SUNY Buffalo's University Archives. Members of Buffalo's Anthropology Department are also not to be overlooked, as their enthusiasm about this project gave me the sense that I was embarking on a truly worthwhile undertaking. Particularly helpful in dealing with the White material at the department's M. E. White Museum were Drs. Margaret Nelson and Lee Hunt. A number of individuals were also very generous with their time and reminiscences. Particular thanks go to Virginia Cummings, William Engelbrecht, William Fenton, Albert Spaulding, Shirley Stout, Elizabeth Tooker, and Ethel White. Donald Grayson has also provided insightful comment on an earlier paper and provided important information on his professional association with White. Any errors of interpretation of these rich data are, of course, my own.

This article first appeared in *The Bulletin*, New York State Archaeological Association, No. 104, pp. 14–20. It is reprinted with permission of the New York State Archaeological Association and editor Charles F. Hayes III.

Chapter 7
Early Women in Southeastern Archaeology: A Preliminary Report on Ongoing Research

Nancy Marie White, Rochelle A. Marrinan, and Hester A. Davis

Serious concern about gender in anthropology and allied social sciences is over twenty years old. There has, however, been a glaring lack of information and interest in the discipline of archaeology. It is possible that some aspects of the current awareness of gender issues are parallel to, or contained within, the concern for multicultural education. It is also possible that the growing number of women in professional archaeology has made this perspective impossible to neglect any longer. For whatever reasons, and here we have considered only a few (but see Wylie 1992; Brumfiel 1992), lately there has been an increased interest in extracting information about gender from the archaeological record and in assessing the role of gender in the history of archaeology. It has been a long wait.

It seems strange that topics such as gender dynamics and recognition of androcentrism in interpretation are not commonplace in the archaeological literature (Gero and Conkey 1991a) given their emphasis in other social sciences. Richard Lee's (1968) work among the !Kung San revealed that the cultural ideal of one hunting society was supported by the real contributions of women's gathering, but such studies have surprisingly not affected archaeological interpretation of sites ranging in time from "Early Man" to the last prehistoric manifestations in the Southeast. In fact, the new volume from the American Anthropological Association entitled *Lords of the Southeast*, edited by Barker and Pauketat (1992), whose subject matter is social inequality, does not even address inequality based on gender.

Some may not question the lumping of two such disparate issues as gender in the archaeological record and women in archaeology, the subject of this paper, because it is all part of the "woman thing." Others may wonder why the two should be discussed together at all. In the Southeast, and elsewhere we believe, the two are inseparable. One's gender, as well as everything else that goes into the enculturation process, is important in doing one's science, whether in field methods, the choice of issues to investigate and sites to excavate, or interpretation of results. Most aspects of being a professional are affected by gender, in ways currently demanding re-examination.

We seek to collect and examine information about the opportunities, contributions, activities, and experiences of women in the field of archaeology in the early years in the Southeastern United States. We want to develop and preserve the history of these early participants and, by doing so, to examine their contributions.

The immediate impetus for this research came from conversations with Hester Davis about some of her early career experiences, and the suggestion that someone should collect that kind of information from the pioneering women themselves. Another impetus for our undertaking was the session on engendering archaeology (organized by Kathleen Bolen and Ruth Trocolli) at the 1991 Southeastern Archaeological Conference (SEAC) meeting. Pat Galloway's paper "Where Have All the Menstrual Huts Gone?" demonstrated the squeamishness of the male establishment in recognizing what was doubtless a common feature of many prehistoric and historic settlements. Keynote speaker Jesse Jennings ended his talk with the observation (non-value-laden) that the single biggest change in archaeology today was the influx of women into the field, and predicted that one day an all-woman crew would be digging somewhere. Such a reality has already been experienced by many of us working in the Southeast, repeatedly, over many years.

Thus began our quest to collect biographical information about the few women who participated in the earliest days of Southeastern archaeology. To date, we have conducted interviews by mail and in person with five archaeologists, and several more are promised. In this paper, we present some preliminary information on many women's careers in Southeastern archaeology. Complementary information on other women can be found in papers by Sullivan and Wurtzburg (both this volume).

The increased interest in gender issues sparked at the 1991 SEAC meetings flavored many discussions there and evoked fascinating anecdotes from people who remembered the archaeology of half a century ago and the few women participants. Before the founding of the

Southeastern Archaeological Conference, a listing of fieldwork conducted in North America was compiled annually by Carl Guthe. Published in *American Anthropologist* from 1928 to 1934, this list provided brief overviews of work written by principal investigators, agency administrators, or institutional representatives. Now it provides us with glimpses of early women fieldworkers.

Earliest Women Fieldworkers in the Southeast

Margaret E. Ashley

Margaret E. Ashley, graduate of Columbia University, may have been the earliest professional woman in Southeastern archaeology. In 1928, Ashley (of Atlanta) reported "an archaeological survey of Georgia begun in July, 1927" (Guthe 1928:504). She listed four counties that had been surveyed and noted, "through public interest, approximately 500 sites (mounds, villages, etc.) have been reported." In 1929, she reported that "a thorough archaeological survey was conducted during the latter part of the year in southwestern Georgia under the direction of Miss Margaret E. Ashley" (Guthe 1929:344). Her field assistant for several projects was Frank Schnell, Sr.

In 1930 Ashley published a brief note relating a Japanese method of rubbing that would allow adequate representation of complicated stamped ceramics. In 1930 Warren K. Moorehead wrote, "Miss Ashley is studying the pottery of the Etowah culture for Phillips Academy, and some time next year a full report embodying both the explorations and her studies will be published" (Guthe 1930:343). In the acknowledgments section of his report on the Etowah site, Moorehead (1932:v) notes, "Miss Margaret E. Ashley joined the survey during its last season, instituted a study of the pottery, and also assisted in fieldwork. Miss Ashley was given workmen to assist in preliminary studies of several mounds and village sites some distance from the central village. We are greatly indebted to her." Her study of Etowah ceramics was published as a part of Moorehead's final report in 1932 (Ashley 1932: 107–136).

Ashley eventually moved from the Southeast to Cambridge, Massachusetts, and redefined herself as a paleoethnobotanist. She had a long affiliation with the Harvard herbarium.

Women Archaeologists in the WPA

We have not yet identified a woman in a supervisory field position in Southeastern archaeology during the WPA-funded excavations of the late 1930s. In fact, the environment for women was often neither encouraging nor hospitable. The correspondence files curated at the Southeast Archeological Center of the National Park Service, in Tallahassee, have provided some documentation regarding this period. In a letter to A. M. Tozzer of the Peabody Museum, Harvard, A. R. Kelly wrote in April of 1936:

> I believe it would facilitate the handling of student instruction in field work to have only men students in the fellowship group this summer at Macon. These young people will be assigned at various times at sites near Macon but remote from each other. It will be impossible for me to be with them the greater part of the time. They will be working with various technicians, archaeological engineers, cataloguers, trowel men on burials and refuse pits, and in the field laboratory. In the evenings I plan to go over details of field technique with the students at my home.
>
> One young woman student is coming to Macon for a few weeks to make studies in satisfaction of requirements for course study in field methods at the University of New Mexico. Her arrangements were made through official channels before I had any information that I might have the archaeological group this summer. Her presence does not affect my general statement concerning the inadvisability of sending women students to Macon. Her home is in Atlanta and she comes on her own responsibility.

We have located pictures of a Miss King photographed at the plane table at Macon. As the dates are reasonable, this may be the University of New Mexico student, but we lack corroborating information.

On the value of women's contributions, passages from a letter from A. R. Kelly to Donald Scott, director of the Peabody Museum, dated January 4, 1938, remind us of the financial inequities in pay and the underlying attitudes about how much a woman should be paid relative to a man:

> Recognizing that any funds which might be available for expediting the Swift Creek studies would probably be limited in amount, I would recommend that the services of my wife be secured for this work as she is much more familiar with the problems concerned than is the person responsible for the tabulations already prepared. Also since she is on the ground and happens to be the wife of the Director and Archaeologist, her services could be secured at a smaller salary than would be the case with a competent graduate research worker who has experience in the handling of statistical work.

The employment of large numbers of African-American women in WPA-funded projects at Irene and Swift Creek is well known (e.g., Claassen 1993). Apparently WPA rules had to be modified to permit these women to do excavation work. Photographs indicate that they wore dresses while digging. Raymond Thompson has told Hester Davis he heard that when New Deal project women were refused jobs with Major Webb in Kentucky because women were not allowed to push wheelbarrows, they asked if they could "tote" the soil instead, which was within the rules. Kelly and Smith (1975:1–2) wrote of the workers at Swift Creek:

Exploration of the Swift Creek site began in March of 1936 and continued into the winter of 1937 when final notes and recordation were made. The project was set up by WPA authorities to employ thirty to forty Negro women as an archaeological field crew under white supervisors trained by A. R. Kelly and J. A. Ford. The project was regarded as an experiment although a similar organization of Negro women workers with white supervisors had performed very well at the Irene site in Savannah, Georgia. [The Swift Creek project was actually the first of the projects to use Black women, predating the Irene site work—ed.] At Macon too, the results were satisfactory; the archaeological excavations were no more exacting physically, than was the farm labor to which most of the workers were accustomed. The trenches and profiles were neat and precise.

We do not get the impression that women archaeologists had much authority in matters that affected archaeology during the WPA era. However, women administrators within the WPA wielded considerable power. In January of 1934, Dr. C. C. Harrold of Macon, then president of the Society for Georgia Archaeology, wrote to A. R. Kelly about the problems of getting WPA funds renewed for work at Macon.

I am afraid that all of us are too sure that our project will be rewritten, and I am not at all sure that it will. The complete revision of the state committee with the concentration of power in the hands of one woman may effect (sic) our chances. Miss Shepperson, the present dictator, is an old friend of mine in charity works, but we have seen nothing of each other in many years. I therefore do not know just how well we may count on her.

A 1937 letterhead of the Works Progress Administration's Atlanta office revealed that Miss Gay Shepperson was still the chief administrator of that office (Ocmulgee Reading File 1937). The crucial role of these women administrators for archaeology projects in the Southeast has also been documented by Claassen (1993) and by Ware (1981).

Other sources of information about women's participation in archaeological research in the Southeast are the publications of the Southeastern Archaeological Conference. An admittedly cursory search was made through newsletters, proceedings, and bulletins of the conference published from 1953 to 1968. During that time, the most consistent women attendees were Madeline Kneberg Lewis, Bettye Broyles, Martha Rolingson, and Adelaide Bullen. Women's numbers were generally low, and the number of papers presented by women was also expectedly low.

Postwar Women Participants in SEAC

We turn now to a consideration of some of the women who were early participants in the Southeastern Archaeological Conference. Our information, except where specifically cited, comes from personal, written, and telephone interviews with the women discussed here.

Madeline Kneberg Lewis

Madeline Kneberg Lewis is famous for her contributions to the archaeology of Tennessee. She was born in Moline, Illinois, and celebrated her 90th birthday in January 1993. Her parents were interior decorators who had immigrated from Sweden as children. As a young woman, Madeline had studied voice. When she was twenty-one the opportunity came to study in Florence, Italy; with five other girls, she set off. The dusty conditions of Florence caused throat and sinus problems and prompted her return to the United States five years later.

Because of her admiration for a friend who was a public health nurse, Madeline decided to study nursing at Columbia Presbyterian Hospital in Chicago. She intended, she said, to use nursing to support her family and as a springboard into medicine. Needing a college degree for medical school admission, she enrolled at the University of Chicago and majored in sociology with a minor in psychology. She continued singing and earned $5 per Sunday as a member of the university choir.

Courses in anthropology led to a fascination with the field. Department head Fay-Cooper Cole was interested in her experiences in Italy and her nursing background, and urged her to go into physical anthropology. In 1932, in the middle of the Depression, he secured her $50 a month from a National Research Council grant to study human hair. This research led to her first professional publications (Kneberg 1935, 1936a, 1936b).

At Chicago she met and worked with some of the great names in anthropology: Franz Weidenreich, A. R. Radcliffe Brown, Fred Eggan, Katherine Dunham, and Robert Redfield. She accepted a temporary position at Beloit College while Paul Nesbitt was on leave. While at Beloit she directed her only field project, the excavation of a conical mound in the Shireland group in the spring of 1937 (Brook and Clark 1937). The crew of seventeen undergraduate students included at least four women and also Hale G. Smith and Andrew Whiteford, who would later become professional archaeologists working in the Southeast.

Her desire to go into medicine was abandoned in the face of her lack of financial resources. She received her M.A. and had passed her preliminary examinations for the doctorate in anthropology at Chicago when a laboratory position in Tennessee was offered. At the age of 35, after three careers, Madeline moved to Knoxville in 1938 to head the WPA-supported laboratory and the cataloging of the ever-increasing TVA collections.

After two years of WPA support, she became an employee of the University of Tennessee and expanded her duties to include teaching. Coming not too long after the Scopes trial, she was told by the president of the university to teach what she thought she should teach. Chicago archaeologist Fay-Cooper Cole assured her that he would testify for her, just as he had for Scopes, if she were arrested.

Madeline supervised the activities of some 30 lab workers. She worked with Thomas M. N. Lewis to produce many landmark publications in Tennessee archaeology (Lewis and Kneberg 1941, 1946, 1958a; Lewis and Lewis 1961). The work drew critical praise from theorists, including John Bennett (1943:211) and Walter Taylor (1948: 7). She says that her favorite major report was *Hiwassee Island*, their first major production, in which the technique of horizontal stripping was employed, a fairly radical departure for the time. Their popular work, *Tribes That Slumber* (1958a), is in its ninth printing.

In 1961, after 23 years of working together, Tom and Madeline decided to marry and retire together. She was 58 years old, and a little tired too, she says, having cared for her mother and sister until their deaths. Tom Lewis died in 1973. Today Madeline lives in Winter Haven, Florida. She raised orchids for a while, gave up bowling a few years ago, and has recently bought an exercise bike and an electric scooter. She reads *Science News* every week.

Madeline Kneberg Lewis says she has seldom felt discrimination or problems associated with being a woman. Her father encouraged her but died young; her mother supported her career choices. She speaks well of colleagues from Chicago and Tennessee. When asked if she felt strange at SEAC meetings, she recalled only memories of headaches from smoke-filled rooms. Andrew Whiteford (1992), now a retired senior anthropologist in the Southwest, who worked in Tennessee during the WPA days, says that Madeline Kneberg did not face any discrimination because she ran the place!

Yulee Lazarus

Yulee Lazarus is a scientist and museum director whose name is synonymous with archaeology in the Florida panhandle town of Fort Walton Beach. She received the A.B. in history from the Florida State

College for Women (now Florida State University) in 1936. She is now in active retirement at age 79. She says that working in the yard of her new house propelled her into archaeology. She and her husband William inquired about the potsherds they found there and made contact with Charles H. Fairbanks and Hale G. Smith at Florida State. With no formal academic training in archaeology, she and Bill worked and studied with Fairbanks and Smith, built up local interest, published professional papers about their findings, and developed the idea for a public museum. Bill Lazarus died in 1965.

In 1967 the city of Fort Walton Beach opened the Temple Mound Museum, next to a Mississippi Period platform mound, hiring Yulee to administer it and continue to conduct research from that base. Among her notable publications are monographs on the Buck Mound (1979) and on Fort Walton Period (Mississippi) pottery (Lazarus and Hawkins 1976), an article in *Florida Anthropologist* (Lazarus 1970) on salvage work in the town, and historic works for local and museum audiences. When the Florida Anthropological Society instituted an award for accomplishments in archaeology by a non-professional and excellence in working with the interested public, they named it after Bill Lazarus and awarded it first to Yulee.

Friendly competition and surprise at an amateur's expertise usually characterized the attitude of male professionals toward Yulee Lazarus, she thinks. She does admit to an occasional negative reaction from a less educated male, and certainly sees some difference in the kinds of contributions women can make. She thinks women can better provide the early training and philosophy of appreciation for archaeology that children need.

Hester Davis

Hester Davis of the Arkansas Archeological Survey has led the country in public archaeology. Dena Dincauze (1992:136) describes her as an archaeologist who has taken "the initiative to speak out on ethical and public issues and assume responsibility for the new administrative and educational tasks in archaeology, achieving considerable power, influence, and renown." Davis has combined scientific research and public archaeology in a fascinating career that is still going strong.

She is a direct descendant of Lucretia Mott, the famous Quaker abolitionist. One grandfather was a Harvard geology professor and her parents were from "old New England families." Her father was a "natural sciences" graduate of Harvard. The family ran a Massachusetts apple farm during the summer and went to Florida in the winter. Her father taught natural history at Rollins College in Winter Park.

There he also directed a natural history museum and organized the founding of the unique Beal-Maltbie Shell Museum, which Hester's mother directed after his death in 1943 until her retirement in the 1960s. Hester is the youngest of five children, all with professional careers (in art, theatre, archaeology, and natural resource conservation).

Hester received the B.A. in history from Rollins College in 1952 and had picked cultural anthropology as a career in graduate school, influenced by Homer Barnett at the University of Oregon, who was just back from using anthropology to help set up the Trust Territories in the Pacific. Given the intellectual orientation of her family, she knew that she would have a life in academia. After two years of graduate work in anthropology at the University of Oregon, she attended Haverford College and received an M.A. there in 1955 in Social and Technical Assistance; she intended to do "relief work" overseas in a cross-cultural situation, but that opportunity did not come. She then completed an M.A. in anthropology at the University of North Carolina, Chapel Hill, conducting her thesis research among the Cherokee (Davis 1957).

In 1950 she went as an undergraduate to New Mexico with the Peabody Museum's Upper Gila Expedition, directed by Charles R. McGimsey III, and returned the next summer to labor in field and lab. In 1952 she was the first woman to work for the River Basin Surveys in North Dakota, as general laborer, photographer, and cook. She joined her brother Mott Davis's field school in Nebraska in the mid-1950s, and in 1956 cooked for the University of Iowa's field school. Her graduate work has all been in cultural anthropology, as was a job at the Iowa School of Medicine doing applied medical anthropology. She says "during a time of 'participant observation' while living and working on a farm in southeast Iowa for a year, . . . I decided I didn't want to work with live people and that I should cash in on my archaeological contacts. I wrote everyone I knew, and McGimsey had a job at the museum" in Fayetteville, Arkansas (Davis 1992). She began there in 1959.

In Arkansas, Hester began with surveys and salvage projects and taught courses in museum methods. She and McGimsey organized the Arkansas Archaeological Society in 1960, and she became the first State Archaeologist in 1967 with the founding of the Arkansas Archeological Survey. Her talents in administration and organization led her to more of such duties, and she became Assistant Director of the University of Arkansas Museum. She was a founding member of the Society of Professional Archaeologists, American Society for Conservation Archaeology, and National Association of State Archaeologists. She has held office in, performed services for, and received awards from dozens of professional institutions and agencies of national and international importance. Her many publications include articles on research in Arkansas and elsewhere, on archaeological professionalism and administration, and on public archaeology.

Asked about her career development, Hester says that, during her undergraduate field experience in New Mexico in the early 1950s, Peabody Museum Director J. O. Brew advised her not to go into archaeology unless she had a special skill such as her sister had, doing art and graphics for archaeologists. Watson Smith, also from the Peabody, suggested she go to Oregon because Luther Cressman was known to take females on his crews. She enjoyed the informal relationships with men in the field and has been able to pursue all her goals in an egalitarian setting in Arkansas. She is also the owner of the famous electric shovel, made for her by one of her non-archaeologist brothers and known to all undergraduates who read Rathje and Schiffer's (1982) introductory archaeology text.

Martha Rolingson

Another major figure in Arkansas archaeology is Martha Rolingson, who continues extensive research at Toltec Mounds Archeological State Park. Martha was born in Wichita and moved to Denver during grade school. Both her parents studied history at the University of Kansas, but her father switched to journalism after his M.A. and worked for various newspapers in Kansas, Oklahoma, and Denver. Her older brother is a chemist.

Martha became fascinated with history and archaeology in high school and declared an anthropology major during her first year at the University of Denver. She went to the 1956 field school directed by Robert Lister at the University of Colorado. She received the B.A. in 1957 from the University of Denver. The following summer, she was an interviewer for a federal Great Plains Health Study and got good experience asking questions of strangers, she says. While teaching public school in Minneapolis for a year, she learned that she did not want to be a teacher and decided to get an M.A. in anthropology. She got a museum position at the University of Kentucky, began graduate work, and welcomed the chance to get a perspective on the East. She never returned to the Southwest.

At Kentucky, Martha worked with Douglas Schwartz in museum exhibits, education, and lab work. She recalls the summer of 1959, processing materials from the field, alone in the lab, while the men were excavating the Tinsley Hill site. Her thesis (Rolingson 1960, 1964) was a study of Paleoindian points, for which she drove all over the state by herself visiting collectors. She was awarded the M.A. without any excavation experience beyond that in Colorado. By 1960, she was a Museum Curator. She wrote an NSF grant with Schwartz to document Paleoindian materials in WPA collections and excavate one site (Rolingson and Schwartz 1966). She did two River Basin Salvage Projects in 1963 by herself, contacting landowners and conducting surface surveying.

Martha then went to the University of Michigan, working with James B. Griffin and James Fitting as teaching and field assistant. She received the Ph.D. in 1967 with a dissertation on Kentucky Archaic shell mound sites (Rolingson 1967). Her dissertation continues to be the best source available for information on the Shell Mound Archaic of Kentucky. Schwartz had asked her to fill in at Kentucky while he took a leave of absence. Thus she taught classes, ran the museum, and directed River Basin Salvage projects.

Rolingson says it was evident that she would not be hired as permanent museum director when Schwartz resigned, so she took a job with the Arkansas Archeological Survey in 1968. She has moved around in the Arkansas system, taught courses and done administrative work, but has always preferred research. She is now the equivalent of a tenured full professor with the Survey. She says the last 24 years have never been dull. She has directed research at Toltec Mounds State Park since 1979.

The young Martha was sometimes told not to go into archaeology, but at other times she was encouraged, and found role models in women such as marine biologist Eugenie Clark. She realized that women were uncommon in archaeology and that most of those women were married to archaeologists. She notes that women in her age group in the profession are few, and says in retrospect that she has "the sense of being caught at the front of a wave. When I started graduate work in 1958 there were few women in archaeology, but by the time I finished in 1968, they were all over the place" (Rolingson 1992:4).

Bettye Broyles

Bettye Broyles, early SEAC participant and major name in the archaeology of the Eastern United States, did fieldwork in West Virginia, Georgia, Mississippi, and elsewhere. She is retired and working hard running a historical society in east Tennessee. Like Indiana Jones, she hates snakes and tells a good story about bashing one that crept out of a bag of potsherds.

Broyles is soon to be interviewed but has already mentioned to us her feelings about being a woman among so many men in the field: "I went my own merry way and ignored them," she said in a 1992 telephone interview. She said that fieldwork was her reason for going into archaeology and she loved working outdoors. Her initial field training was at Angel Mounds, where Glen Black's rule for women was no shorts or halter tops (after someone's halter top came unfastened). Thorne Deuel, director of the Illinois State Museum, told her it was all right for women to be on crews, but not to direct them. In Georgia, A. R. Kelly gave her a whole reservoir to study. One area of her expertise was plane table mapping. At Kolomoki, this skill made mounds visible even when they could not be seen on the ground. Joseph Caldwell (1958), in *Trend and Tradition*, credits Broyles with the illustrations and substantive advice for the manuscript.

Broyles is best known for her excavation of the St. Albans site in West Virginia in the 1960s. At that time she was head of the archaeology section of the Geological and Economic Survey of the state of West Virginia. Her careful excavation resulted in 41 stratigraphic levels that provided the first chronological ordering of dozens of projectile point types.

Other Women Participants

Marion Dunlevy Heimlich, from Nebraska, did pioneering work in Alabama in the 1940s and 1950s (e.g., 1952). She moved to New York where she became a researcher for *Time Magazine*. Before moving to Pennsylvania, Catherine McCann conducted research in the lower South, most notably at the Irene site near Savannah, Georgia, where she did the paleoenvironmental studies and co-authored the final report (Caldwell and McCann 1941). Christine Adcock Wimberly received an A.B. in anthropology from the University of Alabama and spent the WPA era supervising lab work in Birmingham. In later years she was the copy editor for David DeJarnette, was very active in the Alabama Archaeological Society, and wrote *Exploring Prehistoric Alabama Through Archaeology*, which was adopted by some school boards, as well as a book on poisonous snakes.

There are many other women who were in Southeastern archaeology in the decades up to the mid-1960s. Carol Irwin Mason (1992), herself a professional trained at Florida State University and the University of Michigan in the 1950s, mentions how the women in archaeology in those days were much more numerous than some historians of the discipline seem to realize, and were accepted as participants in the field, but often only memorialized in local or regional journals, and now forgotten.

Most of them were not major theoreticians, areal synthesizers, or even famous archaeologists, but neither are most archaeologists any of these things either. What matters is that they were doing prehistoric research, often local, often basic archaeological dog work whose value will endure as part of the cultural historical record. (Mason 1992:97)

Mason (1992:94) recalls, among others, the late Adelaide K. Bullen. She was trained as a physical anthropologist and was a major contributor to archaeology; as she put it, "grinding out site reports for local archaeological journals is not glamorous prehistoric research but the nuts and bolts of the discipline." Bullen was respected as a full colleague by other Florida archaeologists, who did her "the courtesy of disagreeing with her and arguing with her as if she were a real scholar and not merely a woman" (Mason 1992:94).

Reflections

As with much anthropological information, there is great comparability from case to case and yet each case is singular. These women say they faced little discrimination and enjoyed working in a field with men. They all came from intellectually interesting and challenging backgrounds. For each of them, their archaeological work was of extreme importance in life. They also all have, at some point in their careers, often worked in health, education, or other human services.

In writing biographies of 25 pioneering women field naturalists, Bonta (1991:xiii) found that most of them had enlightened and independent parents, all liked men but nearly half never married, and most were childless. Many were associated with or married to supportive males in similar fields. All seemed to feel little or no rivalry but only appreciation for the more powerful males in their fields because they believed the work was all that mattered. These characteristics are remarkably similar to the general profile of the pioneering women Southeastern archaeologists we have so far, although our sample is much smaller.

Certainly the way women are traditionally socialized in our society makes them well suited to field and lab management and the organizational administration so necessary to archaeology (White and Essenpreis 1989, Kelley 1992:88). Other studies (e.g., Gero 1991a) have pointed to the female tendency to excel in tasks perceived as tedious, such as lab analysis of zooarchaeological or ethnobotanical remains, or lithic debitage, and yet our sample shows a wide range of career experiences. Several women excelled at fieldwork despite socialization that might make them fearful of natural and social dangers. All the women seem to have recognized very early the importance of public archaeology and continued to contribute to it in major ways.

It is possible that the early women in the Southeast had few problems because there were just so few of them, and that discriminatory practices came later, perhaps after World War II or in the 1960s and 1970s when so many more women were entering the field. Perhaps we recognize more subtle discrimination today. A mentor who provides equal intellectual opportunity for all graduate students can still end up saying something like, "O.K. Jim, you unpack the field equipment and Nancy, you set up the field kitchen."

So perhaps our work in researching these women is late in coming, but we feel it is important to continue. Role models of all kinds are never out of fashion, of course, nor are female role models in archaeology just for young women embarking on such careers.

As Brumfiel (1992:554) reminds us, "The unstated attitude is, I think, that it really doesn't matter who did what in prehistory as long as the necessary subsistence functions were performed." Given the parallels that women must see in this devaluation of their daily lives and the lives and contributions of their distant and immediate predecessors, it is no wonder that the archaeological literature does not reflect a well-rounded view of past human behavior or of work in the history of archaeology.

Acknowledgments

The authors would like to thank each of the women who agreed to be interviewed. We also thank Lynne Sullivan, Mary Ann Levine, Susan J. Wurtzburg, and Cheryl Claassen, who sent copies of their work and other data, and Ed Lyon, for manuscript excerpts and copies of WPA-era letters. In Tallahassee, the curatorial staff of the Southeast Archeological Center, National Park Service, under the direction of Alan Bohnert, has been very helpful in locating photographs and official correspondence. We are indebted to Ray Williams, who read early drafts and made substantive comments. Jack Walker, National Park Service (retired), provided many fruitful suggestions on information sources.

Chapter 8
Madeline Kneberg Lewis: An Original Southeastern Archaeologist

Lynne P. Sullivan

White et al. and Wurtzburg (both this volume) chronicle the life experiences of several women involved in the archaeology of the Southeast
before the mid-1960s. This essay complements that research by taking
a closer look at the professional accomplishments of one of those
women—Madeline Kneberg Lewis. Mrs. Lewis was one of very few
women working in southeastern archaeology before World War II who
was employed at a supervisory level, and in an academic department,
and one of the even fewer who continued a career in the field after the
war.

The advice Mrs. Lewis now offers younger archaeologists, "try to find
something original" (Lewis 1992), must have guided her own career as
well. Along with her colleague and spouse, Thomas M. N. Lewis,
Madeline encouraged and implemented many innovative approaches
in southeastern archaeology. Her contributions to archaeological research, especially in the Tennessee Valley, continue to influence current
scholarship and her efforts to make archaeology accessible to the public
provide a model that can inform the discipline's present efforts to renew
endeavors in this direction. Mrs. Lewis's work became familiar to me
through my use of materials from a major project in which she was
involved. This project was the New Deal era archaeological research
done in conjunction with construction of a Tennessee Valley Authority
reservoir in the Chickamauga Basin of southeastern Tennessee (Sullivan 1994).

The WPA Years

A job with the Works Progress Administration (WPA) in the Tennessee
Valley initially brought Kneberg to the Southeast from the University

Figure 1. The WPA laboratory at the University of Tennessee. Thomas M. N. Lewis is in the center of the photo and William Webb is in the background. Photo courtesy of the Frank H. McClung Museum.

of Chicago. Thomas M. N. Lewis, the head of the Tennessee WPA program, offered Kneberg the job of running the archaeology lab at the University of Tennessee (Figure 1). At the time, she was working on her doctorate in anthropology at the University of Chicago and was caring for her mother and sister. Lewis hired Kneberg on the recommendation of William Krogman and Fay-Cooper Cole, even though her principal training had been in physical anthropology. Since any job was hard to get during the Depression, Madeline was glad to have the opportunity to do something in anthropology. She bought a car for $700 and moved to Knoxville with her mother and sister (Lewis 1992).

Madeline arrived at the WPA lab in Knoxville in 1938, two years after the fieldwork had begun. Several other University of Chicago alumni were already employed by Lewis to supervise the field crews, including Jesse Jennings, Stuart Neitzel, Charles Fairbanks, Charles Nash, John Alden, and Paul Maynard. Madeline's position as laboratory director involved supervision of about 40 workers and included general oversight of the materials preparation, restoration, and cataloging, as well as analysis. She also served as the project physical anthropologist. Two other University of Chicago students, J. Joe Bauxar and Andrew Whiteford, were employed as the project ethnohistorian and artifact analyst respectively. Another woman, Alice Hendrick, a University of Michigan graduate, was employed as pottery classifier. Other lab staff consisted of WPA laborers.

Under Madeline's direction, the Knoxville lab developed an innovative attribute-based system for artifact classification (see Lewis and Kneberg 1994), a technique for pottery vessel reconstruction, and numerous card files for analytical purposes and collections management. For the Chickamauga Basin project alone, this lab classified over 360,000 pottery sherds and some 100,000 stone, bone, shell, and copper artifacts. They also reconstructed several hundred pottery vessels, and examined all the nearly 2000 skeletons recovered for age, sex, and pathologies.

When asked about Madeline's contributions to the project, several people who worked on the Chickamauga project with her, or who were active in southeastern archaeology at the time, describe her as the dynamic force in the lab and the source of inspiration for much of the analytical work. It was also during the WPA projects that Madeline developed a close working and personal relationship with Tom Lewis, one that was to continue for the duration of their careers, and led to their eventual marriage (Figure 2).

Two years after Madeline's arrival in Tennessee, the University took over her salary and she had the added duty of teaching anthropology (Lewis 1992). The WPA allowed her to hire an administrative assistant to help with the federally required paperwork for the program. Before the work in the Chickamauga Basin was completed, the University of Tennessee began work on three other TVA reservoirs: Watts Bar, Douglas, and Kentucky Lakes. Chapman (1988) estimates that in the six years between 1936 and 1942, University of Tennessee crews excavated 1,577,920 square feet at 62 sites.

The comprehensive approach to site reporting taken by Kneberg and Lewis required long periods of report preparation, a factor that led to a difference of opinion with William Webb. Webb was the director of the Kentucky archaeology program and was instrumental in getting Lewis the Tennessee position. Tom and Madeline were convinced that the final reports should be analytical and thorough in data reporting, but also understood the reasons for Webb's complaints. To comply with contractual obligations, they submitted a large draft report of work in the Chickamauga Basin to the WPA in June of 1941 (Sullivan 1994). They also circulated among professionals a mimeographed copy of the first chapter (Lewis and Kneberg 1941) as a preliminary report which summarized the findings. But, with the entry of the United States into World War II in December of 1941, funding

Figure 2. Madeline Kneberg and Thomas M. N. Lewis at Frank H. McClung Museum before their retirement. Photo courtesy of the Frank H. McClung Museum.

for the WPA projects became unstable. By June of 1942 the program had ended. Tom and Madeline found themselves with huge quantities of unpublished material and increased responsibilities due to the wartime shortage of labor and funds. Since Madeline had trained as a Red Cross nurse before going into anthropology, she was expected to serve during the war, but was allowed to teach home nursing to fulfill the obligation so she could care for her invalid mother. She also taught history to an Air Corps group stationed in Knoxville, and Tom served as the liaison between the corps and the university. They were willing to do whatever was necessary for keeping their jobs during the war, as the university had little money. Archaeology in the southeast essentially ground to a halt during the war (Lewis 1992).

After World War II

From their postwar activities, it is evident that Tom and Madeline realized that, if archaeological research in the state was to continue, a broad-based constituency needed to be developed. They began to advocate a variety of educational programs aimed at the general public. They initiated the *Tennessee Archaeologist* and formed the Tennessee Archaeological Society to promote archaeology in the state and to teach amateurs proper recording techniques. Their co-authored popular book, *Tribes That Slumber* (Lewis and Kneberg 1958a), reflects this concern with public understanding of archaeology. Madeline did most of the writing for this book, and did the illustrations at home at night (Lewis, personal communication 1993).

Tom and Madeline also became the primary proponents for a museum in which to care for and interpret the materials collected by the huge Tennessee WPA projects. This latter goal came to fruition in 1960 with the opening of the Frank H. McClung Museum at the University of Tennessee. In addition, they became consultants for the Eastern band of Cherokees in developing the Oconaluftee interpretive center (Lewis and Kneberg 1954a), and in reconstituting the Cherokee craft of pottery making.

After the war, Madeline began to publish a variety of archaeological reports, books, and articles, some of which were collaborations with Tom. Her first solo archaeological publication, "The Persistent Potsherd," appeared in a 1945 issue of the *Tennessee Archaeologist*, and was aimed at educating the public as to what could be learned about the past from pottery (Kneberg 1945). Her first major collaborative publication with Tom was the report of excavations at one of the Chickamauga Basin sites, *Hiwassee Island* (Lewis and Kneberg 1946). The following year, they jointly authored a monograph on the archaic horizon in western Tennessee, based on the Kentucky Lake work (Lewis and Kneberg 1947).

During the 1950s, Madeline produced a number of publications, including her chapter (Kneberg 1952) on the Tennessee area in Griffin's *Archaeology of Eastern United States*, and several articles in the *Tennessee Archaeologist*, possibly the best known of which is her paper on engraved shell gorgets (Kneberg 1959). Two other major articles dealt with classification problems of projectile points and chipped tone tools (Kneberg 1956, 1957). She and Tom jointly authored several site reports in the *Tennessee Archaeologist* (Lewis and Kneberg 1956, 1957, 1958b), and co-edited a volume of selected papers from the first ten years of this publication (Lewis and Kneberg 1954b). Madeline also served as co-editor of the journal (Tom was the editor) and they began a section entitled "Editors' Notes" in which they reported on various amateur collections, unusual artifacts, and the like.

They remained busy and active in the discipline until their retirement. In 1959, they published a synthetic article in *American Antiquity* on the Archaic in the Middle South (Lewis and Kneberg 1959). In

1961, they married and retired to Florida, and the University of Tennessee Press published their report on one of the WPA excavations in the Kentucky reservoir, the Eva Site (Lewis and Lewis 1961). This was their final publication.

The Research

Many aspects of the research resulting from Madeline's work and her collaboration with Tom Lewis continue to influence archaeological research in the Tennessee Valley. The work was pioneering both in developing the first comprehensive descriptions of archaeological complexes in the region and in attempting to go beyond mere artifact classifications. Unlike much of the work that was being done at the time, Lewis and Kneberg attempted to link artifacts with human behavior. It was this approach that led Walter Taylor (1983:9), to describe the Hiwassee Island report as "possibly the best archaeological report I have had the pleasure of reading."

The work in the Chickamauga Basin reflects the influence of the project's largely University of Chicago-trained staff, who were versed in the "Midwestern Taxonomic Method" for classifying archaeological cultures. The project developed elaborate trait lists for newly defined archaeological complexes. These trait constellations continue to provide the basis for differentiating many of the later prehistoric cultural complexes in the Upper Tennessee Valley. This work also laid the foundations for a plethora of later comparative studies of community plans, mortuary practices, and demography by others. Kneberg's (1959) later study of engraved shell gorgets and their associations derived largely from the Chickamauga work and represents one of the first regional studies of art styles associated with the Southeastern Ceremonial Complex, or Southern Cult as it was then known. Muller's (1966, 1986) subsequent studies of shell gorget styles and of Mississippian symbols in Mud Glyph Cave and the Smiths' (1989) study of shell mask gorgets, build on Madeline's work.

Tom and Madeline's research on the Archaic in western Tennessee also laid groundwork for defining this regional sequence and provided a comprehensive description for the Middle Archaic in the Lower Tennessee Valley (Kneberg 1954; Lewis and Kneberg 1947, 1959; Lewis and Lewis 1961). Their comparative work in this region helped tie models of environmental change to the archaeology and to establish the Eastern Archaic as culturally complex, with rich and varied traditions and material culture.

As can be expected, many of Lewis and Kneberg's conclusions have not stood the test of time, but even some of their mistakes have proved fertile ground for continued research. Their problem in recognizing the Archaic in eastern Tennessee became the subject of major investigations in the Little Tennessee River Valley by Jeff Chapman in the 1970s, which discovered buried Archaic horizons (1984). The puzzle of the absence of burials from Early Mississippian, Hiwassee Island sites led Schroedl (1973, 1978) to question Lewis and Kneberg's attribution of conical burial mounds solely to the Late Woodland, Hamilton complex. He demonstrated, through radiocarbon dating, a longer use span for the mounds that coincided with Hiwassee Island components. Other components of Lewis and Kneberg's work, such as migration theories, ethnic identifications, and dating problems, now are passé or proven invalid, but were common themes and problems of archaeological research at the time (Willey and Sabloff 1974).

The Collaboration: Her Ingredients

As Madeline herself remarked about her collaboration with Tom Lewis, "it's hard to say where a part ends and the other begins" (Lewis 1992). She credits Tom with being more academic, more grammatical, and more knowledgeable about the fieldwork, as well as being the photographer. She states that she "was more for the popular" (Lewis 1992). Based on her own work, I would suggest that Madeline enriched the collaboration with several significant abilities. She was the humanist, the organizer, and the artist. I suspect she also was the more pragmatic and tenacious. Given her background in medicine and the arts, it follows that she would have developed such qualities, and pursuing a career in anthropology while dealing with her familial responsibilities certainly required many of these characteristics.

Not an insignificant contribution to southeastern archaeology at the time is that Madeline brought a humanistic perspective to her work. She states that she "wasn't conscious of any feminine approach" (Lewis 1992). Her desire to make archaeology more people-oriented undoubtedly added the impetus to the collaborative work that sought to take it beyond a classificatory and descriptive procedure. Madeline humanized prehistory by drawing on her own understanding of human nature and by visualizing what everyday life must have been like. Her own writing incorporates an empathy for the ordinary person. For example, in a section of her article in Griffin's (1952) volume she ponders the reasons for the adoption of agriculture, and observes that "the hunter does not take enthusiastically to the hoe, nor does the hunter's wife joyfully add the extra burden of agricultural work to her already staggering responsibilities" (Kneberg 1952:191).

Madeline clearly wanted other people to be able to envision ancient peoples and cultures as she was able to do. This desire to bring the past to life is reflected in the artwork she did for *Hiwassee Island* (1946) and *Tribes That Slumber* (1958a). To attempt this kind of presentation for archaeology at the time she did took some courage because such "popularization" was not considered to be proper archaeology. As Willey and Sabloff (1974:140) note, "excursions into popularization . . . away from recognized and approved procedures were considered 'unsound' and the archaeologist who went too far in this direction was suspect."

The success Madeline and Tom achieved in integrating the academic with the popular is noted in an contemporary endorsement of their work in an issue of the *Pennsylvania Archaeologist*. This acknowledgment appeared in an editorial entitled "Let's put Some Meat on the Bones":

> Individuals who wish to examine a study which combines to an admirable degree the human approach with the sternly academic are advised to examine *Hiwassee Island* by Lewis and Kneberg. . . . Here we see a successful effort to present the various groups inhabiting a site not only as components or foci but also as flesh and blood human beings who "lived, felt dawn, saw sunset glow." In particular, Madeline Kneberg's drawings of various aspects of aboriginal life derived from the archaeological evidence recovered are to be instanced. Most remarkable are her reconstructions of physiognomy based on skeletal remains. In this process she has virtually achieved the suggestion contained in the title of this editorial. (Leslie 1949:2)

The Final Analysis

Many of the contributions Madeline Kneberg Lewis made to southeastern archaeology were rather bold for their time. Her innovations derived from her desire to interpret the past in terms of people and cultures, not just in terms of artifacts. It is this creativity that has allowed her work, including the collaboration with Tom Lewis, to endure and continue to influence archaeological thought in the Tennessee Valley.

Mrs. Lewis's work also can be viewed from her feminine perspective, and as coming from a woman of her time. Today few female archaeologists would be content in the "helpmate" roles she played (such as always being second author on collaborative publications, being a "co-" journal editor, or even being a lab director). Madeline did not rebel against these limitations (nor does she perceive them as such); these merely were the roles that were available to her. But, she was neither timid nor unassertive, as illustrated by a cartoon (Figure 3) based on a presentation Madeline made at the 1959 Southeastern Archaeological Conference (Kneberg 1962). She used all the means available to her to

How many times do I have to show you?

Figure 3. Cartoon originally published in the *Proceedings of the Sixteenth Southeastern Archaeological Conference* (Williams 1962). Reprinted with permission of the Southeastern Archaeological Conference.

influence archaeological thought, either by expressing her ideas directly, by influencing work behind the scenes, or through artistic portrayal. Perhaps some of the most significant lessons to be learned from her career are that the character traits a female archaeologist must possess include a combination of ingenuity and perseverance in the face of limited options, and even more importantly, that feminine perspectives have been and continue to be critical ingredients for ensuring that archaeological interpretations are truly representative of humanity.

Additional Bibliography of Madeline D. Kneberg Lewis

compiled by Lynne P. Sullivan

1935   "Improved Technique for Hair Examination." *American Journal of Physical Anthropology* 20:51–67.

1936a   "Hair Weight as a Racial Criterion." American Journal of Physical Anthropology 21:279–286.

1936b   "Scientific Apparatus and Laboratory Methods. Differential Staining of Thick Sections of Tissues." *Science* 83(2):561–562.

1961   "Four Southeastern Limestone-Tempered Pottery Complexes." *Southeastern Archaeological Conference Newsletter* 7:3–15.

Lewis, Thomas M. N. and Madeline D. Kneberg

1955   "The A.L. LeCroy Collection." *Tennessee Archaeologist* 11(2):75–82.

1955   *The First Tennesseans: An Interpretation of Tennessee Prehistory*. Department of Anthropology, University of Tennessee, Knoxville.

Chapter 9
Down in the Field in Louisiana: An Historical Perspective on the Role of Women in Louisiana Archaeology
Susan J. Wurtzburg

Is there anybody around you could recommend [for a field assistant]? Boas has not mentioned anyone yet. Ladies not wanted.
(Letter 335, dated November 24, 1921, from Sapir to Kroeber; in Golla 1984:387)

I realize that we live in a time when discrimination can land you in jail, but I must risk it and say that you stand a better chance by taking on an inexperienced male volunteer than a female. Digging is, after all, a masculine occupation. . . . One lady volunteer improperly dressed for the occasion can cause havoc throughout the crew as well as damaging the ground on which she walks. High heels and low decolletage are a lethal combination.
(Hume 1987:60)

Introduction

This paper examines the contributions of women to Louisiana archaeology. Some might ask, "Why is a paper on female archaeological work important?" Others, less sympathetic, might query "Why not a topic of historical importance instead of this feminist stuff?" (see Reyman 1992b:72 for his reaction to these comments). The main reasons for examining the careers of women and their contributions to archaeology are: (a) generally the careers of women scholars "follow quite different career tracks than [sic] men; consequently, the history of women in American archaeology is *not* comparable to that of men"

(Reyman 1992b:72); and (b) in many cases, regardless of their value, contributions by women were treated less seriously than those of their male colleagues, and thus, women do not figure significantly in histories of archaeology or their observations in prehistories and histories of regions. We can obtain a more accurate picture of our discipline's past and recover lost data on prehistory through an examination of archaeological contributions by women.

Similar historical studies concerning female archaeological work in other states make it abundantly clear that women did participate in early archaeology, but generally their activities remained unnoticed until recently (papers in Christenson 1989; papers in Gero et al. 1983; papers in Reyman 1992a; papers in Walde and Willows 1991). A case in point is that of southwestern archaeology; it has been demonstrated that women contributed through fieldwork, laboratory work, and publications to understanding of the archaeological remains. For social reasons, however, these contributions were unrecognized for many years (Babcock and Parezo 1988; Bishop and Lange 1991).

In the case of Louisiana, early women archaeologists are not evident in the published sources. For example, the only Louisiana archaeological work written by a woman prior to the 1950s cited in Neuman's *An Introduction to Louisiana Archaeology* (1984:335) is Caroline Dormon's (1934) "Caddo Pottery" article. However, informally archaeologists and geographers mention several Louisiana women who were active in archaeology in addition to Dormon; namely, Margaret Elam Drew, Jo Nichols Evans, Frances Crouser French, Paula Patecek Johnson, Rita Moore Krouse, and Lanier Allingham Simmons (Jon L. Gibson, Hiram F. Gregory, Fred B. Kniffen, and Robert W. Neuman, personal communications, 1991–1992). Unfortunately, not all these women published their work, and thus the degree to which they influenced archaeology within the state is difficult to determine.

Since there is almost no paper trail, the basic question that confronted me at the beginning of this research was how to measure the intensity and nature of female archaeological activity in early- to mid-twentieth-century Louisiana. In addition, if I should find that women did contribute to Louisiana archaeology, I would need to determine why their activities had been ignored. When I first conceived of this research, I assumed that numerous women probably would have been active in the early years of archaeological investigations. This assumption was based on knowledge of the history of archaeology in the Southwest (Babcock and Parezo 1988; Cordell 1991; Preucel and Chesson, this volume; Reyman 1992b) and other areas of the United States (Bender 1991; Levine, Sullivan, White et al., this volume; Mason 1992; B. Williams 1981). However, it now appears that academically-trained women were not involved in Louisiana fieldwork to the same extent as were women in the Southwest. This is not to say that women did not contribute to Louisiana archaeology, but the critical difference is that those women who were active participated as interested amateurs and generally did not obtain advanced graduate training or hold archaeological positions. Thus, as my research developed, it changed in scope, and I began to consider why the women involved in Louisiana archaeology did not have advanced graduate training, and what the implications of this early history were for the development of Louisiana archaeology.

With the goal of understanding the history of women's participation in Louisiana archaeology I divide this work into several sections. The social and educational history of Louisiana women provides the necessary background for interpreting the roles of women in Louisiana archaeology. I then turn to the bibliographic information concerning women who were active in archaeology prior to the mid-1960s. Finally, I deal with the traits held in common by these women, the factors underlying these patterns, and their effects on events in the 1990s. A survey of Louisana archaeologists is presented and provides the data base for discussing recent events.

I now turn to the social and educational history of Louisiana women. I begin this history with events of the nineteenth century since Louisiana archaeology can be considered to originate in 1805 when William Dunbar recorded a Louisiana prehistoric site (Neuman 1984a:6).

Social and Educational History of Louisiana Women

Historically, Louisiana women did not possess many legal rights according to either federal or state laws. In addition to their legal invisibility, American women were generally less educated than their male contemporaries at both the secondary and post-secondary levels. A period of religious revival that lasted from the 1790s to the 1850s promoted the "ideal of the Christian wife, mother, and teacher" (Solomon 1985:16). In the North, this ideal resulted in women going to college to become teachers; in the South, however, the impetus was for women to increase their activities within the church. Even in those cases where women did obtain a college education, their educations generally were more limited than those of the men (Solomon 1985:2) and were often obtained outside the state of Louisiana.

The whole educational system, including primary and secondary schooling, was slow to develop in Louisiana. The educational problems are demonstrated statistically by the fact that "Louisiana was the only state in the United States in which white illiteracy increased between

1880 and 1890, and the only one in which black illiteracy remained above 70 percent in 1890" (Taylor 1984:120).

In all the states, unfortunately, women themselves upheld nineteenth-century values concerning the place of women, and, even when educated, they perpetuated their devaluation. For example, in 1880, Marion Talbot's Boston University graduating address stated that "At the side of man she stands, ready to do not a man's work in a manly way, but a woman's in a womanly way" (Solomon 1985:116).

In Louisiana, two late-nineteenth-century literary events indicated women's changing roles. The earlier of these was initiated by Mrs. E. J. Nicolson, who became the owner and publisher of the New Orleans *Picayune* (Culley 1977:202), a first, both in Louisiana and within the United States. In 1895, she assigned Elizabeth Gilmer to write the "Dorothy Dix Talks," a series of columns concerning women's issues. A few years later, Kate Chopin published *The Awakening* (1988 [1899]). This novel was considered shocking at the time because it describes one woman's rejection of the traditional female roles of wife and mother. The death of the main female protagonist symbolically demonstrated that in Louisiana in the 1890s there was no socially acceptable place for a woman to function outside the home.

Despite breakthroughs on some fronts, female educational advancements were slow. By 1912, women students were admitted into only seven southern universities (Solomon 1985:53). Even the establishment of women's schools, such as Sophie Newcomb in New Orleans, did not ensure that women had equal educational opportunities. In 1906 Newcomb offered only nine scholarships, while its male counterpart Tulane issued 200 (Solomon 1985:72).

From 1935 to 1943, poorer females as well as poorer males were assisted by the National Youth Administration. By this means, more than 620,000 students attended college (Solomon 1985:148). During World War II, women had increased opportunities in traditionally male fields. However, with the end of the war, the Veterans Bill made it more difficult for women to gain access to higher education. In addition, in Louisiana, the traditional "Southern Belle" mystique did not and does not encourage post-graduate study or feminism, "perhaps, because any study of gender inequality would at least implicitly address the full equality of all people, which in turn would challenge attitudes toward race and class as well" (Tucker 1988:52).

Now that some data concerning women's social and educational standing within Louisiana have been presented, I turn to an examination of women who were active in Louisiana archaeology; these women were exceptions to the Louisiana norms presented above. To understand their place in the history of Louisiana archaeology, I examine their individual life stories and then present the traits they held in common. These factors may explain why these women succeeded in influencing archaeologists and the course of archaeological research, although generally they did not publish their work and their names for the most part appear only in volume prefaces, if at all. Published data on most of these women are sparse (e.g., Dundy 1991:27–28, 217–228; Gibson 1984a, 1988; Johnson 1990), and I have relied heavily on personal recollections.

Women Active in Louisiana Archaeology

Caroline Coroneos Dormon (July 19, 1888–November 23, 1971)[1]

Caroline Dormon was born at Briarwood, her family's house in Saline, Louisiana, to Caroline Trotti Sweat Dormon and James Alexander Dormon. She was the sixth of eight children.

The Dormon family had broad interests in the outdoors, and Caroline Dormon inherited a fascination with Native American culture from her father (Johnson 1990:15). In addition, the children were encouraged in literary endeavors by their mother, who published poems and a novel. With this family background, it was not too surprising that Dormon attended a good school; she received a degree in Fine Arts from The Judson in 1907. Later in life, she received an Honorary Doctorate from Louisiana State University (1965).

Caroline Dormon dedicated most of her working life to education in one form or another. She worked as a teacher within the parish school system, and later for the Louisiana Forestry Division and the Department of Conservation. She may have been the first woman hired in forestry in the United States. Her wilderness interests resulted in honors that few women earned, such as her 1930 election as an associate member to the Society of American Foresters (Johnson 1990:49).

In 1917, Caroline Dormon settled at Briarwood, Chestnut, Louisiana. At Briarwood Dormon created a wildflower sanctuary and wrote many publications on horticulture and the environment, in addition to Native American culture: "The Last of the Cane Basket Makers" (1931), "Caddo Pottery" (1934), and *Southern Indian Boy* (1967).

Dormon was similarly active in other anthropological endeavors. An extensive correspondence and collaboration with John R. Swanton (Smithsonian Institution) began with his visit to Louisiana in 1930

1. Information concerning Dormon was obtained from Johnson (1990) unless otherwise indicated.

(Johnson 1990:136). For example, Plate 50 of Swanton's 1987 [1946] publication is a photograph taken by Caroline Dormon. The subject is "Sam Young, or Sesostrie Yauchicant, last speaker of the Tunica language" (Swanton 1987: Plate 50). Other scholars with interests in language also visited Dormon. The linguist Mary Haas spent three days at Dormon's home in 1937 (Johnson 1990:138).

In addition to her anthropological interests, Dormon promoted Louisiana archaeology by assisting many important archaeologists. In 1931, when Winslow M. Walker (Smithsonian Institution) came to Louisiana, he was aided by Caroline Dormon and Cammie G. Henry, who owned Melrose Plantation, in the identification of Caddo sites along the Red River (Neuman 1984a:48). She also helped F. M. Setzler (Smithsonian Institution) when he worked in Louisiana in 1933. James A. Ford (1936:2) acknowledged the assistance of Caroline Dormon, and stated that he was indebted to her for "assistance in investigations in the northern part of the state. Several of the village sites listed were discovered and collected from by Miss Dormon."

In 1932, probably due to an invitation from Walker, she was one of a few dozen participants at the Conference on Southern Pre-History sponsored by the National Research Council in Birmingham, Alabama. In 1936, she was appointed to the De Soto Commission. She served with Hon. W. G. Brorein, Tampa, Florida; . . . Col. John R. Fordyce, Hot Springs, Arkansas; V. Birney Imes, Columbus, Mississippi; Andrew O. Holmes, Memphis, Tennessee; Dr. Walter B. Jones, University of Alabama, Tuscaloosa; and Dr. John R. Swanton, Smithsonian Institution (Swanton 1985:v). Dormon served with Swanton and Fordyce on the fact finding committee (Swanton 1985:vi). Swanton (1985:292) praised Dormon's work in phrases such as, "Miss Dormon's researches have established the probable sites of the provinces of Chaguate and Aguacay at Drake's and Lake Bistineau, and the Naguatex province above Shreveport." That Dormon took an active part in the committee's work is well documented. In addition, she was involved in other committees that influenced the course of archaeology within Louisiana, such as her 1954 appointment to the Historical Sites Commission of the North Louisiana Historical Association.

Caroline Dormon benefited Louisiana archaeology through her activities on its behalf rather than through her formal educational attainments. Her knowledge of the outdoors and her enthusiasm in searching for sites proved useful to professionals. Dormon's assistance to trained archaeologists and anthropologists and her presence on committees ensured a lasting contribution to the field of Louisiana archaeology.

Jo Nichols Evans (July 7, 1896–June 18, 1991)[2]

Jo Nichols Evans was born in Bardwell, Kentucky, in 1896. She was the youngest of six children of Josephine Forée Nichols and John Mahlon Nichols. The family had strong interests in the outdoors, especially in horticulture (Gibson 1988), which prepared her for later horticultural and archaeological endeavors. In later life, Jo Nichols Evans was a prolific writer and published many articles of horticultural interest, in addition to her *Wings in the Night* (1987), which contains archaeological information.

After completing her schooling in Kentucky, Jo Nichols moved to Alexandria, Louisiana, and within a short time, married Uriah Blackshear Evans (August 25, 1914). The young couple continued to live in Alexandria, where he worked as a CPA. Their daughter Marianna was born on December 3, 1916.[3]

By 1928, the Evans had a farm in Grant Parish, and in the 1930s (possibly 1938) they owned Haphazard Plantation near Ferriday, Louisiana. At both these locations, the Evans indulged their interest in archaeology. They collected artifacts from sites, and dug into mounds, many of which have since been destroyed. Their fieldwork was untrained but, fortunately for archaeology, the Evans worked with professional archaeologists to record their sites. As a result of their collaboration with professionals, the Evans projectile point was named in their honor.

Jo Nichols Evans was a friend of Caroline Dormon. The two women shared a delight with horticulture and local archaeology. As a result of this interest, Jo N. Evans assisted Caroline Dormon with her De Soto research. Despite the fact that there were occasional misunderstandings between the two women, they actively collaborated on more than one occasion (Johnson 1990:111–112). For example, Dormon, the Evans, Fred B. Kniffen, and Edward Neild worked to form an archaeological society within the state (Johnson 1990:138).

In 1931 or 1932, Evans, in company with her husband and Caroline Dormon, assisted Winslow Walker's work at the Troyville Site, Jonesville (Evans 1987:13; Gibson 1988:11). Approximately one year later, James Ford and Lary Lovell lived with the Evanses in Alexandria for a

2. Information concerning Jo Nichols Evans is to be found in Gibson (1988), Dundy (1991:27–28, 217–228), Evans (1987), and Johnson (1990:89, 111–112, 138). Unless otherwise indicated, data concerning Evans was obtained from my interviews with Jon L. Gibson, Hiram F. Gregory, and Joan Pitcher, conducted during 1991 and 1992.

3. Marianna Evans Applegate (December 3, 1916–December 1968) graduated from Louisiana State University in 1936 with majors in sociology and anthropology. She had a lifelong interest in archaeology, and was responsible for directing Stuart Neitzel to the Lafayette Mound (Gibson 1988:9).

summer while they excavated the Rougeau Mound (Gibson 1988: 9–10). After that summer, Ford went to Louisiana State University in Baton Rouge with the encouragement of the Evans.

Jo Nichols Evans contributed to Louisiana archaeology through her knowledge of the local environment. A genuine fascination with pre-history spurred her, in company with her husband, to assist many young professional archaeologists who contributed to the written record concerning Louisiana archaeology.

Margaret Elam Drew (December 15, 1919–November, 1977)[4]

Margaret Elam Drew was born to Margaret Taylor Elam and Joseph B. Elam on December 15, 1919 in Mansfield, Louisiana. She and her future husband, R. Harmon Drew, met at Louisiana State University, and married on December 7, 1940. They had three children, Elizabeth Taylor Drew (born 1942), Richard Harmon Drew, Jr. (born 1946), and Margaret Caldwell Drew (born 1950). The youngest child was the catalyst that pushed Margaret Drew into archaeology.

The Drew family resided in Minden, where Margaret Drew became friends with Rita Moore Krouse (see below), and the two women began their archaeological collaboration in 1963. At that time, Caldwell, Drew's youngest daughter, was learning about Native Americans in school. It became apparent to Drew and Krouse how little was known concerning the prehistory of Louisiana. They both began their archaeological endeavors by enrolling in field schools in Texas, reading books, and recording sites in Louisiana.

They took William Haag to the Three Creeks Site (16CL4), about which Haag reportedly said, "I drove up here just to make a couple of little old ladies in white tennis shoes happy, but I knew they didn't know what they were talking about. Temple mounds . . . and there they were" (R. Harmon Drew, personal communication, 1992).

The Three Creeks Site was the most spectacular site they recorded. In addition, over the course of fifteen years, they examined more than fifty other Louisiana sites located in Bienville, Claiborne, and Webster parishes. During this same time period, Drew and Krouse collected surface finds for both Northwestern State University in Natchitoches, Louisiana, and for Louisiana State University, Baton Rouge.

4. Information concerning Margaret Elam Drew was obtained through interviews conducted by the author with Judge R. Harmon Drew, Rita Moore Krouse, and Robert W. Neuman in 1991 and 1992. In addition some data are in Gibson (1984b), and in the records of the Museum of Natural Sciences, Louisiana State University, Baton Rouge, and the Site Record Files of the Division of Archaeology, Office of Cultural Development, Department of Culture, Recreation and Tourism, Baton Rouge.

No doubt because of Margaret Drew's archaeological involvement, her husband, R. Harmon Drew, a member of the House of Representatives in Louisiana, sponsored the bill that formed the Louisiana Archaeological Survey and Antiquities Commission; this bill passed in 1974 (Webb and Duhe 1984:62). Margaret Drew was appointed to the commission in its first year (Gibson 1984a:7), and she became chair of the commission in 1977 (Webb and Duhe 1984:71).

Margaret Elam Drew "will be remembered for her vigorous efforts on behalf of Louisiana archaeology in the private and state government sectors, but perhaps her greatest gift was her infectious enthusiasm" (Gibson 1984a:7, 9). As one half of the Drew-Krouse team, she invested considerable effort in recording sites in north Louisiana, the results of which are readily apparent in the Site Record Files at the Division of Archaeology, Baton Rouge.

Rita Moore Krouse (1921–)[5]

Rita Moore Krouse was born on August 24, 1921, to Mary Moore and Clyde Moore of Equality, Illinois. She grew up in Michigan and Illinois, and graduated from the Masonic School of Nursing in Chicago in 1942. She became an army nurse and married Prescott Krouse on August 3, 1943. They had two children, Patricia C. Krouse (born 1944), and Clyde Francis Krouse (born 1946).

At the end of the war, Rita Krouse and her family moved to Minden, Louisiana, Prescott Krouse's hometown. She met Margaret Drew, and the two women began their archaeological collaboration. Rita Krouse took Introduction to Anthropology and Introduction to Geography through the extension program at Louisiana State University. She remembers Margaret Drew saying "you buy the book and read it and tell me what I have to know." The two women also attended field schools together (see section on Margaret Drew). They recorded sites and submitted site information to Hiram F. Gregory, William Haag, and Robert W. Neuman, among others.

Krouse's interest in archaeology extends to both historic and prehistoric events. In fact, her interest in history predates her involvement in archaeology. Both she and Drew were members of the North Louisiana Historical Association, and Krouse published several articles and

5. Information concerning Rita Moore Krouse was obtained through interviews conducted by the author with Judge R. Harmon Drew and Rita Moore Krouse in 1992. In addition, some data are in the records of the Museum of Natural Sciences, Louisiana State University, Baton Rouge, and the Site Record Files of the Division of Archaeology, Office of Cultural Development, Department of Culture, Recreation and Tourism, Baton Rouge.

a book concerning Louisiana history: *Fragments of a Dream: The Story of Germantown* (1962), "Bayou Dauchite: The Ante-Bellum Lifeline of Claiborne Parish" (1971), "Two Old Claiborne Towns" (1972), and "Communication: An Aspect of the Cultural Development of Early Claiborne Parish to 1860" (1973).

Rita Moore Krouse is proud of her northern heritage, which may have made it easier for her to behave unconventionally in a southern town. Certainly, driving and walking around the countryside searching for prehistoric sites were uncommon activities for Louisiana women in the mid-1960s. However, the end certainly justified the means, for Rita Krouse and Margaret Drew were responsible for locating large numbers of archaeological sites in northern Louisiana.

Frances Crouser French (1928–   )[6]

Frances Crouser French was born in Big Spring, Texas, on August 29, 1928, grew up in Fort Worth, Texas, and graduated from Arlington Heights High School in 1945. By 1948, she was married, and the couple had a daughter, which proved relevant to her later archaeological endeavors.

In 1950, Frances French completed a B.A. in philosophy at Louisiana State University, Baton Rouge. She entered the graduate program in anthropology there, and completed an M.A. in 1952, under the direction of William G. Haag. Graduate school was an especially challenging experience for a married student with a young baby. French took her child with her to work in her "lab" space, which she recalls as markedly inferior to that of the male graduate students. She also remembers her exclusion from archaeological field trips. It was assumed that her female status (with the additional barriers of marriage and motherhood) did not permit her participation on these educational excursions. French believes (personal communication, 1992) that these events occurred because this treatment was considered appropriate within the context of Louisiana archaeology at that time.

Despite this situation, French conducted fieldwork in southern Louisiana, and completed her thesis in 1952, which was titled "The Morton Shell Heap on Weeks Island, Louisiana." This achievement made her the first woman to complete an archaeological M.A. degree in anthropology at Louisiana State University. Despite this achievement, French's

6. Some details of Frances Crouser French's life can be found in her M.A. thesis (1952), and in the *AAA Guide* (1991). Additional information was obtained through an interview with Frances French that I conducted in 1992.

work is not cited in recent archaeological assessments of coastal Louisiana (e.g., papers in Davis 1984; Jeter et al. 1989, Neuman 1984a), and even direct references to the Morton Shell Mound omit mention of French (e.g., Jeter et al. 1989:154; Neuman 1984a:119, 1984b:160–163; Shenkel 1984:44).

Unfortunately French's Morton shell mound research appears only in her M.A. thesis: she did not publish this work. (Later French did publish outside Louisiana archaeology.) After her graduation, French accepted a teaching position in archaeology at Auburn University, Alabama, and worked in Alabama archaeology for a few years. As a direct result of personal experiences within the Alabama archaeological milieu, she switched to cultural anthropology, and finally specialized in the anthropology of law. This change in emphasis spurred French into obtaining her J.D. in 1987, and she now operates a private law practice.

Frances Crouser French contributed to Louisiana archaeology by becoming the first woman to complete an M.A. thesis in archaeology at Louisiana State University, Baton Rouge. At that time, Louisiana higher education in archaeology was solely the preserve of men, and it was important for men and women to see a woman succeed in the M.A. program.

Lanier Allingham Simmons (November 8, 1929–July 30, 1990)[7]

Lanier Allingham Simmons was born on November 8, 1929 to Dorothy Davis Allingham and James Allingham in Lafayette, Louisiana. She attended Newcomb in New Orleans and graduated cum laude and Phi Beta Kappa with a degree in English in 1950. Her involvement with the university did not cease with her graduation, since she was interested in women's activities at Newcomb, and she eventually served on the Tulane Board of Administrators (1971–1986), an unusual honor for a woman in Louisiana.

In 1951, Lanier Allingham married Edward Simmons. They lived in New Orleans and Avery Island, Louisiana. The couple had four children: Edward McIlhenny Simmons, Jr. (born 1953), Ellen Simmons Ball (born 1955), Bradford Simmons Marshall (born 1958), and Lowell

7. Information concerning Lanier Allingham Simmons was obtained through interviews I conducted with Robert W. Neuman, Edward M. Simmons, and Stephen Williams in 1991 and 1992. Additional data are in Anonymous (1971), the records of the Museum of Natural Sciences, Louisiana State University, Baton Rouge, and the Site Record Files of the Division of Archaeology, Office of Cultural Development, Department of Culture, Recreation and Tourism, Baton Rouge.

Simmons Ukrop (born 1962). The presence of these children is important for understanding her life because her family commitments influenced her career decisions.

Two years after her marriage, Lanier Simmons and her husband read *Gods, Graves and Scholars* by C. W. Ceram (1951), and she was fascinated by the information concerning central America. They visited Yucatan and explored some of the Maya sites. By the mid-1960s, she had begun to realize that family responsibilities made it impossible for her to pursue central American archaeology. Therefore her attention turned to the Southeast, and she entered the M.A. program at Louisiana State University, and obtained fieldwork experience, working for two summers on Joffre Coe's project in North Carolina. Later she recorded sites in St. Mary parish (Site Record Files, Division of Archaeology, Baton Rouge).

By the late 1960s, she had completed her M.A. coursework but was unable to finish the degree due to her family responsibilities. However, she maintained her interest in archaeology and remained active on its behalf. Lanier Simmons and her husband were responsible for introducing several archaeologists to the sites along the Louisiana coastline (Robert W. Neuman, Stephen Williams, personal communications, 1992). She and her husband hosted three archaeological meetings at Avery Island. The first conference was organized by Stephen Williams, and the dozen-or-so participants met for a long week-end in May, 1978 to discuss the archaeology of the Lower Mississippi River valley. The second meeting occurred in May, 1979 "in the guise of a conference, but really it was an opportunity to honor Bill [Haag]" (Stephen Williams, personal communication, 1992). For this event, "Lanier Simmons (Mrs. Edward M.), with husband Ned, offered the fabled hospitality of their home on Avery Island on the Louisiana coast to celebrate properly this solemn occasion" (S. Williams 1981). The conference participants produced a volume honoring William Haag (West and Neuman 1981). In 1981, the third Avery Island conference was organized by Dave D. Davis on the prehistory of the Gulf Coast, and the proceedings were published (Davis 1984).

Lanier Simmons participated in several committees that had an impact on the course of archaeology within Louisiana. She served in a leadership role on the Louisiana State Antiquities Commission and Archaeological Survey, as president of the Louisiana Research Foundation, as a board member of the New Orleans Museum of Art, as chair of the Shadows-on-the-Teche Advisory Council, and as a member of the Archaeological Sites Committee of the Friends of the Cabildo. In addition to her committee works, Simmons wrote "Additional Notes on the

Archaeology of Little Pecan Island" (1978) and co-authored *A Bibliography Relative to Indians of the State of Louisiana* (1969) with Robert W. Neuman.

Lanier Allingham Simmons contributed to Louisiana archaeology through "the encouragement of archaeology," because she "cared very deeply about these professionals' work and activity and was knowledgeable about it . . . and why it was important" (Edward M. Simmons, personal communication, 1992). Lanier Simmons had graduate training and fieldwork experience. She supported the work of professional archaeologists and provided an archaeologically informed opinion to fulfil her membership obligations to various groups and committees.

Paula Ann Patecek Johnson (1935–   )[8]

Paula Ann Patecek Johnson was born on May 3, 1935 to Irma Blackwell Patecek and Frank Patecek in Covington, Louisiana. Among her relatives there were some unconventional views. For example, young Paula was told by her grandfather Blackwell that it was important to enjoy life and that it was not necessary for a woman to marry. This same grandfather was interested in both archaeology and Native Americans. No doubt his artifact collecting activities stimulated her curiosity (he died when she was thirty). At age twelve she had an interest in Egyptian archaeology; she expressed her desire to be an Egyptologist to her mother, whose response was that "it was too queer" (Paula Johnson, personal communication, 1992). In 1962, she obtained her B.A. in Education from Louisiana State University, and the following year traveled north to take anthropology courses at the University of Chicago.

She developed an interest in the Maya, and in 1963 traveled to Yucatan to see some of the archaeological sites. Upon her marriage two years later, Paula Patecek Johnson reconciled her desire to do Maya archaeology with the realities of being a Louisiana wife and mother (Jennifer was born in 1968, and Sally in 1971); she realized that she would have to work in the Southeast if she was to continue in archaeology. At that time, few archaeological sites were documented for St. Tammany parish, and so she began to visit them, record information,

8. Information concerning Paula Ann Patecek Johnson was obtained from interviews I conducted with Paula Patecek Johnson, and Robert W. Neuman in 1991 and 1992. Additional data are in the records of the Museum of Natural Sciences, Louisiana State University, Baton Rouge, and the Site Record Files at the Division of Archaeology, Office of Cultural Development, Department of Culture, Recreation and Tourism, Baton Rouge.

and make collections. Around 1967 or 1968, she met Robert W. Neuman at a meeting in Bogalusa, and thereafter informed Neuman about sites. (Both of them retain a vivid memory of a very pregnant [with Sally] Paula Johnson taking Robert Neuman to an archaeological site on a very hot, buggy summer day.) Most of the sites Johnson located were small lithic scatters in the parishes of southeastern Louisiana, such as Washington and St. Tammany. A 1971 news clipping (filed at the Museum of Natural Sciences, LSU) documents Johnson and other members of the St. Tammany Parish Archaeological Society digging into a mound in Covington, Louisiana.

In the mid-1970s she took courses at both the University of New Orleans and Louisiana State University. She had wished to enter the M.A. program in Anthropology at Louisiana State University, but her undergraduate grades prevented her from achieving this goal.

Johnson maintained an interest in archaeology for many years and was a member of the Louisiana Archaeological Society, which was founded in 1974. Paula Johnson met Lanier Simmons through Robert Neuman, but does not recall meeting the other women considered here. Her field activities decreased in volume once her children entered school, and, probably about the mid-1970s, she turned her energies to monitoring and improving the school system.

Johnson published two historical articles: "Oral History Interview: Lawrence Flot" with John Healy (1975) and "The Spring of Abita Builds a Town" (1977). Her assistance is mentioned in Villere's (1980) Abita Springs, Louisiana: Historic Preservation Survey. In addition, Johnson submitted information which led to the placement of the Abita Springs Pavillion on the National Register in 1975.

In conclusion, Paula Patecek Johnson contributed to Louisiana archaeology through her fieldwork. For many years, she documented prehistoric sites in the southeastern portion of the state. In addition, she brought these sites to the attention of professional archaeologists.

Traits in Common Among the Women Active in Louisiana Archaeology

Considering the lengthy history of archaeological investigations in Louisiana, female involvement in data collection was extremely late, not until the 1930s. Caroline Dormon and Jo Evans are the first women who left a record of their archaeological activities. Dormon was active until the 1960s, and Evans until the 1980s.

In the early 1950s, Frances French got her M.A. from Louisiana State University. She was the first woman at Louisiana State University to obtain an anthropology M.A. focused on archaeological fieldwork. Unfortunately, her thesis work is seldom cited, and therefore, she does not seem to have had much ongoing influence within the state. She switched career fields from Louisiana to Alabama archaeology and eventually turned to jurisprudence.

During the 1960s, Margaret Drew, Paula Johnson, Rite Krouse, and Lanier Simmons became active in archaeology, continuing until the 1970s. All seven of these women shared an unusual dedication to archaeology and they also shared several traits that may have facilitated their involvement in a non-traditional field of study:

(1) Generally, their family backgrounds included relatives with interests in the outdoors, ranging from horticulture to Native American culture.

(2) Generally, these women were linked to the upper levels of Louisiana society and played important political roles in the promotion of archaeology.

(3) Generally, they had little formal academic training in archaeology, with the exception of Frances French, who obtained her M.A. and Lanier Simmons who completed her M.A. coursework.

(4) Generally, these women influenced archaeology within the state by assisting formally-trained (male) archaeologists, rather than through their own published fieldwork.

Granted that the past is commonly understood to bear some influence on the present, it is pertinent to investigate current events within the state. I now turn to an examination of the role of gender in women's participation in Louisiana archaeology.

Gender and Archaeology in Louisiana

Among Louisiana archaeologists, there is resistance to the suggestion that gender may play a role in professional success within the state. In this regard, a survey of 50 contract archaeologists who were active in Louisiana in 1991 is informative. Twenty-nine males and 21 females responded to the survey. The major finding was that males generally possessed greater job security (i.e., 56% of the males as opposed to 39% of the females indicated that their jobs were permanent). The survey also demonstrated that men have been involved in contract archaeology for a longer period of time (13% of the male sample and 0% of the female sample had worked at their present company for 11-plus years). Generally, women had lower academic qualifications than men (46% of the males had obtained an M.A. or Ph.D., only 24% of the females were similarly educated). My survey indicated that while the numbers of males and females employed by archaeological consulting firms are approximately equal, still the women are not as well educated and generally hold lower ranked jobs.

My survey suggests a high degree of historical continuity in that the women who work in Louisiana archaeology possess lower educational qualifications than the men employed in the field. This pattern was previously described for both the nineteenth and twentieth centuries in general, and for the period 1930–1960 with regard to seven women working at archaeology. It is depressing that education is an issue today, just as it was fifty years ago. Unfortunately, my survey did not request information concerning financial or family concerns that might have shed light on the factors underlying this enduring pattern.

A disturbing fact is that while there may be few females with Ph.D.s in the Louisiana contract archaeology circuit, such is not the case nationally. During the 1990–1991 academic year, 195 women and 113 men obtained Ph.D. degrees in anthropology (American Anthropological Association 1991). For the 1988–1989 academic year, 152 women and 166 men completed anthropology Ph.D.s (American Anthropological Association 1989). However, of these, only 30 women obtained archaeology degrees, compared to 60 men. (An additional six people's names could not be identified to sex; American Anthropological Association 1989:446–452.) The figures for the previous academic year show new women anthropology Ph.D.s outnumbering men (American Anthropological Association 1988) but a similar underrepresentation of women among the archaeology Ph.D.s. The figures for the Department of Geography and Anthropology, Louisiana State University, indicate that similar numbers of males and females obtain M.A. degrees in archaeology from 1980 onward.

Despite the documented availability of female archaeological Ph.D.s, few women with Ph.D.s are to be found within the state, either in contract, governmental, or academic circles. While it is true that Louisiana does boast a female State Archaeologist, men hold 90 percent of the high-status academic positions in universities (American Anthropological Association 1991). Nationally, statistics indicate a male to female ratio of 3:1 at teaching colleges and 5:1 at research universities (Simeone 1987:31). Thus, the Louisiana 9:1 showing is particularly uninspiring.

However, in keeping with the long standing Louisiana tradition of active women amateurs, there are presently many females involved in non-academic archaeology within the state. These women may participate in non-leadership roles within the contract firms, or they may be found within the ranks of the Louisiana Archaeological Society, and its various Chapters. Pearson's (1985) compilation indicated that the L.A.S. membership was then 31 percent female.

Conclusions

The data presented uphold the contention that women have been and are under-represented in Louisiana professional archaeology. Several factors stemming from Louisiana's social and educational history have resulted in this situation. Educational opportunities, especially for women, were slow to materialize in Louisiana. For many years southern schools did not accept women, and they were late in offering advanced anthropology degrees. In the 1930s, only a few Ph.D.-granting anthropology departments had field archaeology programs, namely California, Chicago, Columbia, Harvard, Pennsylvania, Southern California, and Yale (Guthe 1967:435). None of these institutions was located in the Southeast, although Harvard later developed strong research ties to Louisiana. Interestingly, Columbia University had research connections to the Southwest, and this school produced many female doctorates in the 1930s (Rossiter 1982: Table 7.5). As a result, the history of southwestern archaeology is replete with references to female archaeological scholars. In contrast, the Louisiana case with its Harvard research ties produced no noted women archaeologists with Ph.D.s. Thus, on account of several twists of fate, Louisiana did not promote or attract women to the field of archaeology. Had the educational structure been slightly different, or, had Columbia University devoted a research program to the area, history might have been altered.

Despite the lack of female professional archaeologists, there were a small group of dedicated women (including one professional archaeologist) who worked in archaeology beginning in the 1930s. For the most part, the contributions of the women brought to light here have been forgotten, and a rewriting of the history of Louisiana archaeology is overdue.

As I have suggested, the past influences much of the present, and educators within Louisiana are still struggling to produce graduate-level archaeologists, both male and female. At present, only Tulane University grants anthropology Ph.D.s, while Louisiana State University grants M.A.s, and the University of New Orleans issues B.A.s.

The implications of this research are that (a) we need to promote archaeological education within Louisiana because there is a long history of insufficient education to overcome; (b) we need to encourage women to continue their graduate careers within Louisiana archaeology to attain equal representation within the discipline; (c) we need to recover the survey and collection data generated by those early women archaeologists to enlarge our data base, and (d) we need to rewrite the history of Louisiana archaeology to include these women's contributions.

Acknowledgments

I thank the many people who assisted me in my research: R. Harmon Drew, Frances Crouser French, Jon L. Gibson, Hiram F. Gregory, William G. Haag, Paula Patecek Johnson, Fred B. Kniffen, Rita Moore Krouse, Robert W. Neuman, Joan Pitcher, Don Sepulvado, Edward M. Simmons, Stephen Williams, and all the nameless respondents to my survey of Louisiana archaeologists. Some of this work was completed as part of my duties as Southeastern Regional Archaeologist, Museum of Geoscience, Louisiana State University, Baton Rouge. Portions of this research were presented at the 1992 Annual Meeting of the Louisiana Archaeological Society in Baton Rouge, the 1992 Annual Meeting of the Louisiana Academy of Sciences in Baton Rouge, and the 1992 Gender and Archaeology Conference in Boone, North Carolina.

Chapter 10
Cowgirls with the Blues?
A Study of Women's Publication and
the Citation of Women's Work in
Historical Archaeology

Mary Beaudry and Jacquelyn White

> She's lived to see the world turned upside down
> Hitchin rides out of the blues.
> —Rodney Crowell, as sung by Emmylou Harris[1]

Penned by country music singer-songwriter Rodney Crowell—who was probably at least indirectly inspired by the title of Tom Robbin's book of the same name—*Even Cowgirls Get the Blues* was the title track of Emmylou Harris's 1979 Warner Bros. record album. This musical theme has an archaeological counterpoint of sorts, set forth in an article published in the *Journal of Field Archaeology* in 1981 by Ned Woodall and Philip Perricone. Its ominous title was "The Archeologist as Cowboy: The Consequence of Professional Stereotype."

Woodall and Perricone conducted an "attitudinal survey" that revealed how, a decade ago, the "conservation ethic" had yet to permeate archaeological thinking and practice fully. They attributed this to "a stereotypic self-image fostered by archeological tradition and the nature of archeological research" through which "archeologists view preservationists as being significantly less masculine, less active, less favorable, and weaker than themselves" (Woodall and Perricone 1981: 506). The reason for this, they say, is that

---

1. © 1977 Visa Music ASCAP. Used by permission.

our profession has created a body of myths, legends, and culture heroes serving to generate a self-image. Essentially, this image shows the rugged individual laboring under hardships others could not or would not accept, wresting a romantic prize from forces of destruction, be they federal agencies, pothunters, or the Dim Mists of Antiquity. . . . This vision of the individual counterposed to great forces, struggling to obtain what he values, working virtually alone, but with resourcefulness and energy, also meshes neatly with the traditional Euro-american image of males. The correspondence is marked by other facets of *machismo*, including hard-drinking and womanizing. Maleness is further emphasized by beards, jeans, and work boots . . . and a penchant for cowboy accoutrements when possible (hats, belt buckles, boots, and even, in rare instances, trowel holsters), all serving to merge the profession's hero with the hero of America, the cowboy. (Woodall and Perricone 1981:506–507)

Woodall and Perricone (1981:507) go on to report that their survey showed how preservationists suffered under an image they label as negative, apparently, because it is feminine. They explain that this is an outgrowth of the connotation of preservation as the purview of nineteenth-century "wealthy older females of high social status working to save standing structures of other high-status notables" and, despite all its saving of buildings and raising of funds, preservation is passive: it involves doing nothing, as opposed to fieldwork excavation, which involves risk, danger, and adventure. One way this stereotype is manifested, Woodall and Perricone claim (1981:507), is in the obvious "*overrepresentation* of females in preservation-related pursuits (SHPO staff positions, federal positions created by the preservation legislation of the '60s and '70s, major figures in conservation archaeology in colleges and universities). This, we believe, is in part a consequence of the congruence found between the traditional view of preservationists and the feminine stereotype in our culture" (Woodall and Perricone 1981:507; emphasis ours!). Our public image and our professional self-image dictate that the real archaeologist is a cowboy who digs, that women who want to be real archaeologists must emulate cowboys, and that conservation archaeology, with its anti-machismo overtones, is a more suitable domain for women because it requires less action and less physical effort than fieldwork. While Woodall and Perricone acknowledge that women might want to avoid the feminine stereotype by embracing some of the machismo elements of the stereotypical archaeologist as cowboy, their greatest concern was not how to overcome the feminine stereotype but how to divorce it from historic preservation. If we read them correctly, they saw the feminine connotations of preservation as negative and potentially damaging to a significant growth area of archaeology.

What interests us in the present context is a trend running parallel to the perception of historic preservation as somehow more appropriate a venue for women than for men, that is, the notion that historical archaeology is likewise a field suitable for and, to a certain extent, perhaps even dominated by women. It is difficult to cite hard data; we are speaking of people's impressions. For example, one Texas archaeologist remarked to the authors that he had the impression that historical archaeology was "done by women," although when he thought about it, he acknowledged he had only one historical archaeologist in mind, who happens to be fairly prominent. Perhaps this study can help us move beyond impressionistic characterizations of the field.

This brings us to consider a 1985 article in *American Antiquity* in which Joan Gero discussed the socio-politics of archaeology and documented the "woman-at-home" ideology as one that idealizes women in archaeological roles other than fieldwork.

Corresponding, then, to the stereotyped male, we expect to find the female archaeologist secluded in the base-camp laboratory or museum, sorting and preparing archaeological materials, private, protected, passively receptive, ordering and systematizing, but without recognized contribution to the productive process. The woman-at-home archaeologist must fulfill her stereotypic feminine role by specializing in the analysis of archaeological materials, typologizing, seriating, studying wear or paste or iconographic motifs. She will have to do the archaeological housework. (Gero 1985:344)

Our purpose in this paper is to initiate an examination of women within the field of historical archaeology. What we propose to do here is to explore whether and how the "archaeologist as cowboy" and the "woman-at-home ideology" are manifest in the area of historical archaeology through an examination of the Society for Historical Archaeology and its journal, *Historical Archaeology*. Our idea is to examine the trajectory of women's participation in and influence in the field in part through office-holding in the Society but mainly through publication.[2] The latter, the subject of this paper, we see as a measure both of degree of participation and, somewhat more amorphously, of "authority" through frequency of publication, type of publication (e.g., theory, field report, artifact analysis, etc.), and frequency of citations. Lutz, for example, notes that citation is a form of "'symbolic capital' that confers intellectual legitimacy and boosts professional standing" (as quoted in *Lingua franca* 1991:6). Hence it is important to examine women's publication not just in terms of sheer numbers of articles published but also to discover whether women's work influences the field when it does get

2. We see this as only part of a larger study of women historical archaeologists, a beginning. Beaudry envisions looking at employment among women historical archaeologists as a supplement to this study of publication and citation patterns.

TABLE 1. Summary of Membership in the Society for Historical Archaeology, 1987–1991

	Percent male	Percent female	Percent unknown	Total
Total memberships				
1987	63.8	33.9	2.3	1656
1988	62.0	35.2	2.8	1683
1989	61.1	35.4	2.5	1775
1990	62.5	35.0	2.4	1558[a]
1991	61.2	36.9	1.9	1623
Individual memberships				
1987	66.9	31.3	1.7	1331
1988	64.3	33.0	2.6	1405
1989	65.9	32.0	2.1	1416
1990	66.9	31.4	1.7	1237[a]
1991	65.3	33.1	1.6	1280
Student memberships				
1987	49.3	45.8	4.8	312
1988	49.2	47.3	3.4	264
1989	44.4	51.5	4.1	340
1990	46.6	47.3	6.0	283[a]
1991	46.1	50.9	3.1	293

[a]Raise in annual dues.
Source: Julia G. Costello, "Society for Historical Archaeology Membership Profile, 1987–1991," Manuscript report, 28 March 1992.

published as well as to delineate areas of the field in which women's scholarship has an impact.

Women in the Society for Historical Archaeology

The Society for Historical Archaeology recently undertook to compile data on membership; Immediate Past-President Julia Costello prepared a membership analysis summary (Table 1) that reveals that total individual memberships between 1987[3] and 1990 averaged about 65 percent male and 32 percent female. Of interest is the fact that student memberships are much more closely divided between males and females. Long-term tracking of membership trends might tell us whether these figures mean that ever-increasing numbers of women will continue in the profession beyond graduate school, or indicate that, despite the fact that women and men tend to train for the field in roughly equivalent numbers, more men succeed in finding employment and

3. The SHA does not have computer files for membership prior to 1987. Counts of annual membership lists printed in the Society's newsletter have not been completed.

hence have a reason for maintaining (and a means of affording) membership in the Society for Historical Archaeology.

The SHA journal, *Historical Archaeology*, has had four editors in its history (see below). The post of Editor is a presidential appointment; the Editor appoints sub-editors, members of the editorial advisory committee, and editorial assistants. Under the editorship of Ronald Michael (1978–   ), the Editorial Advisory Board has grown as the field and the journal have expanded and includes increasing numbers of women. A group of Associate Editors assist Michael in the review process; in 1990, two women served as Associate Editors. Roderick Sprague has served as Book Review Editor since 1977, succeeding Kathleen Gilmore, who served in that post from 1974–1976, and Lyle Stone (1968–1973). A general observation can be made that as the representation of women on the editorial staff has increased, the appearance in the journal of articles and reviews by women has increased in frequency. This could be no more than a coincidence and not really a "warming trend" based on the presence of females, because the Editor and sub-editors undertake most of the solicitation for articles and reviews.

Women in *Historical Archaeology*

To examine patterns of women's publication in historical archaeology, we focus on the journal of the Society for Historical Archaeology (1967–1990) because it long has been the major outlet for publications in this field. Deagan's survey of "Where Historical Archaeologists are Publishing" (1989) revealed that fully 71 percent of peer-reviewed journal articles on historical archaeology appeared in *Historical Archaeology*. The journal was established almost immediately on the heels of the formation of the Society, and, initially, presented the proceedings of the early SHA meetings. John Cotter was the first editor of the journal, David Armour was editor from 1968–1973, John Coombes from 1974–1977, and Ronald L. Michael since 1977. In 24 years of publication, 35 issues of the journal have appeared, and 320 articles and 312 book reviews have been published.

Content Analysis

Following is a year-by-year discussion of the contents of the journal in terms of women's participation (Table 2). Information is presented on total number of articles and book reviews per issue, on topics of articles and reviews by women, and on patterns of citation. It is relevant to note that tabulation of bibliographic citations as male or female is likely

TABLE 2. Content Analysis of *Historical Archaeology*

Vol.	Woman author/ total articles	Women's cites/total cites/junior women	Women/ reviewers	Books by women/books reviewed
1	0/19	2/99/2	0/0	0/0
2	2/9	8/79/1	0/9	3/17
3	0/18	1/72/0	0/8	2/9
4	0/9	27/102/1	2/18	3/18
5	2/9	10/107/2	0/16	2/16[a]
6	1/7	26/213/6	1/12	2/12
7	1/10	5/48/1	2/11	1/13
8	2/7	14/83/3	1/9	1/9
9	2/9	3/190/0	0/7	1/7[a]
10	4/15	21/199/7	2/5	3/5
11	5/16	14/204/6	1/4	0/4
12	5/8	32/161/3	3/8	5/9[a]
13	2/6	13/134/5	0/5	1/5[a]
14	0/6	18/204/3	1/9	3/9[a]
15(1)	7/10	55/339/13	4/8	2/8
15(2)	2/4	24/249/3	1/8	4/8
16	0/1	0/23/0	0/0	0/0
17(1)	9/8	48/244/6	3/12	4/12
17(2)	3/10	39/312/11	1/10	3/10[a]
18(1)	3/8	52/301/16	2/11	2/11[a]
18(2)	3/10	30/175/2	3/11	4/11[a]
19(1)	3/11	25/196/9	1/10	2/10[a]
19(2)	3/10	28/283/10	1/10	2/10[a]
20(1)	2/7	58/249/22	6/10	4/10
20(2)	2/7	60/163/19	4/11	2/11[a]
21(1)	3/8	38/305/13	3/11	5/12[a]
21(2)	3/7	78/330/17	2/11	2/11[a]
22(1)	1/12	39/236/9	7/20	8/23[a]
22(2)	2/6	43/157/12	1/17	2/17
23(1)	6/12	78/277/26	3/10	1/10
23(2)	6/7	83/343/20	3/9	7/10
24(1)	4/7	59/198/19	0/8	1/8
24(2)	3/14	41/179/16	0/0	0/0
24(3)	1/7	159/453/36	1/5	1/5
24(4)	7/11	103/450/37	0/0	0/0

[a] Includes work or works (e.g., site report) with a woman junior author.

skewed by a number of factors, including the fact that historical archaeologists inevitably cite large numbers of documents and historical works, as well as many items attributed to "Anonymous." Virginia Woolf notwithstanding, we did not feel safe assuming that "anonymous was a woman" and hence have not counted such entries as female. No doubt we have also assigned gender mistakenly in several instances, and perhaps our figures are better characterized as "female" vs. "not female" authors rather than "male" as opposed to "female" authors. In tabulating citations,[4] we counted each bibliographic entry as a separate citation (i.e., we counted each item by any given author or set of authors once) and included women junior authors in the totals for women authors; female junior authorship thus appears in our figures as a proportion of total female authorship.[5] We note, however, that we did not tabulate instances of males as junior authors when females were senior authors.[6]

Volume 1 of *Historical Archaeology* contained 19 articles, all by men; topics included military sites of several periods, eighteenth-century cemeteries, and the post-1800 fur trade. While early journal articles tended to have pretty sparse bibliographies—understandably, given the paucity of material available—in this issue only two women were cited. The current research section of the journal listed no work by women.

In Volume 2 (1968) the first articles by women appear. These articles were "The Archaeologist's Guide to 19th Century American Glass" by Dessamae Lorrain and "The Archaeology of Mass-Produced Footwear" by Adrienne Anderson. The topics tackled in these first articles by women, artifact identification and classification, provide a preview of the sort of articles women published in the journal in the ensuing years. Lorrain cited two women out of ten references, and Anderson cited only men. A single listing in the current research section described a project directed by a woman.

Volume 3 (1969) had a couple of articles that are embarrassing, even given the time, for their sexist language and sex-stereotyping.[7] Only one article by women is found in a list of 40 recent publications.

4. We did not count the listings of publications included with memorials as citations.

5. Our count of women junior authors perhaps over-represents women in a certain sense: multiple women junior authors each were counted on multi-authored works.

6. This of course would be an important element of a comprehensive equity study. We were interested in looking at women's participation and framed our study accordingly. It is of interest to note that we observed several instances of citations in which junior/senior authorship had been reversed. What we mean by this is that the senior woman author was demoted to junior authorship, no doubt inadvertently, by the person citing the work. This most frequently occurred when the work cited was by a wife/husband team, but the fact that we picked up repeated examples of this sort of slip-up has, we feel, considerable implications for the way women's work is perceived. Another related practice we observed, albeit infrequently, is that occasionally those citing wife/husband teams fail to use the woman's surname if it is the same as her husband's. We expect that the recent addition of a full-time copy editor to the journal editorial staff will render such digressions from the established bibliographic format extinct.

7. John Rick's editorial, "Man and Superman" and Stanley South's "Wanted! An Historic Archaeologist"—both of which could have been textual candidates for a *Ms.* "No Comment" section. South (p. 74) characterizes the sought-for archaeologist as "an individual with an uncommon amount of common sense; a tool user, a chain saw user, an

Volume 4 offered a book review by Margaret Brown of Audrey Noël Hume's booklet, *Glass in Colonial Williamsburg's Archaeological Collections*. Schuyler's article "Historical and Historic Sites Archaeology as Anthropology: Basic Definitions and Relationships," cited one woman in 25 references. This begs the question whether women were writing and publishing about theory and method and issues of self-definition for the fledgling field of historical archaeology. The answer, it appears, is that they were not. Schuyler's thought piece is itself in a minority, as men writing for the journal continued to focus on forts and gunflints. Eighteen of 211 recent publications had women as authors, of whom almost 50 percent were junior authors.

Volume 5 contained articles by Olive Jones, who wrote "Glass Bottles: Push-ups and Pontil Marks," citing four women out of 15 references, and by Carol Mason, who commented on "Gunflints and Chronology at Ocmulgee National Monument," citing two women out of nine references. Three out of 54 recent publications listed were by women, two of whom were co-authors with men.

In Volume 6 Kathleen Deagan published an excavation report about Fig Springs in Florida, citing four women out of 31 references, and Virginia Harrington reviewed a book in conjunction with her husband, J. C. Harrington. Of 26 citations to works by women, 21 appear in Karklins's and Sprague's article on glass trade beads in North America, which cited 138 total references. In six instances these women were junior authors. Seventeen of 131 recent publications listed were by women; one-third of these were written in conjunction with men.

One of the 10 articles published in Volume 7 (1973) was by a woman. Jennifer Leighton wrote "Photography of Glass Artifacts from Historic Sites: A Useful Technique." Book reviews were penned by Margaret Brown for Good's report on the Guebert site, and Joan Townsend for Van Stone's *Nushagak*. Six of 128 recent publications listed were by women.

A big year for women in the SHA was 1974: Kathleen Gilmore was the first woman on the staff of the journal (as Review Editor) and was elected to the Board of Directors, and Susan Jackson became an associate editor. In Volume 8, Florence Lister and Robert Lister published "Maiolica in Colonial Spanish America" and Alice Wood wrote about "Jesuit" rings from western New York. Nine of a total of 14 references to work by women were cited in the articles written by women. Twenty-

---

ax man, a carpenter, a mechanic, a tractor driver; an action man—an engineer. He should be an observer, a searcher, a doer, a craftsman—an artist." This characterization of historical archaeologist as "cowboy of all trades" was clearly not aimed at women.

one of 152 recent publications listed were written by women, four in conjunction with men. Joan Townsend reviewed a report on Fort Enterprise.

In 1975 (Volume 9) Joanne Bowen wrote "Probate Inventories: An Evaluation from the Perspective of Zooarchaeology and Agricultural History at Mott Farm," and Elizabeth Sanford wrote "Conservation of Artifacts: A Question of Survival." These articles seem to be indicative of the type of articles women were getting published and the areas in which they were working. Twenty-three of 73 recent publications listed were by women.[8] The listing of recent publications ended with this issue.

Volume 10 (1976) saw a rise in the number of female contributors. Joyce McKay wrote "The Coalescence of History and Archaeology," the first theoretical article by a woman. Janet Spector wrote on "The Interpretive Potential of Glass Trade Beads in Historic Archaeology," Carol Mason on "Jesuit Rings from Rock Island, Wisconsin," and Florence Lister was senior author with Robert Lister on an article entitled "Italian Presence in Tin-glazed Ceramics of Spanish America." Nine of the 21 women cited were acknowledged by women authors. Dorris Olds reviewed Kathleen Deagan's *Archaeology at the National Greek Orthodox Shrine*, and Julia Costello reviewed *Excavations at the Tubac Presidio* by Lynette Shenk and George Teague.

Ten years after the first publication of the journal, Volume 11 offered five articles and one book review by a woman. Barbara Butler reviewed Ralph Lewis's *Manual for Museums*. Lynne Sussman wrote "Changes in Pearlware Dinnerware, 1780–1830," and Shiela Minni wrote "A Note on Foundation Preparation in Permafrost." Amanda Watlington served as senior author with Donald Jackson for an article on "Simple Methods and Materials for Preparing Drawings for Publication," while Marsha Kelly was junior author with Roger Kelly of an article on pressed brick bands and Sarah Peabody Turnbaugh was junior author with William Turnbaugh on "Alternative Applications of the Mean Ceramic Date Concept for Interpreting Human Behavior."

In these first ten years, as far as contributions are concerned, the journal moved from no representation of women to approximately one-third representation of women. The citation ratio is far less cheering, however. While they may not have published as much as men, women simply are not cited in proportion to the frequency with which they *have* published (as revealed in the lists of recent publications). We would expect to see a dramatic increase in citations of women's work as

8. After 1975, current research and recent publication listings appeared in the Society's newsletter.

they publish more often, but such is not the case. Out of a total of 106 books reviewed in the journal's first 10 years of publication, only 13 works with women authors were reviewed; in three instances, the women were junior authors on multi-authored site reports.

In 1978 (Volume 12) Florence Lister was senior author with Robert Lister for "The First Mexican Maiolicas: Imported and Locally Produced." Also published were articles by Kathleen Deagan, "The Material Assemblage of 16th Century Spanish Florida"; Dorothy Griffiths, "Use-Marks on Historic Ceramics: A Preliminary Study"; Shawn Bonath, "An Evaluation of the Mean Ceramic Date Formula as Applied to South's Majolica Model"; and Lynne Sussman, "British Military Tableware, 1760–1830." The common denominator of all of the contributions by women archaeologists is a focus on artifact identification or analysis, especially ceramic analysis. Gail Fowler reviewed Audrey Noël Hume's *Archaeology and the Colonial Gardener*, Noël Hume reviewed two books on English pottery by Jo Draper, and Mary Good reviewed a report by Byron Sudbury on a French contact site in Oklahoma. Also of note is John Cotter's review of Lynne Lewis's book, *Drayton Hall*.

Susan Henry wrote about terra cotta tobacco pipes from the Pamplin pipe factory in Virginia, and Kathryn Kimrey-Lees was junior author on an article about Colono ceramics in Volume 13.

In Volume 14 Priscilla Wegars reviewed *The Ceramics of Lower Fort Garry* by Lynne Sussman. Women were co-authors of two of the other publications that were reviewed.

After 1980 the journal became a biannual publication. In 1981, Volume 15, no. 1 had 10 articles. Caroline Carley reported on the evidence of fever epidemics at nineteenth-century fur trade posts, Katherine Singley provided advice on artifact conservation, Barbara Stark wrote about a survey of sites in the Papaloapan estuarine delta, Florence Lister was senior author with Robert Lister on an article about recycling of Spanish pots and potsherds, Jane Busch offered an introduction to tin cans, and Sarah Bridges and Nan Rothschild were junior authors with Bert Salwen in a discussion of the research value of small samples. Thirty-three of 55 citations of women's writing were in articles by women. Kathleen Gilmore reviewed a report on the Fort Sam Houston project, Stephanie Rodeffer reviewed *Colonial Life on the Georgia Coast*, by Nicholas Honerkamp, Shirley Gorenstein reviewed a historic structures and furnishings report on Fort Stanwix (note that the table of contents lists Gorenstein as reviewer of Cynthia Price's *19th Century Ceramics . . . in the Ozark Border Region*, which was actually reviewed by Steven Baker), and Roselle Henn reviewed Vernon Baker's *Black Lucy's Garden*.

Olive Jones wrote about essence of peppermint bottles, and Frances

Mathien reported on a remote sensing project at Chalmette National Historical Park in Volume 15, no. 2. Olive Dickason reviewed a report on Canadian blockhouses by Richard Young, while James Bradley reviewed Susan Gibson's (editor), *Burr's Hill: A 17th-Century Wampanoag Burial Ground in Warren, Rhode Island*, John Combes reviewed Alice Kehoe's *François' House: An Early Fur Trade Post on the Saskatchewan River*, and James Tuck reviewed contributions to the Parks Canada *History and Archaeology* series by Jeanne Alyluia (glassware) and Barbara Wade (cutlery). Hence publications by women were highly visible in both numbers of Volume 15.

Volume 16 (1982) was a special edition authored by William Gates and Dana Omerod, both presumably men, devoted to the potteries of East Liverpool, Ohio. Gates and Omerod cited 23 references, none of whose authors were female.

In 1983, Volume 17, no. 1 had eight articles, four with a woman as senior author, five as junior author, for a total of nine women authors! (There were also 9 male authors.) Articles by women as sole author were on redwares (Sarah Turnbaugh) and bottles (Olive Jones), while co-authored pieces were on ceramic typology (Mary Beaudry, Janet Long, Henry Miller, Fraser Neiman, and Garry Stone), faunal remains (Peter Schulz and Sherri Gust), a Peruvian roadside structure (Colleen Beck, Eric Deeds, Sheila Pozorski, and Thomas Pozorski), western milling sites (Roger Kelly and Marsha Kelly), and conservation of water-logged artifacts (Mark Denton and Joan Gardner). Carol Ruppé reviewed *A Bibliography of Glass Trade Beads in North America*, Martha Latta reviewed *Mr. Thomas McVey's Dwelling House* by Roger Grange, and Patricia Netherly reviewed *Language and Lore of the Long Island Indians*.

Volume 17, no. 2 had 10 articles. Elizabeth Reitz coauthored with Nicholas Honerkamp an article on British colonial subsistence in the southeastern United States, Susan Kent wrote about differential rates of culture change based on a Navaho case study, and Donna Seifert contributed a memorial to Charles Di Peso. Olive Jones reviewed *Bottles on the Western Frontier*, by Rex Wilson, and three works were reviewed with women junior authors.

Articles with women authors in 1984, Volume 18, no. 1 included those by Bente Bittman and Gerda Alcaide (*oficinas* in northern Chile), Florence Lister and Robert Lister on the potter's quarter of colonial Puebla, Mexico, and Lois Feister (building materials at Crown Point barracks). Caroline Carley reviewed a multi-authored issue of Canadian Historic Sites *Occasional Papers in Archaeology and History*, and Sarah Turnbaugh reviewed Susan Myers monograph on early nineteenth-century ceramic production in Philadelphia.

In Volume 18, no. 2 Julia King reported on ceramic variability in seventeenth-century St. Augustine, George Miller and Catherine Sullivan discussed machine-made glass bottles, and Diana Rockman and Nan Rothschild compared and contrasted assemblages from urban vs. rural tavern sites. Georgeanna Greer reviewed the Gates and Omerud work published as Volume 16, nos. 1 & 2; Julia Costello reviewed Frierman's report on the Ontiveros Adobe; and Birgitta Wallace reviewed Story's edited volume, *Early European Settlement and Exploitation in Atlantic Canada.*

In Volume 19, no. 1 (1985) Kathleen Deagan and Michael Scardaville wrote about the archaeology of Hispanic sites, Pam Crabtree discussed methods in historical zooarchaeology, and Olive Jones published a memorial to Iain Walker. Olive Jones reviewed Deiss's *The Development and Application of a Chronology for American Glass.*

Volume 19, no. 2 had 10 articles. Hetty Jo Brumbach wrote about recent fur trade sites, Cynthia Price reported on faunal remains at the Widow Harris site, and Kathleen Deagan wrote a memorial for Charles Fairbanks. Sarah Peabody Turnbaugh reviewed the catalog of the exhibit, *Unearthing New England's Past: The Ceramic Evidence.*

In 1986, Volume 20, no. 1 contained seven articles. Martha Zierden and Jeanne Calhoun discussed urban adaptations in colonial Charleston, and Bonne McEwan wrote about domestic adaptation at Puerto Real, Haiti. Book reviews numbered 10, with a grand total of six of these by women. Carol Ruppé reviewed Dobyns's *Spanish Colonial Frontier Research*, Roberta Greenwood reviewed Chartkoff and Chartkoff's *The Archaeology of California*, Priscilla Wegars reviewed the first issue of the *Australian Journal of Historical Archaeology*, Ann Morgan Smart reviewed Diana Roussel's book on the Castleford pottery, Georgeanna Greer reviewed a special issue of *Winterthur Portfolio* devoted to marketing of ceramics, and Olive Jones reviewed *Glass and Archaeology.*

Volume 20, no. 2 had two articles by women, on historical land use (Mary Beaudry) and contrasting patterns of faunal remains on urban vs. rural sites (Elizabeth Reitz); a third article on estimates of vessel "populations" from minimum vessel counts by George L. Miller included an appendix by Meridith Moodey. Carrel Cowan-Ricks reviewed *Exploring Buried Buxton*; Rochelle Marrinan reviewed Deagan's *Spanish St. Augustine*; Mary Beaudry reviewed a bibliography of seventeenth-century Chesapeake archaeology; and Kathleen Deagan reviewed *Historical Archaeology of the Eastern United States*, edited by Neuman.

Volume 21, no. 1 (1987) had eight articles. The articles by women authors dealt with burials from the Santa Barbara Presidio chapel (Julia Costello and Phillip Walker), bottle reuse (Jane Busch), and an unusual pipestem from Maryland (Julia King and Dennis Pogue). Roberta Greenwood reviewed Felton and Schulz's *The Diaz Collection*, Priscilla Wegars reviewed a site report on a Chinese laundry, and Kathryn Lang reviewed *Remember Thou Art Dust*.

Suzanne Spencer-Wood's lead article presented an overview of domestic reform movement sites in Boston and Cambridge in Volume 21, no. 2. Julia King and Henry Miller discussed midden analysis of plow zone contexts, and Eugene Hattori and Marna Thompson wrote about dendrochronological analysis on mining sites in Nevada. Carol Ruppé reviewed a bibliography of underwater archaeology, and Julia Curtis reviewed Petersen's *Mackinac and the Porcelain City*. Spencer-Wood's article represents the first appearance in the journal of an explicitly feminist approach to historical archaeology.

In 1989 only one of the dozen articles published in Volume 22, no. 1 was by a woman, Kathleen Deagan's "Neither History nor Prehistory: The Questions That Count in Historical Archaeology." It was part of the plenary session for the 1987 SHA meetings. Apart from standing out as the sole woman-authored piece among the articles in this issue, Deagan's essay takes on added significance as one of *only two* articles that can be counted as "theoretical" position statements by women appearing in the journal between 1967 and 1990. This issue contained a very large number of book reviews and women reviewers. (Here we have the lone instance of a woman junior author of a book review: William and Nancy Buckles's review of a catalog of lighting devices from the Parks Canada collections). Cynthia Price reviewed a report on historical settlement in Missouri, Carol Ruppé reviewed Ward's edited volume, *Forgotten Places and Things*, Evelyn Tidlow reviewed *Mortuary Variability*, Donna Seifert reviewed Lister and Lister's work on sixteenth century maiolica in the Valley of Mexico, Priscilla Wegars reviewed two books on bottles, and Kathleen Gilmore reviewed Hoover and Costello's report on their excavations at Mission San Antonio.

Volume 22, no. 2 was a special theme issue devoted to research on the seventeenth-century Chesapeake, compiled and edited by Henry Miller and Julia King; it contained five articles as well as a brief introduction by Miller and King; Julia King's comparative midden analysis of two sites in St. Mary's City was the only contribution authored by a woman. In this issue, a 27 percent frequency of citation of work by women is relatively high and no doubt reflects the strong contribution women scholars such as Lorena Walsh, Barbara Carson, and Lois Carr have made in the areas of economic and material history of the Chesapeake. Susan Henry reviewed a report on excavations at the Lincoln home site.

Most of Volume 23, no. 1 comprised a set of papers on landscape archaeology compiled by Faith Harrington, who contributed an article on the Sherburne houselot in Portsmouth, New Hampshire, in addition to a very brief introduction to the papers. Other papers with women authors included an analysis of the built environment in Lowell (Mary Beaudry), the landscape of Jack London's "beauty ranch" (Adrian Praetzellis and Mary Praetzellis), comments on the landscape papers (Patricia Rubertone), and an analysis of ceramics and status on plantation sites (William Adams and Sarah Boling). Mary Beaudry reviewed Fitzhugh's *Cultures in Contact,* Judith Liu reviewed Lydon's *Chinese Gold: The Chinese in the Monterey Bay Region,* and Olga Klimko reviewed Kenyon's *History of James Bay.*

The articles with women authors in Volume 23, no. 2 were varied in subject matter: pewter as missing artifact (Ann Martin), Spanish colonial wineries of Peru (Prudence Rice and Greg Smith), seed analysis on historical sites (Naomi Miller), wealth and status in northeastern Missouri (Michael O'Brien and Teresita Majewski), faunal remains from antebellum Arkansas (Leslie Stewart-Abernathy and Barbara Ruff), and computer-assisted artifact illustration (William Adams and Sarah Boling). Mary Beaudry reviewed two California site reports; Ann Martin reviewed Charlotte Wilcoxen's book on Dutch ceramics in seventeenth century North America; and Carol Ruppé reviewed Catherine Sullivan's publication on artifacts from the wreck of the *Machault.*

The 1990s opened with another expansion in the journal; beginning with Volume 24, *Historical Archaeology* became a quarterly. The move to quarterly publication was viewed by the SHA Board of Directors as evidence that the field was reaching maturity; submissions to the journal were growing steadily, and the practice initiated in 1987 of soliciting entire symposia from the annual meetings was paying off with publication of "theme" issues (Volume 22, no. 2) or parts of issues (as in Volume 22, no. 1 and Volume 23, no. 1). The transition to four numbers could not be effected wholly through new submissions or solicitation of groups of papers, however, so the Editorial Advisory Board moved to incorporate the Society's annual Special Publication series into the quarterly format while maintaining separate publication of its other series (proceedings of the underwater archaeology papers from the SHA annual meetings and the archaeology of the immigrant experience bibliographies) and readers.

Volume 24, no. 1 had 7 articles. Charles Cheek and Amy Friedlander wrote about ceramics and faunal analysis in interpreting ethnicity and the use of space in late nineteenth and early twentieth century Washington, DC, Gerald Kelso and Mary Beaudry reported on

results of pollen analysis in Boston, Elizabeth Honeysett and Peter
Schulz discussed seeds from a site in Sacramento, and Nan Rothschild
published a memorial to Bert Salwen. Olive Jones's *Cylindrical English
Wine and Beer Bottles* was the only book reviewed that was authored by a
woman.

In Volume 24, no. 2 there were 14 articles. Six of the articles are
grouped thematically as "Methodological Approaches to Assessing the
Archaeological Significance of Historic Sites." These are essays with
far-flung ramifications for all practitioners in the field. All the essays,
however, are by male authors. The implications of this fact will be
drawn out in the concluding section. Articles by women dealt with site
abandonment behavior (Susan Kent), identification of a group of cannon (Pandora Snethkamp et al.), and gunflints (Nancy Kenmotsu).

Volume 24, no. 3 contained Anne Yentsch's "Minimum Vessel Lists
as Evidence of Change in Folk and Courtly Traditions of Food Use."
Yentsch cited 166 sources, 76 by women. Mary Beaudry reviewed
Leone and Potter's edited book, *The Recovery of Meaning*.

Volume 24, no. 4 was a special issue edited by Charles Orser, Jr.,
Historical Archaeology on Southern Plantations and Farms, and contained
10 articles and an introduction by Orser. Doreen Cooper was junior
author with Kenneth Brown for "Structural Continuity in an African-
American Slave and Tenant Community"; Linda Stine wrote "Social
Inequality and Turn-of-the-Century Farmsteads: Issues of Class, Sta-
tus, Ethnicy, and Race"; Shawn Carlson, "The Persistence of Traditional Lifeways in Central Texas"; Claudia Holland, "Tenant Farms of
the Past, Present, and Future: An Ethnoarchaeological View"; Theresa
Singleton "The Archaeology of the Plantation South: A Review of
Approaches and Goals"; Jean Howson, "Social Relations and Material
Culture: A Critique of the Archaeology of Plantation Slavery"; and
Amy Friedlander, "Beyond Regionalism: History, Archaeology, and
the Future." By any measure, women make substantial and substantive
contributions in this volume. The citation pattern is therefore especially interesting; one might predict that women authors will cite more
sources by women (based on the reasonable assumption that, at the
very least, they would cite their own work even if it is not being cited by
others). They do not (Table 2).

It is not safe to assume that women will break the pattern and cite
their sisters more frequently than do men. Yentsch is singlehandedly
responsible for bringing the citation of women's work up to the level of
34 percent in Volume 24, no. 3, and Spencer-Wood cites the majority of
works by women in Volume 21, no. 2. There is another pattern of
interest, however, that emerges informally from the raw data: women

authors appear, on the average, to cite more sources than do men authors.[9] Does this means that women writers are drawing on a broader range of material than their male counterparts? Could it indicate that women have less confidence and go to greater lengths to support their statements by citing more sources? It is difficult to tell without closer examination of the data and perhaps careful consideration of whether certain topics on which women publish (foodways and culinary history, for example) have far larger bodies of literature than topics on which men are more likely to publish, although this is certainly not the case with military sites. It is also apparent that the field has grown quite rapidly since 1967 with the founding of the journal *Historical Archaeology*—the literature in historical archaeology has expanded to the point where it is difficult for anyone to keep up with it— one result is longer reference lists in articles appearing in the journal.

Summary and Some Observations

In 24 years of publication, female authors of articles and book reviews in *Historical Archaeology* increased from 0 in 1967 to one-third in 1977, to about one-half in the late 1980s; in 1990, 23 (48%) out of 47 articles and reviews were by women.

In 1977 one-eighth of citations were to works by women; this improved to one-third in 1987. Women cited other women more than men cited women, but this could result from the fact that women authors cite more sources on average than male authors do. The topic of an article had a decided effect on how many women were cited (cf. Lutz 1990; see also Gero 1991b). In historical archaeology, the areas in which women have published most are ceramic analysis, bead research, and other artifact studies, as well as urban archaeology, faunal analysis, and paleoethnobotany (Victor and Beaudry 1992:17, 21 and Figure 12). Citation patterns in any materials analysis field can be tricky to decipher; specialists often feel no need to cite work in their area (topically or geographically) if the analytical methods employed by other researchers are not directly comparable to their own. Other

9. Admittedly it is difficult to use the data in their present form to support this directly. The observation is based on the clear evidence that in an average journal issue containing 7 articles, the higher the proportion of women authors to men, the greater the total number of references cited. Even though we have presented here only the totals, we do have the raw counts broken down by article/author for all issues except Vol. 24, no. 4, which has all the references grouped at the end, so there is no way of tracing citation patterns without checking back and forth between the reference list and each article. This is especially frustrating given that women are so well represented as authors in this issue.

studies hence may be perceived as irrelevant even if to the non-specialist they seem to be on the same topic.[10] Such an attitude (in the humble opinion of the authors) serves only to justify the further politicization of the already treacherous area of citation practices.

Published work by women can be given recognition and legitimacy by review in a journal's book review section, even if the review is not a positive one. What gets reviewed, however, is not controlled by the authors of works, but results from selections made by the book review editor among works sent by publishers and authors for review and depends upon reviewers actually producing the reviews (not all prospective reviewers fulfill their obligation). From 1967 to 1990, a total of 331 works were reviewed in *Historical Archaeology*; of these, 79 had a woman as sole, senior, co-, or junior author (the latter two categories being more frequent). Thus just under one-fourth of the total number of works reviewed had women authors. While this is perhaps a lower ratio of female : male publication than one might wish (especially given the greater than one-third representation of women among the SHA membership), it is a higher proportion of females to males than that for publication in the journal itself. What is more, it is higher than the ratio of female to male book reviewers (54 women out of a total of 313 reviewers, or 18%) during the journal's first 24 years. The works by women that were reviewed were, for the most part, monograph site reports or artifact studies, and perhaps indicate that women working in historical archaeology have concentrated more on careful data gathering and reporting than on writing topical articles and thought pieces. Or it may reflect anxiety over peer review, though it is clear that there is great variability in review of monograph reports before they are published.

Many women published in conjunction with men, and, in the early years, appeared far more often as junior than as senior authors when there was more than one author. Our figures show that about one-fourth of the time women contributed journal articles they were listed as junior authors and, of the total works with women authors cited in all articles, 30–50 percent of such citations list a woman or women as junior authors. We did not examine issues of collaboration and mentorship closely in this study; we only looked at how often women who co-authored were listed as junior author. There are certainly more constructive ways to approach this matter in order to address questions of how women get their work into print. How often do mentors (male or female) provide student authors with their first opportunity to pub-

---

10. At least this is the rationale Beaudry in her role as editor (of two books and the journal *Northeast Historical Archaeology*) has been offered on several occasions.

lish? How frequent is collaboration between men and women versus among women? How often are women independent authors/researchers? Do some women reach this stage only after initial efforts at collaboration? Counting instances of junior authorship as a percentage of total publications by women did not permit us to answer these questions, but such a count could permit us to address them, and other questions, in the future.

Returning to our opening discussion of how so many have the impression that historical archaeology, with its undeniable links to and firm roots in the historic preservation movement, is a welcoming and open field for women, our findings surprise us a bit. One is tempted to draw the conclusion that Woodall and Perricone's desire for historic preservation to take on a more macho image has come to pass as we note with some dismay the absence of women authors among the essays on site significance that appear in Volume 24, no. 2, of *Historical Archaeology*. Even if women are employed in CRM archaeology in great numbers and are highly visible in some regards, if publication implies or confers "authority," they and their potential contributions have been left out in this instance.

We suspect that there is a lingering ambivalence about the relationship between historical archaeology and historic preservation. Anyone involved in preservation-oriented archaeology soon becomes aware that it is anything but a passive pursuit for hobbyists and do-gooders. But the image of "little old ladies in tennis shoes" persists, it seems, despite the fact that the movers and shakers in the CRM field are mostly men.

It would be facile to attribute the *initial* lack of publications by women in *Historical Archaeology* directly and solely to the sex/gender system at work in mid-twentieth-century North America. This system maintains a gender hierarchy that consistently and systematically undervalues the work and skills of women (see Gero 1985). While it does *seem* that women have often been shunted into non-fieldwork activities—the women's work of historical archaeology is not unlike the "women's work" of prehistoric archaeology: faunal analysis, artifact identification and classification (e.g., glass and glass beads, ceramic typologies, etc.), botanical analysis—these "housekeeping" activities are critical to the field.[11] Artifact analyses are far from the sole province of women. The troubling point is that a great deal of very basic, foundation-laying work done by women (and by men) often does not

11. It should be noted that in a recent survey of the SHA membership, women reported "fieldwork" more frequently than any other task they performed as part of their jobs (Chester, Rothschild, and Wall 1992).

get cited. It is, however, particularly galling that in our field, historical research often gets ranked with the housewifely chores. Site reports by women are few and far between; articles on theory are rare indeed. Nevertheless, our content analysis of the journal reveals that women have published fairly frequently and have made some important contributions through the work they publish in the journal, all the more impressive when we consider just how few women members of SHA submit manuscripts for review.

Admittedly the editorial policy of the journal affects what gets published:[12] *Historical Archaeology* has never published much in the way of theory, and the yardstick for publication is "is it archaeological enough?" Hence much of the work by women who have not specialized in fieldwork may not get published unless it either relates directly to someone else's fieldwork (by classifying, and/or analyzing artifacts, plant, or animal remains from a site), or is likely to be of general but nevertheless direct use in artifact identification and classification. Other areas in which women archaeologists are especially active, such as public education and historic preservation, have a tidy fit with the ideals of the sex/gender system but seem to provide fewer publication opportunities and hence are devalued in academic arenas and, we suspect, in the discipline at large.

Truth be told, women cannot be published if women do not submit articles for review. Ronald Michael, editor of *Historical Archaeology*, kindly provided those data on submissions he had available, which cover 1988 through early 1991.[13] Sixty-seven manuscripts were submitted for review over a 39-month period. Of these, twenty-one (31%) had a female as senior author. After the review process was complete, five articles with female senior authors and 14 manuscripts with male senior authors had been rejected. The figures reveal that during this period women submitted manuscripts for review one-third as often as did men, and that these were rejected 24 percent of the time as opposed to an approximate 30 percent rejection rate for male-as-senior-author manuscripts. It is clear that work by women is reviewed favorably in about 3 out of 4 cases; one cannot claim that the journal fosters a

12. It is not altogether clear what the overall effect of editorial policy, explicit or otherwise, might have on either rate of submission or rate of publication by women. At least one woman author reports withdrawing an article accepted for publication because she was asked to eliminate use of the first person. She noted that she did not view herself as a radical feminist, but that she was talking about her own conclusions, based on her own research, and could not bring herself to objectify her work by use of passive voice or impersonal constructions. See Young-Bruehl 1991 for a general discussion of this topic vis á vis feminist scholarship.

13. Letter to Mary Beaudry from Ronald L. Michael, March 27, 1991. Michael further reports that up to 50 manuscripts may have been in limbo (returned for revision less than 18 months previously, considered dead but not officially declared so) or in copy editing and do not show up in the figures presented here.

"chilly climate" for women.[14] The main reason their work appears less often than work by men is that it is submitted far less often. What is more, a slight discrepancy in the rate of return after an author has been asked to revise a manuscript reveals another factor contributing to women's lower frequency of publication: of 16 manuscripts accepted pending revision, three women authors failed to revise after 18 months with 81 percent resubmitting, while 27 of 32 male authors (84%), resubmitted. This discrepancy appears very small based on these figures, but it may reflect a broader pattern[15] in which women who have worked up the courage to submit a manuscript find the (usually anonymous) review process less than congenial.

We have noted that demographics cannot account for the disparity in frequency of publication by men and by women in historical archaeology's major journal. While there are more men than women historical archaeologists holding academic posts, the number of academic slots occupied by bona fide historical archaeologists is minuscule. Hence academic, tenure-related pressure to "publish or perish" cannot explain women historical archaeologists' low rate of manuscript submission. The approximate 30 percent submission rate is very close to parity for females if looked at in terms of total manuscripts the journal reviews. In terms of total SHA membership (see Table 1), however, both males and females submit manuscripts in shockingly small numbers; if we average the membership totals for the years 1988–1990 (the years for which we have manuscript submission figures), we learn that 0.01 percent of the female membership submitted articles during this time period, as opposed to 2.75 percent of the male membership. Articles by women comprised only 17 percent of the total number published in the journal from 1967–1990.

A study of women's research performance in the sciences, reported in *Scientific American* (Cole and Zuckerman 1987), revealed that, overall, women publish less than their male counterparts regardless of their family situation, professional status, etc. (married women publish as much as their unmarried female colleagues do, but neither publish as much as men). It seems likely that, whatever the reason, this condition obtains in historical archaeology: that is, up until quite recently, women

14. Results of the SHA membership survey support the conclusion that the "attempt rate" for women is considerably below that for men; women and men who do submit manuscripts for publication both report a high rate of "success," however (see Chester, Rothschild, and Wall 1992).

15. A pattern observed by Beaudry as a journal editor: women seem more likely to perceive an acceptance with request for extensive revision as tantamount to a rejection. Males are more likely to question the reviewers' judgement and return the manuscript indicating they've revised as much as they intend to and express to the editor in quite vivid terms their objections to reviewers' criticisms. Women who've gotten the hang of the publishing game behave similarly.

historical archaeologists have sought to publish less often than males in the SHA journal and elsewhere (although see Deagan 1989) by submitting fewer manuscripts for review and hence have not been represented in print in proportion to their numbers in the field.

We conclude that women in historical archaeology, would-be cowboys or otherwise, have found in historical archaeology a climate somewhat less chilly than that for women in other fields and other areas of archaeology (cf. Wylie and Backhouse 1991). Not everything is perfect and the situation can improve. But improvement along the lines of women's publication has to be a bootstrap operation. It should be of concern to both men and women that publication—communication with professional colleagues of one's work and one's ideas—is not at the very core of our identity as historical archaeologists. If it were, both men and women would publish more often, and, what's more, many more voices would be heard. Or, at least we hope they will be heard. Citation practices are also a matter of concern and are another area where what is needed is a conscious effort to take all relevant work into account in preparing one's own manuscripts while taking care to avoid the pitfall of padding a reference list or relying on a well-worn handful of prominent, oft-cited sources.

It is altogether possible that via the 1991 and 1992 volumes of _Historical Archaeology_ the journal (and, presumably, the field as a whole) has entered a new era that will result in a steady increase in publication by women historical archaeologists. A special issue on gender (Volume 25, no. 4), edited by Donna J. Seifert, and another on postprocessual approaches to material culture analysis in historical archaeology (Volume 26, no. 3), edited by Barbara J. Little and Paul A. Shackel, together offer a range of new approaches to historical archaeology. The very fact that the journal is increasingly open to the exploration of themes arising out of post-modernist thought and critique may be an indication of further changes to come.

Acknowledgments

This article originated in a class paper by Jacquelyn White (White 1990) and was revised and expanded by Beaudry. It has gone through at least two incarnations as a conference paper, having been presented at the 1991 meetings of the Society for Historical Archaeology and in expanded form at the 1992 American Anthropological Association meetings. We thank Julia Costello and Ronald Michael for providing figures on SHA membership and manuscript submissions. We could not have established a context for our analysis without their help. We also thank Cheryl Claassen for her careful and constructive editing.

Chapter 11
Women in Mesoamerican Archaeology: Why Are the Best Men Winning?

Anabel Ford

Having achieved my majority amidst the active women's movement of the 1970s and having participated, if only vicariously, in a number of women's "encounter" groups in college, I was turned off by the nature of discussions and the expression of anger. I was aware of the issues and concerns of the women's movement (Degler 1981), but I could not relate to it. I felt that any issue of women specifically should be an issue of gender generally. Besides, it appeared to me that the increased awareness of women's issues was, indeed, resulting in progress. Affirmative action was coming to campuses (cf. Menges and Exum 1983) and there was hope in the future. Believing in the ideals of democracy, I knew that I would succeed by doing the best job I could. If I did not succeed, I just was not doing my best. That was two decades ago. I plodded forward isolated from the reality that any issue of gender was an issue of equality for women.

The background data I synthesize on the status of women in academia demonstrate how false my perceptions were and provide the necessary basis for a more detailed examination of the status of women in Mesoamerican archaeology as represented in the American Anthropological Association *Guide to Departments* (1989). While one can present figures that demonstrate significant progress, the stark reality is that women are underrepresented, underemployed, and underutilized in almost every aspect of the academic setting. The data on women in academia supporting these conclusions are overwhelming.

In examining this problem, it is important to consider the barriers to and constraints on a more equitable distribution of women in academia (Menges and Exum 1983). Obviously, the availability (or unavailability as the case may be) of faculty positions in North America continues to be a significant *first* obstacle to the representation of women on university and college faculties, as a review of the advertised archaeology positions in the *Anthropology Newsletter* over the past decades can demonstrate. So, while women have been an increasing fraction of the Ph.D. pool in all fields of the social sciences, including Mesoamerican archaeology, the number of available positions in the last two decades has not followed the same pace.

But there certainly are other factors at work in the under-utilization of women academics. To address these factors, I fielded a questionnaire that solicited basic information on career, research, and personal issues that, in combination, could isolate the constraints on women's careers in Mesoamerican archaeology. The constraints and barriers to academic women's career progress inevitably relate to their other roles in life, such as spouse and parent. Yet these other roles need not be the constraint they are perceived to be. Since women are the minority in academia, it is increasingly clear to me that the essential and ideal goal of equality can only be achieved through women's united voice.

Visibility of Women in Academia

Since the dawn of affirmative action in the United States two decades ago, major changes can be seen in the visibility of women in academia, particularly in the proportion of students seeking college and post-graduate education. The number of Ph.D.s awarded to women has more than doubled, although today they represent around 40 percent of all Ph.D.s in the social sciences (Chamberlain 1988:227; Simeone 1987:29). Despite the increasing pool of women Ph.D.s, women are still outnumbered on faculties 3:1 and 5:1 at research universities (Simeone 1987:31; see also Menges and Exum 1983). The gap widens as one moves up the ladder (Table 1) and the implication is that women tend not to advance in the system (Chamberlain 1988:215–217; Menges and Exum 1983:124, 139). Chamberlain's field-by-field survey demonstrated that women were well represented at the assistant professor level, but their rate of promotion was 25 to 50 percent lower than that of their male counterparts. The harshest cases are characteristic of the top research universities (Chamberlain 1988:214). This finding brings into question attitudes at hiring. When a department hires a woman, is it to fulfill Affirmative Action mandates and create a "revolving door" where there is no real consideration of promotion (Simeone 1987:33), or are women falling short on their own merit? Evidence suggests that the latter is far from the case (see Chamberlain 1988:209–213).

TABLE 1. Proportion of Ladder Faculty at Teaching Colleges and Research Universities in the United States (after Chamberlain 1988:56)

	Assistant professor	Associate professor	Full professor	N
Total	32%	32%	36%	353,359
Women	51%	31%	18%	78,377
Men	28%	32%	41%	274,982
Proportion of women to men at colleges and universities				
Number	113,330	111,887	128,142	
Women	35%	22%	11%	
Men	65%	78%	89%	

Advancing within the system is dependent on a number of factors, but research and publication stand prominently among the criteria (Astin and Bayer 1979). While the number of articles published by women in social science rose from 16 to 24 percent between the late 1960s and 1970s (Simeone 1987:55), it appears that, overall, women tend to publish fewer articles than men (Astin and Bayer 1979; Simeone 1987:37). But this statistic should not be taken at face value.

More recent studies are illuminating. Productivity, as measured by publication, increases with rank, regardless of sex (Chamberlain 1988: 265–266). Furthermore, while the number of publications by men was *slightly* greater than that of women, the productivity of married women, especially in the social sciences, exceeded that of single women of any rank (Chamberlain 1988:266). Thus the long-held perception that marriage inhibits productivity among women is false.

Other factors also must come into play. Productivity is affected by the research atmosphere, access to support, and the availability of research assistants. Whether one is at a research university or at a teaching college is relevant to research and publication. It goes without saying that research universities foster research productivity while teaching colleges concentrate on teaching. It is not surprising, then, that women may be less productive in the publication arena as their numbers are greater in the teaching setting by at least 10 percent (Simeone 1987:31).

There is another serious dimension that needs to be addressed: unemployed or under-employed Ph.D.s. Either state seems to be the cumulative effect of a long-term trend of career deflection from the normal academic track (Aisenberg and Harrington 1988). The trajectory of attrition among women is high all along the academic course, beginning with college graduates (Table 2).

Once in graduate school, women make up some 50 percent of the graduate students. There is a 25 percent attrition among women be-

TABLE 2. Students Continuing in Postgraduate Studies (after Simeone 1987:8)

	"A" grade average	"B" grade average
Women	47%	22%
Men	70%	45%

tween graduate school matriculation and the achievement of the Ph.D. Further loss from 20 to 50 percent occurs in the move from Ph.D. into the professional academic setting. What accounts for this attrition or deflection from the traditional academic career track? While some fields may be growing, it is not the case in the social sciences. If faculties are not growing, then there will be few opportunities to hire anyone, man or woman. The lack of growth, however, does not adequately explain the whole picture.

Research has demonstrated that a higher proportion of women Ph.D.s are unemployed than are men Ph.D.s (Simeone 1987:120–122). While there were a variety of reasons cited for unemployment, 57 percent of the women indicated that family commitments restricted employment while *none* of the men referred to such commitments as causes of unemployment (Simeone 1987:121). Although personal commitments of women in academia tend to inhibit development of their careers, women still continue to maintain links with their profession (Aisenberg and Harrington 1988). The maintenance of professional ties is significant, because it demonstrates that there is a clear commitment to their academic career.

The Status of Women in Mesoamerican Archaeology

Do women Mesoamerican archaeologists in academic settings reflect or defy the generalities just presented? In evaluating the status of women in the subdiscipline of Mesoamerican archaeology, I created a database from the *AAA Guide to Departments* and flagged individuals listing Mesoamerican archaeology among their specialties. Positions listed in the current *AAA Guide* include regular ladder (tenure track) faculty and affiliated adjunct and research faculty, as well as public sector archaeologists. I also reviewed and tabulated the dissertation titles in Mesoamerican archaeology for the last decade, as listed in the *AAA Guides* (1979–1989). These combined efforts provided the background data on proportions of women and men Ph.D.s in Mesoamerican archaeol-

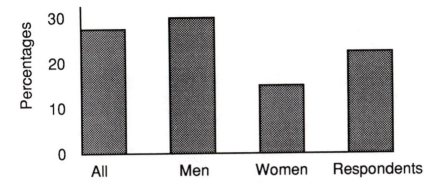

Figure 1. Percentage of Mesoamerican archaeologists affiliated with top-30 institutions.

ogy over the last decade and the representation of women and men in Mesoamerican archaeology on faculties today.

Mesoamerican archaeology is a robust subfield and is widely represented at academic institutions. There are 216 individuals in the *AAA Guides* listing some aspect of Mesoamerican archaeology as their focus; of these, 77 percent are males and 23 percent are females. These proportions are comparable to the representation of all women in academia (Chamberlain 1988:59).

From this exercise, it was immediately evident that women are still a distinct minority in the profession, even though their proportional representation has increased over the years. Moreover, the representation of women on faculties drops from 23 percent to only 17 percent when top universities are considered alone (Figure 1). This difference is even greater when one considers that 50 percent of women in Mesoamerican archaeology are affiliated and not ladder faculty. This figure of affiliated faculty women is 60 percent greater than that for affiliated faculty men (Figure 2).

These data become even more depressing when we consider the positions held by Ph.D.s of the last decade. Of the 106 Ph.Ds. granted to archaeologists specializing in Mesoamerica between 1979 and 1989, 40 percent were awarded to women (Figure 3). Further, of those women, only 48 percent were listed in the 1989 *AAA Guide*, and less than 25 percent of them were in ladder faculty positions (Figure 3), a figure lower than the representation of women in ladder faculty positions in the early 1960s (Bernard 1964:214)! These percentages are quite different for the same cohort of men (Figure 3). Fifty-nine per-

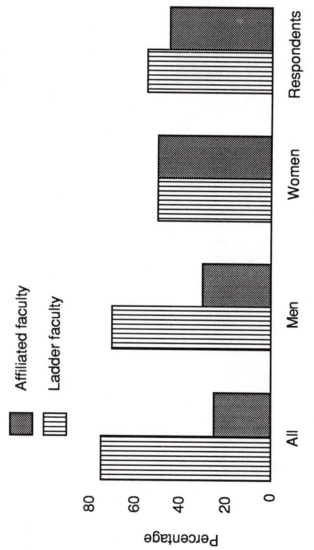

Figure 2. Distribution of faculty positions in Mesoamerican archaeology (percent).

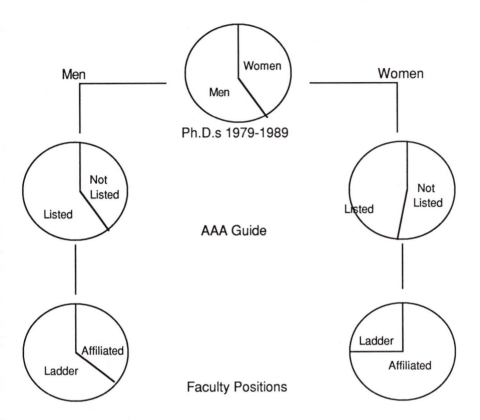

Figure 3. Ph.D.s in Mesoamerican archaeology, 1979–1989.

cent of the graduates from that decade are listed in the 1989 *AAA Guide*
and 74 percent of them are in ladder positions. So, while women are
increasing their visibility, their numbers are not significantly increasing
in the desired ladder tracks (cf. Menges and Exum 1983). In fact, when
considering Ph.Ds of the last decade, only 15 percent of *all* ladder
positions are occupied by women; this is their representation from the
40 percent availability pool (Figure 3). Thus, while the ratio of women
to men Ph.Ds over the last decade is 2:3, the representation of the same
group of women on ladder faculties is 1:6! Indeed, it appears that it is
by their own tenacity that women are visible at all.

All women listed in the *AAA Guide* who indicated a Mesoamerican
archaeology specialty were sent a questionnaire soliciting information
on their career, research, and personal background. Included with the
questionnaire was a list of all the women in the *AAA Guide* as well as
women with dissertation titles focusing on Mesoamerica who were

missing from the 1989 *AAA Guide,* in an attempt to locate them. A number of women who obtained Ph.D.s in the last decade were "found" in this manner and sent questionnaires. Thirty-seven women answered the survey.

The questionnaire was designed to collect data that could be compared with more general studies of women in academia (Acker 1977; Aisenberg and Harrington 1988; Bernard 1964; Chamberlain 1988; Itow 1989; Kramer and Stark 1988; Menges and Exum 1983; Simeone 1987). In addition, the questions were set up to go beyond and somewhat deeper than usual in surveys in an effort to isolate issues that were often left unexplored. The questionnaire itself was two pages long. Most questions were relatively simple to answer and concerned basic facts about career, research, and domestic life. In each major category there were questions about perceptions and feelings; they are important data as they track relationships between career, research, and domestic arenas. Queries were included on compromises, effects of gender, acceptance by colleagues, meeting attendance, proposal submission, grants, awards, and types of publications. The pool of questions provided a balance between feelings and facts, and these two realms can be compared with each other to illuminate the common paths of different women.

The return rate for the questionnaire was overwhelming, as if this was something long-awaited. There was greater than an 80 percent return within one month from a single mailing in September 1989. There was good representation in all categories of affiliated and ladder faculty distributed differentially over the generations of scholars (1980s Ph.D.s, 65%; 1970s Ph.D.s, 30%; 1960s Ph.D.s, 7%), the younger and largest generation being the most responsive to my probing. The majority of my respondents were in ladder positions. (Some faculty in research and adjunct positions were not in residence at their listed institutional affiliations and so were prevented from responding by the deadline.)

There was considerable interest in the issues raised in the questionnaire, and there was an effort to explain aspects of certain responses. In many ways, the response was like a flood-gate opening. I got the kind of return one could only hope for, far above the normal expected return of 10 to 20 percent. Furthermore, there was a real interest in the questions, and respondents made an effort to amplify and explain answers rather than to demur. The fullness of the responses gives me confidence in the results. The results of the questionnaire are at once predictable and surprising, sobering and heartening.

The Respondents: Women in Mesoamerican Archaeology

The women in Mesoamerican archaeology who participated in the survey come from Canada, the United States, and Mexico, and almost all of them have been educated in the United States. They are women who got their degrees between 1967 and 1989, with a median age of 31 at the time of the Ph.D award. This average age is younger than the median age (33) of women Ph.Ds in 1969 (Bernard 1964:113) as well as the median age (35) in 1986 (Chamberlain 1988:257). Three-quarters of the Ph.D.s (78%) came from the top 30 universities as listed in Kramer and Stark (1988).

The personal profile of these women tells one chapter of their story (Figure 4). While over three-quarters (76%) of the group have long-term commitments to a partner, less than half (44%) have no children. Data from the early 1960s showed that only 48 percent of women in academia were married (Bernard 1964:113), and in the mid-1970s, 46 percent of women in academia had children (Acker 1977:288). Interestingly, more than four-fifths (82%) of the partners were in tenured positions in 1989, suggesting a mutual understanding of career commitments. Even so, family commitments weighed heavily on these women, as almost three-quarters (73%) felt that personal commitments affected their career, about half felt that they had compromised their careers for personal reasons (54%), and almost half felt that geography played a major role in career decisions (49%). Data collected in the 1970s showed that 67 percent of the academic women surveyed had a "spouse-first" orientation (Acker 1977) while the surveys of Whittlesey (1991 and this volume) from 1991 and 1992 show that these concerns are shared by women archaeologists in general.

These perceived constraints have obvious impacts on women's careers and have an underlying association with the high proportion of women in affiliated faculty positions. The constraints also illustrate why many women are under- or unemployed (Aisenberg and Harrington 1982; Simeone 1987:121) or sought non-academic positions (Whittlesey, this volume). Despite the identified obstacles, almost three-quarters of the women in Mesoamerican archaeology (73%) are in the same position they were at the time of their Ph.D. award, be it a ladder or affiliated position. A large majority are satisfied with their jobs (72%) and 51 percent are holding positions that were directly related to their Ph.D.s.

Career progress in academia is largely measured through research

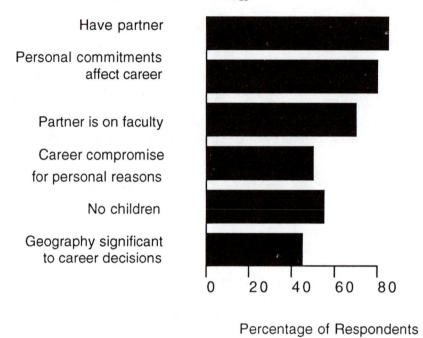

Have partner

Personal commitments
affect career

Partner is on faculty

Career compromise
for personal reasons

No children

Geography significant
to career decisions

0   2 0   4 0   6 0   8 0

Percentage of Respondents

Figure 4. Profile of respondents' personal data.

and publication, although teaching and service activities are relevant as
well. There has been a general perception that women publish less
than do men (Astin and Bayer 1979; Simeone 1978:37; Beaudry and
White, this volume), and that publication is linked to the many demands that women have on their time outside their careers. While
more recent research suggests that this is not so obviously the case
(Chamberlain 1988:266), it must be borne in mind that women comprise a higher proportion of the teaching college faculties than of the
research university faculties (Simeone 1987:46) thus reducing time for
participation in research and publication and doing both without research assistants. Such is also the case among Mesoamerican archaeologists, where 17 percent of all women faculty are in positions at the top
30 universities (Figure 1) and 36 percent are at colleges where only
a BA is offered. These figures include ladder and affiliated faculty
women. The percentage of women at the top 30 universities drops to
10 percent if only ladder faculty are included, only a third of the
proportion of faculty men at the top 30 universities (Figure 1).

These data have immediate impact on the education of future Mesoamerican archaeologists (cf. Moore 1982; Rich 1986; Speizer 1981).

Women are more visible in settings that are focused on undergraduate programs and less visible as role models and mentors to the majority of Ph.D students in their subfield. Seventy-six percent of the Ph.D.s in Mesoamerican archeology come from the top 30 universities where women represent only 10 percent of the ladder faculty. National agencies, such as the National Science Foundation, have recognized this problem and have promoted target programs for women, including the prestigious Visiting Professorship for Women program. Promoting visiting professorships, however, is merely a transient measure, effective only during the term of the grant, and does not solve the problem.

When examining the proportions of women and men Mesoamerican archaeologists, the case of underrepresentation of women is most obvious. Hiring is the first major obstacle. Despite their nearly equal representation in the Ph.D. pool over the last decade, they are significantly underrepresented among the ladder positions at universities and colleges (Figure 2). Since the selection process is dominated by men, it is not difficult to see that women could have problems at hiring. Examples of the subtle prejudices that women candidates can face is epitomized in an explanation one woman received after she was not selected for a position at a prominent university. A committee member stated that the interview dinner with the male candidate "was so comfortable and easy." It is no surprise that a search committee of several men would be more at ease with a man than a woman. How often might "ease with candidate" affect hiring?

Women Mesoamericanists are best represented at the assistant professor level, where there are two men for every one woman (2:1). The representation of women shifts dramatically with tenured positions where there are six men for each woman (6:1). These data mirror the distribution of women across disciplines in all of academia (Table 1). Women are being hired but are not making the same progress as men in moving up the ladder.

The lack of representation of women on faculties is a distinct disadvantage to women students. Basic opportunities that are theoretically available can be denied to them. Women archaeology students at one major university complained that while they represented half the graduate students and half the teaching assistant appointments, they were never afforded the opportunity to be TAs for introductory archaeology courses. The limited teaching opportunities in archaeology had been the case for over five years, even though there are two introductory courses taught each year and two teaching assistants each time the course was taught. They attributed this to the lack of women archaeologists on the faculty and to men tending to select men as TAs with whom to work. Another case example occurred when a student added a woman faculty member to her doctoral committee. She later encountered this committee member in the women's bathroom. The student was amazed at this chance meeting: "I had never met a faculty member in the bathroom before!" This chance meeting was her first informal encounter with a faculty member and, in an odd way, underscores the importance of role models and mentors in one's career (Speizer 1981).

The distribution of women between research universities and teaching colleges has an impact on women's participation in research and publication. Since graduate programs are integral to active research, teaching at an institution not offering advanced degrees is an obvious disadvantage that women face. Using the data presented on NSF funding of archaeology (e.g., Gero 1983, 1985; Kramer and Stark 1988; Yellen 1983) as one monitor of research activity indicates that women are having a difficult time getting research support. Only 34 percent of the surveyed women in Mesoamerican archaeology had received NSF support, but that represents two-thirds of those who had applied. These figures demonstrate how few women apply for and receive NSF support, but the proportions of this subset appear higher than the overall data (Yellen 1983:60–61). While a relatively small fraction of women surveyed had applied for and received funds from NSF, 94 percent have applied for intra- and other extramural grants (median 5 proposals) and 81 percent have been successful.

There has been the feeling that women are generally pushed toward the laboratory setting (Gero 1983, 1985). However, nearly all the women surveyed (97%) indicated that they participated in fieldwork as well as lab work. Further, an equal proportion of women indicated that they had been involved in fieldwork for their dissertations. There remain, however, some prejudices about women in the field, and several anecdotes are worth mentioning here. One woman in Mesoamerican archaeology mentioned that she had repeatedly had outside reviewers of NSF proposals question her qualifications as a fieldworker. In a different context, another Mesoamerican archaeologist revealed that one NSF review of her proposal had suggested that she obtain a Vietnam war veteran as a "body guard" while she was in the field. These comments are clearly uncalled for and irrelevant, and should be actively discouraged and dismissed.

Another major professional arena is that of publication. Based on my tabulation, the representation of women Mesoamerican archaeologists as authors over the last ten years in *American Antiquity* is only 16 percent of the total. This figure is lower than their representation on university and college faculties by one-third. Yet the data on Mesoamerican women in my survey suggest that they are deeply involved and active in disseminating research results. Nearly all have presented papers (median 8) and published articles (median 6) in the last five years. In addition, a great majority (78%) have unpublished manuscripts (median 3) on their current research. In sum, women in Mesoamerican archaeology (1) are active in research, (2) participate in professional meetings, and (3) publish their results. Furthermore, 87 percent perceive that their research and publication efforts are accepted. Thus, while compromises are freely acknowledged, they have not been seen as a brick wall because these women are clearly active participants in their profession.

A complex picture of women at work in Mesoamerican archaeology is presented by these data. On the one hand, women are a minority of all Mesoamerican archaeology faculty; they are a majority of the affiliated, as opposed to ladder, faculty (Figure 2); they are underrepresented at top research universities (Figure 1); and they represent only 15 percent of the ladder positions filled in the last decade. On the other hand, these women comprise a very intellectually active group. They are submitting research proposals, supporting field and laboratory studies, presenting results at meetings, and publishing articles and books. These professional activities have been undertaken despite the myriad of commitments and compromises these women face as they juggle their personal and career goals (Figure 4). These women present a strong statement on the status of women in general, and represent an inspiration for a united voice against discrimination and underutilization that must be heard.

Conclusions

We are reaching a new threshold on the issue of women in academia. While there have been major efforts to correct the blatant discrimination against women with Affirmative Action programs for hiring (cf. Menges and Exum 1983), more subtle and insidious discrimination remains essentially unchecked (Aisenberg and Harrington 1988). Judgment is generally more harsh at the hiring stage and promotion up the academic ladder is more difficult for women than for men (Chamberlain 1988). Protective devices focusing on aspects of research and publication can be used to promote objective standards for subjective decisions on competence and achievement, especially where women are concerned. Where 70 to 90 percent of the judging faculties are men, these subtle prejudices gain power. Academic women, including women in Mesoamerican archaeology, need to educate themselves on these facts and mobilize themselves to address these inequalities actively.

Women's networks can have a major impact on these subtle sources of prejudice and discrimination (Aisenberg and Harrington 1988; Simeone 1987). Such networks should function at the local level, such as the Affiliated Faculty Women at U. C. Santa Barbara, as well as at the national level, such as the American Association of University Women. In addition, such networks should be a part of national scholarly meetings—for example, the network meeting I organized at the 1989 Society for American Archaeology meetings in Atlanta, which grew out of an invitational Pushy Broads dinner group and has been followed annually by an open reception for women in archaeology. These networks should explicitly seek to include students to provide role models and promote the student-professional transition (Moore 1982; Speizer 1981). More than sharing information, ideas, and interests, a network of women archaeologists that would cross-cut schools and subfields could serve as a conduit for linking women in different universities and colleges into an advocacy group that could speak for the majority of women.

Acknowledgments

This paper was made possible only by the women in Mesoamerican archaeology who took time from their busy schedules to respond to my intrusive query. I have tried to present the data in an objective manner, but I am moved by my own status as a woman in Mesoamerican archaeology. Consequently, the interpretations and opinions expressed herein, while guided by my colleagues, are entirely my own.

Chapter 12
Male Hunting Camp or Female Processing Station? An Evolution Within a Discipline

Tracy Sweely

It takes a certain kind of person to endure the range of grueling conditions of archaeological fieldwork and analysis, to retain the passion for the meticulous acquisition of knowledge from the past. As I have discovered since my first field experience, it also takes a certain kind of *woman* to endure a specific brand of "grueling conditions" in order not only to retain that passion, but also to establish and maintain a unique and necessary perspective. The sexism women are subjected to in the field, in the lab, or in the office is very much a given in our society. But it is not an immutable given, for how we react to sexist behavior in the workplace can be an effective way to transcend it. To respond constructively is the responsibility of our generation of female scholars. This is particularly relevant to the field of archaeology. In our attempts to transcend the androcentric basis and integrate ourselves into the field, to establish and define a past of our own, a female past, we have essentially redefined prehistory. Innovative female anthropologists, because of their unique perspective, have confronted the foundations laid down by the "old guard" and have begun to establish new and revolutionary methodologies and interpretations of the archaeological record. Among the many women who have helped to build this revolution in the conceptualization of prehistory is Janet Spector (1983; Spector and Whelan 1989), who has in various publications contributed greatly to the establishment of a method of gender analysis. Another important figure is Margaret Conkey, who, in addition to contributing to methodology, has critically revealed the sexist and socio-political motivations for traditional narrations of human origins (Conkey and Williams 1991). In the first collection of articles entirely devoted to gender and the field of archaeology, *Engendering Archaeology: Women and Prehistory*, edited by Joan Gero and Margaret Conkey (1991), traditional dogmatic concepts of interpretation are challenged on all fronts by a range of "possibilities" advanced by the gendered perspectives of a number of innovative researchers.

Since the advancement of gendered perspectives in that book and in other publications, supporters of an engendered past have begun to visualize alternative interpretations of sites processed by the cultural resource management programs for which they work. These interpretive changes have paralleled an increase in the number of women participants in the process of recovery and analysis of prehistoric data. Now, as we use our positions to promote more gender balanced notions of the past, we can feel resistance associated with "making too much" of gender. This resistance became personalized for me during a recent field season. Near the completion of an excavation, my female supervisor presented the idea that the site may have been a "female" processing station. The opposition to the idea, while not overt, was indicated by the profound silence on the part of the fieldworkers present, which was explained as a resistance to the idea of "sexing" a site. The androcentric foundations on which archaeological interpretation is formulated will continually influence the images of *who* created the material remains we find. The sex of the "who" imagined in most cases will be male until a gendered perspective is integrated into traditional modes of interpretation (Conkey and Spector 1984).

As women in a traditionally male field, using our positions to further a more gender balanced perspective has not been an easy responsibility to embrace. The ability to take on that responsibility evolved from a long procession of "grueling" experiences that began the day we walked onto our first archaeological dig. This paper explores my personal evolution as a female participant in the field of archaeology. The range of experiences I have confronted in my career as an archaeologist reflects the progress of women as participants in this field.

Training a Woman Field Archaeologist

In the Beginning

When I participated on my first dig I was sophomore at the University of Oregon, filled with all the naïveté and excitement that a young woman's first archaeological dig can inspire. I knew that I was about to participate in the process of solving a mystery. The solution would reveal an as yet unknown kind of life, one that would have occurred in the distant past. To extract and understand the scant remains left after a multitude of processes occurring over many hundreds or perhaps thousands of years depended completely on my abilities, and those of the people I would work with. And it is the glamor and mystique associated with the discipline that encourages students, despite the often absurdly boring manner in which it is taught, to strive one day to say "*I* am an archaeologist."

So it was that I joined the virtually all male field team on the side of a soon-to-be-straightened highway. From the beginning there was the standard relationship between my "supervisor/instructor" and me as "employee/student" that can only be characterized as "paternal." He gave the information he felt necessary to impart, and I took it. And while every aspect of site excavation was under way, in the 7+ days that we were there, I basically learned only how to screen. I believe that the limited amount of information and experience offered to me regarding basic archaeological techniques, was due to the fact that I was a woman. It is important to note here that, at the time, being a typical young woman, I was as passive as I had been socialized to be. The thought of requesting more information, about survey and site layout, for example, never entered my mind. In addition, the practical development of my skills was not encouraged. I distinctly recall that on the token occasion when I was actually allowed to dig a level in the test pit, I was left feeling a strong sense of inadequacy, because the assumption of both my supervisor and myself was that a woman obviously could not dig effectively.

Fortunately I was not persuaded by the experience to end my career then and there. Instead I did what I believe many young women who come to this point in the field resolve to do—work harder. I recall thinking that I *had* to keep up with the men if I was ever going to get anywhere in the field of my dreams. But, as I soon discovered, the harder I worked the less I was *allowed* to keep up with them.

Learning the Ropes

Having obtained some experience from my first dig, I was teamed up with two men considered to be qualified and competent. For the most part, I again took on the role of screener. But emboldened by my new resolution to work harder, I expressed my interest in digging, carrying my share of our work as a team. I suddenly became well aware of how hard one has to work to keep two screeners busy and to keep the work under control and flowing. It can be a very physically demanding aspect of contract work. But this case had an exceptional quality about it. While I was not aware of it at the time, I can see now that my teammates were suddenly doing all that they could to keep me as busy as possible. Indeed, it seemed that while they kept me occupied with the physical aspect of actual digging, they offered very little explanation of the "process" of excavation. One incident in particular has convinced me that it was no illusion. I was digging and they were screening at a steady pace when I was overcome by the call of nature. In order not to disturb our work flow I prepared four large buckets of soil that ordinarily would have kept them busy for more than 10 minutes. Upon my return less than four minutes later, I found all the buckets empty and my teammates waiting with empty screens, irritated at the interruption. I now understand why my teammates were willing to sacrifice the integrity of our unit by not screening the dirt adequately, if at all, in order to make my job as difficult as possible. I have considered this incident for years since its occurrence, and just as women do in other professions I initially doubted and blamed myself. If only I had returned more quickly? If only I could dig faster? If only I had a bigger bladder? What the real question should be here is: would they have done this to a man? Would they have repressed the development of my abilities by circumscribing my contributions as a participating member of our team if I were a man? Would they have sacrificed their own credibility in order to subjugate me if I were a man? Or, would they have attempted to supersede their own levels of proficiency in order to present an image that a man in my position could aspire to? I would contend that since I was a woman, and in no traditional sense able to attain that image, it was not worth their while to expend such energy. Circumscribing my role could be explained as a response to the increasing threat of women in a previously male dominated field. The view of women as threatening is even more apparent in settings where a female supervisor is present. A majority of the women supervisors I surveyed reported at least one experience of having their directions ignored or purposefully misconstrued by male workers. The female supervisors all felt that, had they been male, these men would not have challenged their authority.

There is no way to become proficient in fieldwork other than to be taught basic principles and encouraged in the practice of them. I learned to what extent my own skills in basic archaeological method had suffered when I began work on my fourth dig at the Honokahua Burial site on Maui, Hawaii.

The Light at the End

Honokahua was the place where I learned proper archaeological method, by the seat of my pants. Field technicians were each entirely responsible for their own unit areas, which contained on the average close to 70 cubic meters of ground. It was quite a rude awakening suddenly to find myself in a position of vast responsibility and possessing very little understanding of what exactly needed to be done. I owe it entirely to the character of the crew at Honokahua that I was (1) able to realize the extent to which I had been denied crucial knowledge concerning methods of archaeological field work, and (2) given the opportunity to learn.

The major difference between the crew at Honokahua and those of the previous digs I had participated in was that it had more women than men working as field technicians. More important than this was the fact that, though the consulting firm itself was headed by two men, the primary field supervisor was a woman. These two points did not matter much to me at the time, as I was completely overwhelmed at being directed to a unit area, told to lay out units, write thorough notes, describe soils, map, sketch, take samples, and exhume individuals, as fast as possible—all this when I had only relatively recently mastered the line level! It is with great thanks to the women working directly around me that I was able to learn the techniques of excavation while simultaneously collecting good information. They readily offered instruction and willingly answered my questions. While I was not the fastest technician in the field, in time I was also not the slowest, and by the end of my time at Honokahua I had earned, from the primary field supervisor, the comment that I had been one of the best people working there. Coming from her it meant a great deal. Here was the first woman I had encountered who had reached such a high position in the field of archaeology. There were many inspiring women at this site, all of whom showed me that being female did not mean I could not go as far as I wanted. I also realized that I could go in any direction that I wished. The two people responsible for bone analysis were women. One of the site photographers was a woman. And a few of the women were returning to school to specialize in various areas. The possibilities I was exposed to were ultimately inspiring to me and reaffirmed a hope that had been waning since my first dig.

The cause of my wavering resolve to continue in archaeology had been the frequency of incidents like those previously described. Until recently I had only suspected that the cause of my co-workers' behavior towards me lay in the fact that I was a woman. In order to discover to what extent other women experienced similar situations, I administered a survey to individuals and programs in cultural resource management throughout the country. The results of this survey show that indeed the skills and participation of women fieldworkers have not been cultivated to the same degree as those of their male colleagues.

The Surveys

My experience at Honokahua was, I believe, unusual. Archaeological field teams have traditionally consisted mostly of men. After collecting surveys from a dozen programs, the inception of most being in the mid 1970s, I found that more men have been employed in positions of responsibility, such as field supervisor and project director, than women. Indeed only an average of 30 percent of the directors of the programs I surveyed have been women. The rate was slightly higher for field supervisors at 34 percent. This is compatible with a statistic of 35 percent female participation in British archaeology, cited in a recent article by Roberta Gilchrist (1991). In addition to a circumscribed participation, the active suppression of women's talents in the field and the lack of interest in instructing women in field skills is evident in the fact that women fieldworkers generally lack as wide a range of skills when compared to men of equal or even less experience. By skills I mean knowledge of and experience with the use of survey equipment, cameras and other technical equipment, mapping and artifact analysis. In the survey of individuals, it was found among fieldworkers that women consistently report obtaining fewer skills during their first field experience than do men.[1] From a list of 19 skills, women reported having learned, during their first field experience, an average of six while men reported having learned an average of eight. In addition, the average number of skills women currently possess was found to be fewer, even if they had the same number of months of field experience (Figure 1). From the same list of skills, women reported having an average of 12 where men reported having an average of 14. Be it due to lack of initiative or lack of opportunity, women learn less during their initial field experiences and receive fewer opportunities through-out the duration of their field careers. The reasons for the lack of women's participation in the field of archaeology and beyond are vast, variable, debatable, and far from being included in the scope of this paper. But just as the roles of women in society are even now changing,

---

1. The survey of individual skills here is admittedly problematic. There is the problem of possible over-reporting by males and under-reporting by females due to a general disparity in confidence level between the sexes. According to Dweck et al. (as cited in Bernstein et al. 1991) boys are taught that their errors are due to oversight or something beyond their control, whereas girls are taught to believe that their errors are the result of their own inabilities. As children grow and experience the many "errors" associated with the learning process, the idea that mistakes are due to inherent inability will be reinforced in females. Even when girls are aware of their intelligence they will generally continue to perceive of themselves as incapable when they are confronted with difficulty (Licht and Dweck 1984). The same response may follow when their intelligence is called into question, as in a survey that asks whether or not one can perform a given task with confidence.

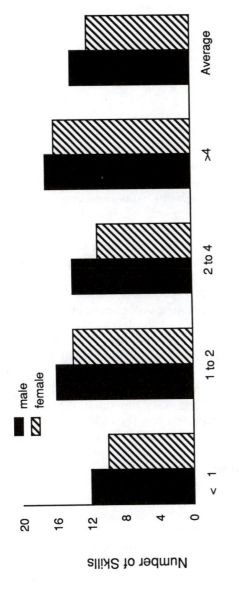

Figure 1. Number of skills possessed by fieldworkers.

so is the role of women in the field of archaeology. Women are employed in key positions in cultural resource management programs in appreciable numbers. These key positions afford the opportunities for advancing more gender-balanced fieldwork and ideas of the past. But changing basic conceptual patterns in interpretation—indeed any kind of basic change—is rife with resistance. This resistance became particularly clear to me during my first field season with a consulting archaeology program in Vermont.

Epilogue

During my first season in Vermont, I was reading the flood of literature on feminist anthropology and specifically feminist archaeology. Inspired by these readings, I began to look for practical ways to apply the concepts to the work I was doing. I found support and receptivity to the ideas in my female supervisor, who also became inspired by the idea of engendering archaeological interpretations. At the conclusion of the data recovery phase of a site where a predominance of quartz scrapers was found, my supervisor offered a preliminary interpretation to the field crew. Based on the associations of that particular class of artifacts, she suggested that possibly the site was a place where women might have gathered to process hides. The response of the field crew to this was indeed surprising to me, as I had been submerged in the new and promising feminist interpretations. The majority of the crew was silent, except for those who offered mumbled rejections to "sexing" a site. Still others supported the idea that, even with the proportions of artifact types represented, the site could still be a male hunting camp. Later my supervisor told me of additional resistance offered from her male colleagues. They discouraged her from integrating the gendered perspective into the report because of the lack of ethnographic evidence of a female processing station. Indeed, the argument whether the site was a female processing station or a male hunting camp is definitely debatable. But more important, this argument symbolizes the confrontational context in which we all, as feminist anthropologists and as employees of cultural resource management programs, now stand. It was, at one time, our cause simply to add women to images of the prehistoric world. While this is still a necessary and important facet of our cause, moving beyond it will allow for the growth of the entire discipline. What of the other possibilities? A female hunting camp? A male processing station? Or, exactly *who* was doing what here? There is as much uncertainty in calling a site female as calling it male. The only reason it is more acceptable to call a site male is that we have been doing it for so long. Consciously engendering prehistoric interpretations, where we can, not only allows for greater possibilities in our reconstructions of the prehistoric world, but it also helps us see exactly *where we can* engender archaeological data. Proponents of a gendered perspective have a rough road ahead, when we consider the resistance we are up against. Obtaining and holding positions from which we can offer interpretations in cultural resource management programs is a prerequisite. Considering the total number of sites that will be processed, these are key positions to hold that should not, indeed, will not be wasted.

Acknowledgments

I would like to especially thank my dearest friend and partner in the world of academics, Casey Walsh, for his most intelligent and insightful suggestions upon reading the first draft of this paper. I would also like to thank my supervisors Geraldine Kochan and Nora Sheehan for their unlimited support and most patient assessments of each rendition. I indeed have no idea what I would have done without Thomas Haviland to help me in converting the files for this paper and with general computing. My greatest appreciation goes to Kevin Donald, my West Coast Connection, for his help in implementing the surveys in that area. Finally, I would like to thank all the people who participated in the survey.

Chapter 13
Women in Contract Archaeology

Barbara Avery Garrow, Patrick H. Garrow,
and Pat A. Thomas

Contract archaeology in the United States is a product of the environmental movement of the 1960s and 1970s. The laws and regulations passed as a result of that movement addressed both cultural and natural resources, and required that the impacts of projects conducted with federal permits or funding be assessed prior to construction. Cultural resources were defined to include archaeological resources, as well as standing structures and areas of historical significance.

The professional archaeological community in the United States was not prepared to meet the unprecedented demand for professional services created by the environmental laws and regulations. The initial demand for services was primarily met by universities, but it soon became evident that those institutions could not provide the type of service demanded by tight and inflexible construction schedules. Most universities that were engaged in contract archaeology in the 1970s had either stopped doing contracts or deemphasized contract work by the 1980s.

Private sector contract archaeology programs had been established in most regions of the country by the late 1970s. Those firms progressively conducted more contract projects through time, and dominated archaeological contracting by the early to mid-1980s. The overwhelming majority of contract projects are currently undertaken by private sector firms, although a few universities have retained sizable contract programs.

No statistics are currently available concerning the numbers of archaeologists employed in contract archaeology programs, but it is evident that the majority of all archaeologists in the country are directly or indirectly involved in contracting. Published data are also unavailable on both the relative proportions of women employed in contract archaeology and the positions they hold within contract programs. Employee data for private sector contract archaeology firms are more difficult to access than similar information for public institutions, as private firms are not compelled to make employee data available to the public at any level.

The following paper is based on analysis of the employee and recent applicant records of Garrow & Associates, Inc., a private sector contract archaeology firm. The records of that firm were used since they were available to the researchers, and included a data base of 991 individuals. Insights into the role of women in contract archaeology are provided by this analysis, and the results are compared to available statistics concerning the role of women in American archaeology from published sources.

The Data Base

Garrow & Associates, Inc. was incorporated in 1983 and is a Woman Business Enterprise (WBE). The size of the firm's staff has fluctuated greatly since 1983, with a high of 176 and a low of two staff members. The firm's staff fluctuates with contract needs, although a core staff is now maintained that consists of senior archaeologists, field directors, and support staff.

The employee data base used for this paper was derived from Garrow & Associates employee files. Those files did not include resumes for all applicants, as resumes of applicants not hired standardly are retained only for two years. The employee records include the applicant's name, job title, date of first hire, and marital status in all cases. Date of birth was added to the basic employee form in 1986. The highest educational degree achieved, years of work experience, and publication record at initial hire were abstracted from employee resumes when they were available. Gender was not recorded on employment forms or on the resumes received, but was determined in each case from study of each employee's or applicant's name and from the personal knowledge of current staff.

Most of the individuals hired by the firm were employed on a project-to-project basis, although all employees were hired with the same staff benefits, such as group medical and life insurance, and accrual of paid vacation and sick leave, as members of the core staff. The only individuals hired as subcontractors for projects were those specialists such as geomorphologists, faunal or floral analysts, or the like who clearly met legal criteria for subcontractors. No subcontractors were included in the employee or applicant data bases used for this paper.

Figure 1 reflects the date of first hire by gender of all employees. That figure reflects the steady growth experienced by the firm from 1983 to 1984, and the extremely large number of new hires in 1985. The spike in new hires in 1985 resulted from the need to staff a large project in Georgia and a second large project in Maryland. New hires in 1985 included equal numbers of males and females. The very low number of new hires in 1986 was not necessarily reflective of the company's workload in that year, as most staffing needs were accommodated by retaining persons employed in 1985 or rehiring those initially hired at that time. The year 1987 marked the worst single year in the firm's history since its startup, but exhibited an increase in new hires over 1986. The increase in new hires in 1989 and 1990 that culminated in 1991 reflects a major project in Vermont and New Hampshire followed by an even larger project in New York and Connecticut. The new hires for those projects were predominantly male, but both men and women who previously worked for the firm were rehired. The low level of new hires in 1992 reflects completion of the large New York and Connecticut project and retention or rehire of staff who had previously worked for the firm, similar to that occurring in 1986.

The applicant portion of the data base was based on information taken from resumes received during 1991 and 1992 from persons who were not hired. Resumes were available for all applicants, and level of education, past experience, and publication record were available in all instances. Age at time of application and marital status could not often be determined. Gender was assigned based on study of the applicants' names, and could be determined in all but five instances.

The total sample available for this study consists of 991 individuals. That sample includes 596 present or former employees and 395 applicants. Females represent 238 employees and 159 applicants, or 40.1 percent of the data base. Five applicants (0.5%) were gender-ambiguous, and the remaining 59.33 percent (n = 589) were male.

The total employee and applicant data base includes a small number of biologists, as well as administrative and other technical support staff. Those individuals were retained in the data base to present a total picture of the firm. Staff are clearly delineated by position in the analyses that follow.

The cultural resource employees of Garrow & Associates are assigned to job positions and given salaries based on written job descriptions. The staff levels and requirements used by the firm are presented in Table 1.

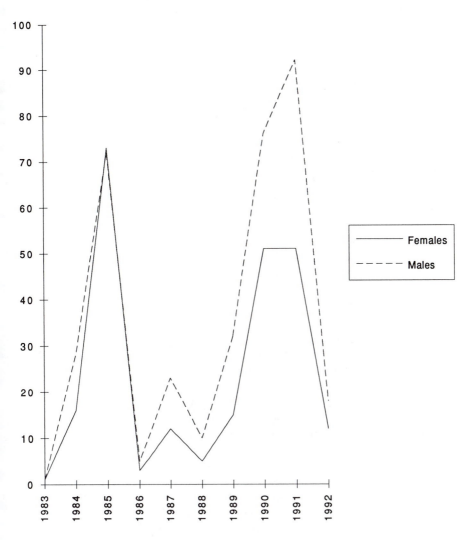

Figure 1. Employees by year of first hire by gender.

The job levels range from entry level technicians with no experience or education at the Technician I level to senior historians and archaeologists. Level I technicians have rarely been hired in the past, and are not differentiated from level II technicians in the following analyses. Historian technicians have also been rare in the firm, and historians at all levels have been combined into a single "historian" category for purposes of this analysis. Evidence of a publication record is required

TABLE 1. Staff Levels and Qualifications

	Degree required	Substitute exper.?	Exper. required[d]	Publication record
Field Tech. I[a]	None		None	No
Lab Technician I[a]	None		None	No
Field Tech. II	B.A. or B.S.	Yes	1	No
Lab Technician II	B.A. or B.S.	Yes	1	No
Historian Tech.[a]	B.A.	Yes	1	No
Senior Field Tech.	B.A. or B.S.	Yes	3	No
Senior Lab Tech.	B.A. or B.S.	Yes	3	No
Lab Director[b]	M.A.	No	3	Yes
Historian	M.A.	No	3	Yes
Archaeologist I	M.A.[c]	No	3	Yes
Archaeologist II	M.A.	No	5	Yes
Senior Historian	M.A.	No	5	Yes
Sr. Archaeologist	M.A.	No	7	Yes

[a]This category has rarely been used.
[b]This job description has been followed for new hires, although experience has been substituted for degrees for long-term staff.
[c]M.A. candidates also accepted.
[d]Expressed in years.

beginning at the laboratory director level, as persons of that level and above are expected to participate in report writing.

Table 2 reflects the firm's employees by job level at first hire and by gender. Women accounted for 40.1 percent of all employees, but were poorly represented at the level of Archaeologist I and above. The administrative staff was 93.8 percent female, and included all persons hired to provide administrative management for the firm. Women dominated all three laboratory positions, and all laboratory director positions filled through new hires were filled by women. Historian positions were nearly equally filled by males and females, with three women and four men initially hired as historians.

The relatively low proportions of women in upper level technical positions within the firm is also reflected in Figure 2, which presents a breakdown of age at initial hire by gender. The age at initial hire was available for 434 of the 596 former or current employees, with less complete age data available from 1983–1985. The age data base includes 163 (37.6%) females and 271 (62.4%) males.

Figure 2 demonstrates that the proportion of women in the sample peaks within the 21–25 age group, of which 42.9 percent is female. The proportion of women to men within the staff declined through the 26–30 to 36–40 age group, 38.1 percent and 24 percent respectively. The number of women exceeds the number of men in the 46–50 age

TABLE 2. Employees by Level and Gender

	Female no.	Female %	Male no.	Male %	Totals
Undefined	5	55.6	4	44.4	9
Admin.	15	93.8	1	6.3	16
Biologist	7	50.0	7	50.0	14
Project Manag.	0	0.0	1	100	1
Report Coord.	0	0.0	1	100	1
Editor	1	100	0	0.0	1
Graphics	1	25.0	3	75.0	4
Other Spec.	0	0.0	4	100	4
Field Tech.	148	39.8	224	60.2	372
Lab Tech.	22	61.1	14	38.9	36
Field Sr. Tech.	20	28.6	50	71.4	70
Lab Sr. Tech.	4	66.7	2	33.3	6
Lab Director	4	100	0	0.0	4
Sr. Tech/Arch.	0	0.0	1	100	1
Historian	3	42.9	4	57.1	7
Arch. I	2	16.7	10	83.3	12
Arch II	7	26.9	19	73.1	26
Sr. Arch.	0	0.0	12	100	12
Totals	239	40.1	357	59.9	596

group, although the total number of employees in that category (n = 13) was small. The oldest employee of the firm at initial hire was a 72-year-old woman who was hired as a field technician.

The employee data base is presented by gender, level, and mean age by level in Table 3. The mean age of all 434 employees recorded by age at initial hire was 29.6 years, which probably reflects an attempt by the firm to hire experienced personnel at each level. The mean ages of men and women hired as field technicians was virtually identical, while female laboratory technicians were older than the men hired for the same position. Men hired as senior laboratory technicians were older (by two years) than women hired for the same position, a pattern that was evident for both historians (6 years) and entry level archaeologists (5.5 years). Men hired for the Archaeologist II position were also older than the women hired for that position. In fact, of positions that had both male and female employees in the subgroup, the men were in all cases virtually equal in age or older than the females except for the class of lab technician, where the mean age of the females in this group was four years older than their male counterparts. The female field senior technicians were not only younger than the male field senior technicians, but they were also younger than the female lab technicians. The 11 senior archaeologists had a mean age of 39 years, and all were male. The 14 administrative staff members had a mean age of 34

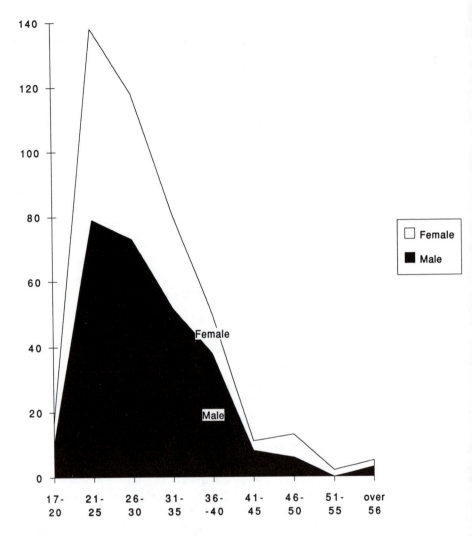

Figure 2. Employees by age at initial hire.

years, and was the group with the oldest female mean age. That group also happens to be all female.

The experience level of applicants and employees at initial hire by gender is reflected in Figure 3. As previously mentioned, the firm has rarely hired individuals without experience, and that fact is well reflected in Figure 3. The firm has received applications from more males than females who totally lack experience, but has hired inex-

TABLE 3. Employees by Level, Gender, and Mean Age

	Female no.	Female mean age	Male no.	Male mean age
Admin.	14	34.0		
Biologist	7	31.4	6	32.5
Project manager				
Report c'rdinator			1	31.0
Editor	1	22.0		
Graphics			3	27.3
Other specialist			3	29.3
Field technician	90	28.8	164	28.5
Lab technician	18	28.9	12	24.8
Field sr. tech	16	26.8	41	31.3
Lab. sr. tech	4	28.0	2	30.5
Lab. director	3	31.3		
Sr. tech./arch.			1	24.0
Historian	1	28.0	3	34.0
Archaeologist I	2	27.0	8	32.5
Archaeologist II	7	32.4	16	35.4
Sr. archaeologist			11	39.0
Totals	163	29.3	271	29.9

perienced males and females in approximately equal numbers. The proportion of males to females hired with one to two years of experience is virtually the same as the proportion of male and female applicants with the same level of experience. The proportion of female employees to applicants with three to four years experience is lower than males with the same experience levels, but the total number in each class is small, and the differences may not be significant. Conversely, females with five to six years experience were hired in higher proportion to applicants than males, but again, the total numbers involved are small. The numbers of female employees and applicants in the data base drops off sharply after six years of experience, although the numbers of males and females employed by the firm with nine to ten years of experience is virtually identical. Very few women are represented in the data base as either employees or applicants with more than ten years experience. The number of male employees has a corresponding drop after fourteen years experience. The individuals with the greatest amount of experience in the entire sample were a male Ph.D. applicant with thirty years experience and a female administrative employee.

A factor studied that was independent of experience or education was marital status. That factor could not be determined for most applicants, but it was recorded for all but four employees. Marital status was available for 238 female employees, of whom 21.3 percent

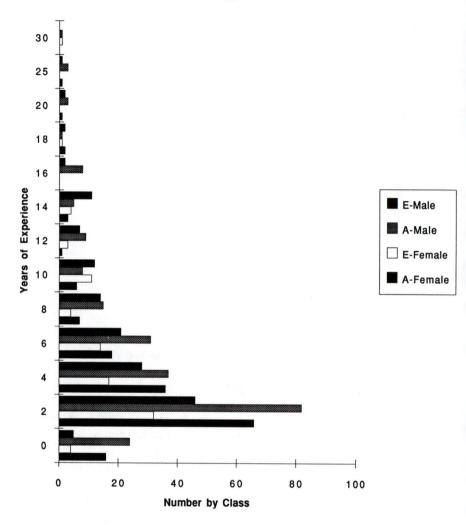

Figure 3. Experience of applicants and employees at initial hire.

were married. A total of 23.5 percent of the 357 male employees for whom marital status was known were married. The percentages of married versus single employees seems low for a population with a mean age of 29.6 years old, but it maybe reflective of the lack of long term employment security of most members of the sample or of general population trends to postpone marriage or to remain unmarried. The indication of divorce was coded as single, while separated was

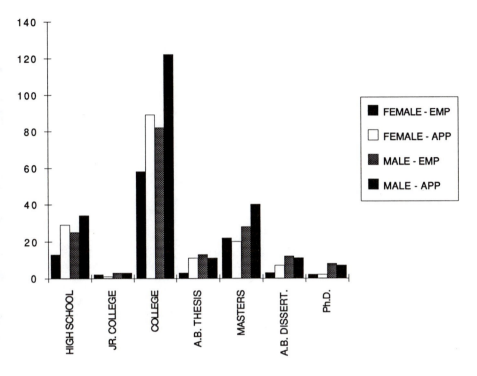

Figure 4. Education by level of employees and applicants.

counted as married; both instances were infrequent and not considered a contributing factor.

The educational level of employees and applicants is presented in Figure 4. Education level could not be determined for 320 former employees and three applicants, as employee resumes are retained only for two years after the last date of hire. A total of 38 employees (females n = 13, males n = 25) had a high school degree, although most of those individuals had attended college but had not graduated. In contrast, 63 applicants (females n = 29, males n = 34) had a high school degree, and lack of a college degree probably played a role in their failure to achieve employment with the firm. The junior college level of education refers only to those individuals with A.A. degrees, and included only five employees (females n = 2, males n = 3) and four applicants (females n = 1, males n = 3). An undergraduate education was the highest education level achieved by an overwhelming majority of both employees (females n = 58, males n = 82) and applicants

TABLE 4. Employee Publications by Education and Gender

	F 0–2	M 0–2	F 3	M 3	F 4	M 4
Book, mono.						
Report	3	6	2	3		
Article	2			1		
Pres'ted pap	1		1	3		
APA		1	2	1		
BA		1				
BR			1			
BRA						1
BRPA					1	
RA		3		3		
RPA	3	1	1	1		
RAPA			1	4		4
All		1		2	2	9
Totals	9	13	9	17	3	14

Key: F = female; M = male; 0–2 = high school or undergraduate; 3 = M.A. and M.A. candidate; 4 = Ph.D. and Ph.D. candidate. APA = published article and presented paper; BA = book or monograph and published article; BR = book or monograph and report; BRA = book or monograph, report, and published article; BRPA = book or monograph, report, and presented paper; RA = report and published article; RPA = report and presented paper; RAPA = report, published article, and presented paper; and all = all types

(females n = 89, males n = 122) in the data base. Employees who were M.A. candidates included three women and 13 men. The female employee category at that level differed markedly from applicants, as 11 female applicants were M.A. candidates. A total of 22 female and 28 male employees had M.A. degrees versus 20 female and 40 male applicants. The employees who were Ph.D. candidates included three females and 12 males, while the applicants at that level included seven females and 11 males. Staff members who were hired with completed Ph.D. degrees included two females and eight males, while the applicants included two females and seven males.

The breakdown of staff and applicants by degree is somewhat misleading. As an example, one female hired with a Ph.D. in hand had a degree in cultural anthropology with no prior experience in archaeology. That individual was hired as a field technician and subsequently filled positions as a laboratory technician and as a historical researcher. The other woman who had a Ph.D. at initial hire was hired as a laboratory director for a major project, and was unavailable for other project employment due to prior commitments. Further, at least some applicants sought positions at a time when none were available, and at least some lacked the requisite experience or publications required for senior technical positions.

TABLE 5. Applicant Publications by Education and Gender

	F 0–2	M 0–2	F 3	M 3	F 4	M 4
Book, mono.					1	
Report	2	2	2	7	3	
Article		3		2	1	1
Pres'ted pap	3	3				
APA	3	1		1		2
BA			1	1		
BR						
BRA						1
BRPA						
RA			1	4		
RPA			1			
RAPA		1		5	5	4
All		2	1	1	1	2
Totals	8	10	6	21	11	10

For key see Table 4.

The publication record of the individuals hired by the firm by degree level and gender provides additional insights into the nature of the employee data base. Table 4 presents publications by educational level for cultural resource employees, while the same data for applicants are provided in Table 5. Only 15.14 percent of the total data base of employees at first hire and applicants over the last two years had publication experience.

Table 4 demonstrates an expected relationship, as the majority of individuals with publications of all types also held or were candidates for graduate degrees. A total of 22 staff members with high school or undergraduate degrees claimed to have presented papers or publications. Two claimed books or monographs, while the remainder claimed reports, published papers, and/or presented papers. The remaining 43 individuals with publications were either M.A. or Ph.D. candidates or had graduate degrees.

Table 5 reflects the publication record of applicants. Resumes were available on virtually all 395 applicants, and there is little question that all applicants with publications had resumes on file, as applicants who lacked resumes tended to lack experience totally or to lack education beyond high school. A total of 18 applicants with undergraduate degrees claimed publications, and at least two of those claimed each type of publication. Forty-eight applicants holding graduate degrees claimed publications, and five claimed each type of publication. Seventeen of the 48 (35.4%) applicants with graduate degrees who claimed publications were women, as opposed to 12 of 43 (27.9%) of the employees in the same categories.

TABLE 6. Gender of SOPA Members by Region of the United States in 1992

	Female no.	Female %	Male no.	Male %	Unknown no.	Unknown %	Totals
Northeast	7	43.8	9	56.2	0	0.0	16
Mid Atl.	23	26.1	60	68.2	5	5.7	88
South	31	37.4	46	55.4	6	7.2	83
Midwest	19	30.2	42	66.6	2	3.2	63
Plains	0	0.0	18	75.0	6	25.0	24
S'west	65	26.2	173	69.8	10	4.0	248
N'west	3	15.0	15	75.0	2	10.0	20
Alaska	0	0.0	4	100	0	0.0	4
Hawaii	2	40.0	3	60.0	0	0.0	5
Total	150	27.2	370	67.2	31	5.6	551

Comparisons

The Garrow & Associates, Inc. employee and applicant data base provided detailed information concerning a number of data categories. Unfortunately, similarly detailed data are not currently available from other sources. Stark (1991:190–191) compiled gender data from the 1985, 1987, and 1988 SOPA (Society of Professional Archaeologists) guides, and found that women accounted for approximately 20 percent of the membership in each year. The 1992 SOPA Directory (SOPA 1992) was compiled by region and gender for this paper, and the results are presented in Table 6.

Study of the 1992 SOPA guide indicates that the percentage of women SOPA members increased to 27.2 percent from approximately 20 percent in 1985–1988. Female SOPA members accounted for 43.8 percent of the membership from the Northeast, but were not represented in the Plains (although some of the gender-ambiguous names were almost certainly female) or Alaska. Female membership was greater than 27.2 percent in Hawaii (40.0%), the south (37.4%), and the midwest (30.2%), and less than 27.2 percent in all other areas.

SOPA membership by emphases and gender are presented in Table 7. The total number of person-emphases is well beyond the total SOPA membership because any given SOPA member can be certified in multiple emphases. Historical Archaeology (31.2%) and Documents Research (44.8%) were the only emphases in which women were represented in numbers greater than their 27.2 percent membership in SOPA. Further, women were certified in only 21.3 percent of the total emphases, which is well below the proportionate membership of women in the organization. This implies that SOPA women are either more narrowly focused than SOPA men, or that they have less experi-

TABLE 7. 1992 SOPA Emphases by Gender

	Female no.	Female %	Male no.	Male %	Unknown no.	Unknown %	Totals
Field	132	24.1	389	71.0	27	4.9	548
Collect'ns	28	20.1	104	74.8	7	5.1	139
Theretical	15	14.9	80	79.2	6	5.9	101
Arc. adm.	13	11.8	93	84.6	4	3.6	110
CRM	13	14.6	70	78.7	6	6.7	89
Museology	15	17.9	65	77.4	4	4.7	84
Teaching	28	18.4	115	75.7	9	5.9	152
Urwt. sur.	0	0.0	11	91.7	1	8.3	12
His. arc.	44	31.2	94	66.7	3	2.1	141
Arc. & sci.	5	17.9	22	78.6	1	3.6	28
Urwt. arc.	1	9.1	10	90.9	0	0.0	11
Documents	13	44.8	16	55.2	0	0.0	29
Total	307	21.3	1069	74.0	68	4.7	1444

Key: Field = field research; Collect'ns = collections research; Theretical = theoretical or archival research; Arc. Adm. = archaeological administration; CRM = archaeological resource management; Urwt. Sur. = underwater survey; His. Arc. = historical archaeology; Arc. & Sci. = archeometric and natural science research; Urwt. Arc. = underwater archaeology; Documents = documents research

ence and therefore exhibit a more narrow range of expertise than SOPA men. The recent increase in the proportion of SOPA women to SOPA men in the organization argues in favor of the latter interpretation.

A second point of comparison was derived from a study of gender in Canadian archaeology published by Kelley (1991:197). Kelley found that 49 percent of graduate students in departments of anthropology in 20 Canadian university departments were women. Twenty-five percent of the graduate students in anthropology specialized in archaeology, within which field only 17 percent were women. This study underscores that a much lower percentage of women in Canada are selecting archaeology as a specialty within anthropology than are men, although the percentage of women to men in anthropology graduate departments is approximately equal.

Levine (1991:181) cites data from a study conducted by Kramer and Stark (1988:11) that indicated, based on analyses of the *Dissertation Abstracts International* and the *AAA Guide*, that women were awarded 36 percent of the archaeology Ph.D.s from 1976 to 1986. That number is somewhat more impressive than the numbers generated from the Canadian study, but 40 percent of women versus 27 percent of men specialized in Old World archaeology.

An additional issue germane to the current study is the representation of women on university faculties. Levine (1991:182) points out that Kramer and Stark (1988) found that only 15 percent of the archaeology faculty among the top 30 institutions that granted Ph.D.s in archaeology were women. This is a particularly telling statistic, given the mentor system that operates within American archaeology, and may be the single most important factor in the low representation of women with graduate degrees and extensive experience within the field.

Interpretations and Suggestions for Future Research

No single theoretical umbrella can serve as a complete explanatory system for any given social phenomenon under study, particularly one as complicated as the effect of gender in the workplace. Gender is created within a particular social and institutional structure and varies as does that structure. Gender also is created with and maintained by symbolic and ideological elements. Within this structural, social, ideological, and symbolic complex known as culture, human motivation exists and human action occurs. People have goals that are influenced by ideological constructs, or cultural models, and that are constrained by structural realities, some of which they may try to circumvent and some of which they may not. Individuals set goals, strategize, make choices, form alliance networks, and negotiate with others within the conditions provided by their culture and mediated by their own idiosyncratic responses to them. Elements of different theoretical approaches can be used to examine different components of a given social phenomenon.

In explaining the discrepancy in the numbers of men and women in archaeology, several approaches could be and have been taken, although investigations into this situation are fairly new. We suggest three possible areas for further research that taken together involve structural, social, ideological, and symbolic elements. The first is what Reskin and Hartmann (1986:53) term sex typing of occupations and professions. The second is the mentor system as it operates in archaeology. The third is two encompassing cultural models that provide contradictory beliefs to women and men in archaeology as well as society as a whole, and that perhaps strongly influence the first two suggested areas of investigation.

Occupational Sex Typing

Occupational sex typing involves, often at an early age, imparting beliefs about traits and behaviors that are expected of females and males in the workplace, and also the structuring of their experiences to reflect and reproduce those beliefs (Reskin and Hartmann 1986:58–61). Archaeology seems to possess two gender related popular images. The first is the "cowboys of science" image (Gero 1985:342); the Indiana Jones romantic adventurer image. It is populated by men conducting fieldwork in the outdoors. Characterizing archaeologists as the cowboys of science is interesting symbolism that evokes images of the raw, untamed exploits of the TV western cowboy on the one hand, and the controlled, precise investigation and technological advancement sought after by the dedicated scientist on the other. Both the cowboy and the scientist are stereotypically male. The cowgirls of science do not readily come to mind for most people.

The other image is of the female archaeologist, often with spindly bird legs, atrociously thick glasses, stringy hair tied back in a bun, and wearing a moldy wool suit, working in a musty lab or museum piecing together and classifying obscure artifacts that have merit only when an amulet or charm is needed to counteract the curse of the mummy on the late night fright show. So we can't say the archaeologist is singularly gender typed the way that the firefighter or nurse is. Most people can picture either a man or a woman as an archaeologist without too much trouble. Occupational sex typing is at work because the picture of each is very different, and they contrast with each other so completely: the mobile adventurous male doing fieldwork and the sedentary, unimaginative female working in the lab.

The question is whether these gender typed popular images affect what real archaeologists actually do. Gero (1985:347) looked at the percentages of males and females doing field related research and the percentages of those doing non-field related research in three areas: (1) Mesoamerican archaeological research; (2) dissertation research in archaeology; and (3) National Science Foundation funded projects in archaeology. What she found for the years 1979–1980 was that

males, who represent 74% of the total sample of archaeologists . . . account for 83% of all the current Mesoamerican field research, 81% of the dissertations based on field research, and 93% of all the NSF field research projects. Females on the other hand, representing 26% of the total sample . . . , undertake 45% of the current Mesoamerican non-field research, 46% of the non-field based dissertations, and 27% of the NSF non-field research.

Gero concluded that archaeological field research fulfills a male stereotype, and that field research, and so too, the male stereotype, is favored by the prestigious National Science Foundation. This conclusion was supported by Yellen's (1983:60–62) findings that during the same time period, 1979–1980, 35 percent males and 15 percent females received field related grants. Females were somewhat more successful (28%) if they proposed non-field related projects. The success rate remained unchanged for males whether they asked for field related funds or non-field related funds. Also, not surprisingly, men's applications received funding appreciably more often than those of women. That was not the case in cultural anthropology or in physical anthropology. Stark (1991:188) has shown that women in archaeology are also more often excluded from prestigious university positions. Women do not have the same access as men in archaeology to prestigious institutions for funding or for learning.

The stereotypical male activity of fieldwork is valued and stressed in archaeology and might even be considered its hallmark, while more stereotypical female activities such as lab work and analysis are less prestigious and less valued (Conkey 1991:26). Women seem to be more successful in archaeology if they follow these more stereotypically feminine, less prestigious pursuits. Whether a woman decides to slip comfortably into the gender typed niche created for her by the subculture of archaeology and its attendant beliefs and practices and the structure they reinforce, or decides to try a less traveled road and aspire to a position of influence and prestige, may come down to whether she can acquire a mentor and, if she can acquire one, whether the sponsorship will be limited.

Mentors

Having a mentor or sponsor who is established and influential in the profession, and who will help establish professional networks, instill accepted values and behavior, impart technical expertise, and provide official and/or professional endorsement is a common strategy and practice for most neophytes endeavoring to enter a profession. When men hold the majority of influential, high status positions in a profession, women must look to them for sponsorship (Reskin and Hartmann 1986:55). However, men may not want to invest in female proteges if they believe that women might marry and drop out; that they may not be mentally, physically, or emotionally capable of doing what is required; that having to work closely with women will precipitate logistical, professional, and personal complications; or that having a female protege may lower their status. And when women do have a mentor at the postgraduate level, the sponsorship can be limited so that they are not groomed for influential leadership positions but are channeled into less prestigious ones (Reskin and Hartmann 1986:56). In the case of archaeology, it is at this point in their careers that the greatest number of women drop out (Stark 1991:192).

The reluctance of men to sponsor women fully may account for Stark's (1991:192) observation that the position of women is improving in non-academic areas of archaeology, such as cultural resources management and the government sector, but that women are still less likely to secure faculty positions in prestigious university departments than are men. If men control the networks that influence these departments, then the reluctance of men to sponsor women, or their tendency to give only limited sponsorship to women would explain in part the underrepresentation of women in more prestigious and influential academic positions.

Although female mentors are not unknown and they are important in helping establish their proteges in the profession (Goldstein 1979: 407–410), the fact remains that there are fewer of them in archaeology because fewer women hold positions that allow them to be effective mentors. So, the question arises whether female mentors are as beneficial as male mentors. The answer seems to be that usually they are not. In order to narrow the discrepancy in numbers between women and men in archaeology and the discrepancy in the quality and prestige they enjoy, there will not only have to be more women, there will have to be more women in influential positions willing to sponsor other women on more than a limited basis.

The mentor/protege relationship is a type of alliance in the social context of archaeology. Ideally the mentor instructs, introduces, and endorses the protege. In turn the protege assists, supports, and is loyal to the mentor. Brumfiel (1992:551–553) argues that alliance networks are organized on the basis of gender, class, and faction, and that people within these alliances carry on negotiations with people belonging to other alliances who may have different goals and may be operating within the same or different environmental, structural, and/or social opportunities and constraints. This characterization is true of the alliances and networks formed in archaeology that affect women. But there is another type of negotiation that also occurs. That is the negotiation that individuals carry on with themselves when they must, perhaps unknowingly, reconcile two conflicting and personally accepted ideologies.

Contradictory Cultural Models

Individuals make choices based on their personal goals and priorities and the existing structural conditions, which include opportunities and constraints. Goals and priorities are at least partially formed by beliefs about how things should be. In turn, these beliefs are segments of larger, more complex culturally shared models of the world. Cultural models structure our world so that we see, hear, and think about certain things in certain ways, and those ways of observing and thinking seem so natural that we do not question them. Several different cultural models exist in any society at any one time so that some may carry beliefs that conflict with beliefs embodied in other cultural models (Quinn 1985:7).

The Nurturant Wife/Mother cum Super Mom ideal is an elaborate network of beliefs that is part of the cultural model of Female Domesticity that reached its peak in the 1950s and is still powerfully persuasive in our society. The ideal is the woman who devotes herself to her spouse and children, their well being, and their comfort. The partial acceptance of the Gender Equity cultural model encompasses a complex of beliefs about the equality of women and men. At that point the Nurturant Wife/Mother was given permission by most of society to be also Super Mom who works outside the home and strives for equal pay, then comes home and devotes herself to her spouse and children, their well being, and their comfort by spending six more hours of her day producing happy full stomachs and a sparkling, dustless, tidy house.

Part of the Gender Equity model has been accepted. The part that engenders beliefs that a woman may earn a salary, have a job or profession, and leave the kids during the day, or forgo having children at all has been more or less accepted. Other parts of the model have not been accepted so readily by men or women. One part that has been accepted somewhat in theory, but not often in practice, is the part that endows men with as much responsibility as women for being nurturing, supportive, and domestic. Those beliefs have not been sufficiently well accepted so that we can think about them without having to consider whether they are appropriate or not in particular situations.

The result may be that a woman will believe she should be able to hold the same job at the same pay as a man does based on the accepted beliefs involving gender equity in the workplace. However, if that job requires frequent travel and separation from spouse and/or children, long and unpredictable work hours so that child care becomes a problem, geographic mobility, and difficulty in taking time off to handle family emergencies, the woman will have to choose the cultural model with which she is most comfortable. The Nurturant Wife/Mother cum Super Mom model will vie with the Gender Equity model.

Individuals become creative in resolving this kind of conflict, but the conflict is there, and women make choices according to their situational constraints and to which beliefs hold more power for them. There is always a lag in the acceptance and discard of cultural models in a society. And they do not gain or lose acceptance all at once. Individuals accept and discard different parts of cultural models at different rates.

What this negotiation means for women in archaeology is that some women will be able to make the ideological adjustment necessary to reconcile a healthy personal life with the special demands that positions in the discipline require. Those demands are particularly rigorous if they choose field related projects. But, as has been demonstrated, the field is the place to go if one seeks influence and prestige. Other women in archaeology will adhere to other sets of beliefs that have more persuasiveness for them. They may choose the less powerful positions or they may choose to drop out all together. It is to be hoped that more and more women will become part of the first group.

The data we have presented are probably fairly representative of the situation for women in contract archaeology. Usually we have to fill positions fairly quickly, so we are limited by the available pool of qualified people whether they be women or men. What we have often found is that there are fewer qualified women available than men. We have also offered some approaches based on parts of larger theoretical models to try to help explain that situation as well as the situation for women in general.

What we have presented in an attempt to explain our data is not a comprehensive theoretical approach to studying the influence of gender in archaeology, but a suggestion for further investigations. We believe that following this course of action will provide insights into the structural, social, ideological, and symbolic components of gender and how they operate in our field. Then maybe we can decide what to do about those elements we wish to change.

Chapter 14
Academic Alternatives: Gender and Cultural Resource Management in Arizona

Stephanie M. Whittlesey

The archaeological profession has been radically altered within the last decade. With the expansion of cultural preservation legislation, the widespread financial woes within the state university system coupled with intense competition for federal research support, and the need to comply with affirmative action rulings, the ways in which archaeology is carried out and the characteristics of the people who conduct it have been radically and irrevocably altered. Not so long ago, academic teaching and research positions were perceived by most archaeologists as the only acceptable professional goal. Whereas other options have always been available in the form of museums, federal, state, and similar nonacademic positions, these options have been perceived as less desirable and accompanied by lower professional standing and status. Today this perception no longer holds.

The research presented in this paper begins with the notion that gender influences career pathways. In a previous study (Whittlesey 1991), I examined the extent to which nonprofessional responsibilities that are largely gender-based influence professional success. In this paper, I examine the role that gender plays in determining academic versus nonacademic career choices, its influences on roles and responsibilities within nonacademic positions, professional rank and salary differentials, and influences upon professional mobility. The results of my study indicate that, although women in the state of Arizona have made remarkably successful ventures into nonacademic career tracks, this progress is marred by continuing disparities between men and women professionals in salary and rank.

Methods

Based on its success in previous research, I used a questionnaire format to collect data. Questionnaires were mailed to 51 professional archaeologists in nonacademic positions in the state of Arizona; individuals presently pursuing graduate degrees, including those completing dissertations, were excluded because their career paths remain incomplete. An attempt was made to select an approximately equal number of men and women in similar positions within a broad range of professional options. Although the sample is small, it represents an excellent cross-section of nonacademic professional situations within the state.

The questionnaire was brief (21 items) and formatted; to facilitate analyzing the data, only one open-ended response was elicited. Self-addressed, stamped envelopes were provided for responses, and the response rate was good; 25 women and 18 men answered (a response rate of nearly 84 percent). Of these, one response from a woman was eliminated because she now works in New Mexico, for a final group of 24 women and 18 men. Most respondents answered completely, but several declined to answer one or more questions. For this reason, the frequencies vary in the accompanying tables.

Results

Professional Roles

In examining professional role distinctions, the first difference noted is that women work for a greater variety of employers than men. Most of the male respondents were employed either by a federal or state agency (38.9 percent) or a private cultural resource management firm (33.3 percent). Although this pattern also holds among women, employers of female respondents included universities, other governmental agencies, and private environmental/engineering consulting firms; the percentage of nonprofit museum employers was also higher. More of the male respondents were self-employed, however.

Professional Responsibilities

Table 1 reports professional responsibilities among women and men. Respondents were asked to rank their three primary job responsibilities by percentage of time spent on each task. Gender-based distinctions are evident. Whereas men and women report that management or administration is their primary responsibility, the figures differ

TABLE 1. Ranking of Three Primary Job Responsibilities by Percentage of Time Spent on Each Task

| Task | Gender and Task Rank | | | | | |
| | Men | | | Women | | |
	Primary	Secondary	Tertiary	Primary	Secondary	Tertiary
Management/administration	13	—	2	10	5	—
Archival research	—	1	1	—	2	1
Fieldwork	1	3	5	1	1	5
Laboratory work	—	1	—	—	2	—
Drafting	—	—	—	—	—	1
Editorial/report production	—	4	3	5	2	3
Specialized analysis	—	1	—	2	2	2
Writing	3	6	4	2	5	5
Cartography	1	—	—	—	—	—
Report review	—	1	—	—	—	—
General research	—	—	1	—	—	—
Public education/outreach	—	—	1	—	1	1
Compliance	—	—	—	1	—	—
Curation	—	—	—	1	—	—
Technical assistance	—	—	—	—	1	—
None	—	1	1	—	1	4

greatly; although nearly 72 percent of the men report managerial duties as their primary task, this is true for only about 45 percent of the women. Secondary job responsibilities show an interesting shift; the most frequently reported secondary task among men was writing (35.3 percent), followed closely by editorial tasks and report preparation, whereas among women it was evenly divided between management or administration and writing (23 percent). Two tasks are reported with equal frequency as the third most important job responsibility by men and women alike: writing and fieldwork.

An equal number of women and men supervise other people. Women, however, tend to supervise fewer people; half of the male respondents supervise between one and five individuals, with a range up to 35; about one-fourth of the women supervise only one other person.

An unexpected finding was the difference in terms of graduate education among men and women reporting management and administration as their primary responsibility. Of the men listing managerial tasks as primary duties, 46 percent held M.A. degrees, 46 percent held Ph.D.s, and 8 percent had a B.A. degree. Among the women, however, 70 percent held M.A. degrees, and 8 percent held a doctorate.

As I reported in 1991, women have made the shift out of the laboratory into performing other kinds of tasks. However, many more of the respondents who reported specialized analysis (such as ceramic, lithic, and paleobotanical analysis) as one of their primary job responsibilities are women.

The women Ph.D.s hold highly responsible but diversified management and administrative positions. Of the seven respondents with doctorates, one was half-time director of archaeology at a nonprofit research and education institution and a half-time, self-employed consultant; one was a manager of cultural resources services at a private environmental and engineering services firm; one was a principal investigator at a private cultural resource management firm; two were editors or assistant editors of a national journal; and one was director of a nonprofit research foundation and museum. The seventh respondent until recently held an important position in the State Historic Preservation Office and had moved into combined private cultural resource management and teaching. These women reported editorial work or report production most frequently as their primary job responsibility, followed by management and writing.

Salary

No one is unaware by now that salary, rank, and role differentials exist between men and women within the profession. Numerous studies have demonstrated gender-based distinctions within academic archaeology (for example, Kramer and Stark 1988). It is disconcerting, although not unexpected, that similar differentials exist in nonacademic settings. Table 2 presents salary by gender and academic degree. Respondents in part-time positions are excluded, and these were the only individuals to report annual incomes of less than $10,000. Nearly equal and low percentages of women and men report annual incomes between $10,000–20,000. Men most frequently report incomes greater than $40,000, whereas the women most frequently earn between $20,000–30,000 per year.

Although 57.1 percent of the men with Ph.D.s earn more than $40,000 per year, only one-third of the women Ph.D.s represent this upper income bracket. Holding a doctoral degree, therefore, apparently does not advance women's salaries as much as among men. Furthermore, women have equivalent or longer tenure in their present positions as men.

These data suggest that women as a group are spending nearly as much time on managerial, administrative, and supervisory tasks as men, but that this is not reflected in equitable salaries. Further, the study suggests that job tenure and education are not as frequently rewarded with salary increases among women as among men. Similar

TABLE 2. Education (Degree) by Annual Salary and Gender

Annual salary	Men				Women			
	B.A.	M.A.	Ph.D.	Total	B.A.	M.A.	Ph.D.	Total
$10–20,000	—	—	1	1 (6.2%)	1	—	—	1 (5.3%)
$20–30,000	—	1	1	2(12.5%)	2	3	3	8(42.1%)
$30–40,000	1	4	1	6(37.5%)	—	5	1	6(31.6%)
> $40,000	1	2	4	7(43.8%)	—	2	2	4(21.0%)
Total	2	7	7	16	3	10	6	19

findings are reported by England (1992a, 1992b), who discovered that jobs filled by men pay more, although they may demand no more skill or difficult working conditions than comparable jobs held by women.

Gender, Personal Roles and Responsibilities, and Career Pathways

In a previous study (Whittlesey 1991), I demonstrated that marital status and family responsibilities are factors influencing professional success among men as well as women archaeologists. In the present study I posed a related question: do personal roles and responsibilities influence career pathways, and are women affected more than men?

Approximately equal numbers of female and male respondents were married (about 61 and 67 percent). Slightly more of the men reported children living at home than women (about 40 percent). Most important, few of the men in committed relationships are paired with archaeologists, contrasted with about half of the women. This appears to be a significant factor influencing professional mobility among women. The data also suggest that women may be consciously choosing careers over parenthood more frequently than men, and that this choice may also be related to the higher frequency of same-profession spouses.

Respondents were asked to rank their reasons for choosing non-academic careers (Table 3). Both men and women targeted better opportunities for research and better salaries as primary and secondary reasons, but women twice as often indicated an inability to relocate. Asked to answer why they were unable to relocate, men and women alike most frequently indicated that their spouse's job was the responsible factor, followed by a preference for their present location and personal responsibilities. These data are more striking in light of the fact that men marry nonarchaeologists and women marry archaeologists.

Men more frequently than women also appear to remain locked in their preference for academic positions, despite their selection of a

TABLE 3. Respondents' Reasons for Choosing Nonacademic Career Paths by Gender

| | Reason Rank | | | | | |
| | Men | | | Women | | |
Reason	Primary	Secondary	Tertiary	Primary	Secondary	Tertiary
Unable to relocate	—	1	2	1	3	3
Better opportunities for research	5	4	1	5	3	2
Dislike teaching	—	3	1	2	2	2
No academic positions available	2	3	1	5	2	1
Prefer self-employ-ment/direction	2	1	2	1	1	2
Better salary/benefits	—	4	3	1	6	3
Lack necessary degree	—	1	3	1	1	1
Financial	2	—	—	—	—	—
Not selected	1	—	—	—	—	—
Tired of school	1	—	—	—	—	—
Dislike of academic en-vironment	1	—	—	3	1	—
Prefer wide range of responsibilities/chal-lenges	2	—	—	—	—	—
Personal responsibili-ties	—	—	—	1	—	—
Job available when needed	—	—	—	1	—	—
Opportunity to begin new program	—	—	—	1	—	—
None/no response	1	—	4	—	2	8

nonacademic career. About 22 percent of the male respondents indicated that they would prefer an academic position if one were available, contrasted with only 16.7 percent of the women. In answering a question concerning why they would prefer an academic position if one were available to them, men more frequently indicated that they would receive a better salary or benefits in an academic position while women listed their enjoyment of teaching most frequently.

Responses to the open-ended question concerning reasons for choosing nonacademic career paths proved instructive. Men and women alike appear to have balanced the pros and cons of academic versus nonacademic lifestyles. Men indicated that although they disliked the atmosphere, bureaucracy, isolation, and competition of academic life, they would have enjoyed teaching or what they perceived to be better opportunities to pursue their own research. Others enjoy the research opportunities of cultural resource management, but dislike the poor benefits. Most perceive that cultural resource management positions afford a much broader range of opportunities, and are challenged by their responsibilities in many areas, including research, environmental preservation, public education, media contact, and program expansion. Women listed a range of similar reasons for choosing a nonacademic career, most frequently suggesting that they preferred the more relaxed, noncompetitive atmosphere and ability to employ a hands-on approach provided by nonacademic positions. However, women alone indicated that the nonacademic career they had chosen provided the freedom and flexibility they needed to cope with their personal responsibilities.

Discussion

To summarize my findings, I discovered that women work in more varied nonacademic settings than men, and that fewer women than men hold advanced graduate degrees (compare Whittlesey 1991). Although an approximately equal number of male and female archaeologists are married, many more women than men are also married to or seriously involved with archaeologists, a factor that appears to influence their mobility. Marked disparities exist in salary by gender, although men and women perform much the same range of tasks. Those salary differentials are not explained by duration of job tenure, or by differences in education. Reasons for choosing nonacademic career tracks differ somewhat by gender, with women respondents appearing to be more frequently hampered by personal responsibilities and inability to relocate in search of job opportunities than are men, perhaps largely due to their marriages to same-profession spouses. Men apparently still prefer academic positions more than women.

The results of this study neither confirm or refute the notion that gender influences choice of career pathways. Whereas it is evident that men appear to prefer academic positions more than women, both have learned that nonacademic positions can prove challenging and rewarding despite the fact that the academic setting may have been their first choice. Two facts stand out as most unsettling: first, women may be hampered more than men in their career decisions by nonprofessional, personal factors such as family responsibilities; and second, affirmative action regulations appear to have made little impact on private industry and governmental agencies. Women still make less than men while performing the same tasks. This second fact is extremely disturbing, because about 40 percent of all respondents in this survey were employed by federal, state, county, or municipal governments. It can only be speculated that this situation will change as more employers are challenged by parity demands, and as the collapse of university-based CRM archaeological research is intensified along with the continued alteration of university faculty composition. This study is clearly provisional and based on a small sample; my conclusions must remain tentative. I envision a larger, future study with sufficient size to compare professional positions more closely in terms of responsibilities, education and experience of individuals filling the positions, and similar factors that remain incompletely understood. This study does provide a direction for further inquiry, however, and a basis for examining gender-based influences on professional career pathways.

Chapter 15
Women and Archaeology in Australia

Wendy Beck

Australian archaeologists claim that their archaeology aims to establish the history of occupation of regions and the ecological relationship of people with their environments, and to document relationships between the material evidence and past activities (e.g., Golson 1986; McBryde 1986). Very little of this research is concerned with social matters at all, let alone with gendering archaeology, mostly as a result of the implicit and explicit ecosystems approach adopted by Australian archaeologists (Brumfiel 1992). Here I want to draw attention to the recently evolving links between Australian women as prehistorians and women in Australian prehistory. I will briefly illustrate these links by introducing a feminist archaeological project that I have been working on for the last five years. The Coonabarabran project aims to generate a more inclusive archaeology than that currently written in Australia, one that is inclusive of people in the present and the past.

Australian prehistoric archaeology is unusual because it represents an entire continent that was occupied by people who lived solely by gathering, hunting, and fishing until contact with Europeans about 200 years ago, and these lifestyles could be observed in some parts of Australia until the early twentieth century. Therefore Australian archaeology is at the interface of the social and natural sciences, drawing many of its intellectual traditions from history and to a lesser extent anthropology, while at the same time drawing increasingly on the use of evidence from the natural sciences. The subject matter as well as the methods lie at this interface; a theme that echoes through much research is the relative influences of natural and cultural factors in prehistoric change. This position at the interface is one of particular interest to feminist scholars as well (Beck and Head 1989).

Women as Prehistorians

A basic question is whether and to what extent views of the subject matter and views of gender in Australian prehistory are influenced by the participation of women in the discipline. In order to appreciate this issue fully it is necessary to examine some quantitative measures of participation. What follows here is not intended to be an exhaustive account but merely an introduction to the Australian scene, particularly as it applies to the university context.

Prehistory as a discipline is relatively new. In terms of academic recognition it is largely the product of the last two or three decades, reinforced by the enactment of various pieces of cultural resource legislation the the late 1960s and 1970s. The discipline thus has been expanding at a time when women's workforce participation has also been increasing. Federal legislation in the form of the Affirmative Action (Equal Employment Opportunity for Women) Act was passed in 1986 and this has applied to both university and government archaeological employers. The newness of the discipline has meant that there are relatively large proportions of young people in it and that students can make a mark fairly early in their careers (Beck and Head 1989).

There are generally three types of employment open to archaeological graduates: as university teachers and researchers, as private consultants, and as cultural resource managers in government cultural heritage agencies such as the National Parks and Wildlife Service, museums, and the Victorian Archaeological survey (Hope 1993). The overall number of archaeologists in Australia is small; there are nine university departments granting Ph.D.s in prehistoric archaeology, and the number of workers in public archaeology is higher than that in the academic sector (Goulding et al. 1993). In 1991 there were 325 members of the Australian Archaeological Association, which is the main body for professional and student archaeologists. Of these, about 100 would be full-time students. The proportion of women who were members in 1991 was 47 percent compared with 44 percent in 1985 and the trend has been for the proportion of women to increase slightly over time.

There are different patterns of women's participation in the three types of archaeological employment. Cultural resource management is dominated by women, at least in some Australian states (McGowan 1991). The status of cultural resource management, however, is very low both in the community outside archaeology (for example, the natural resources managers) and in the academic archaeological community (Clarke 1993). "If these issues are not very important then they can be safely left to the girls" (McGowan 1991) is an attitude that has led to the marginalization of CRM practitioners within government organizations (Hope 1993) and in private archaeological consulting. Consultant archaeologists mostly undertake Aboriginal site surveys as part of environmental impact assessments for large public and private land development proposals. The 1990 membership of the Australian Association of Consulting Archaeologists was 64 percent women, an increase of 13 percent since 1985 (Hope 1993).

For the academic career path, both as university students and as staff, the situation for women is rather different. Although women earned 57 percent of Australian undergraduate degrees in 1990, the general rate of completion of Ph.D. degrees in 1990 was still much lower than that of men (36 percent women) (DEET 1992). I suspect that this situation reflects the case for archaeology graduates, also. Of the four Ph.D.s granted since 1985 by the University of New England, only one has been awarded to a woman. Figures calculated for the period 1980–86 indicate that 28 percent of doctoral graduates were female (Beck and Head 1989). A Ph.D. is practically essential for university employment, but this is less true for the other two categories of employment. About 25 percent of all academics employed in Australian tertiary institutions are women. Australian Archaeological Association figures over the last five years indicate similar proportions, in that 17 to 28 percent of academic archaeologists are women (Beck and Head 1989) and this low proportion of women employed by universities partly reflects the low completion rates for Ph.D.s. It should also be noted that only about half of these women have tenured appointments (Gale and Lindemann 1989), but it may be that women are gaining employment in universities in about the same numbers as they are gaining doctorates (cf. Kelley and Hill 1991). In general these statistics are similar to figures for United States universities (Stark 1991).

Low participation by women in collegiate tracks is, I think, due to problems within the culture of university life that discourage women from achieving higher degrees. In surveys of U.S. graduate students, more women than men reported feelings of powerlessness, pressure, isolation, and low self-esteem during their university training (Widnall 1988). In my own university, there have been several outbursts by staff in the weekly newspaper during the last twelve months criticizing institutional gender equity programs. Other issues of the same publication have championed the adherence of academics to the generic use of the word "man" despite the university's recommended "Guide to Language Usage." Women students may feel that their concerns are ignored and they may be discouraged from further study by the general university environment, especially further study in the "apprenticeship" mode where research degrees like the Ph.D. rely on close cooperation between staff member and student (see Widnall 1988 for further analysis).

So, the overall picture in Australian archaeology is one where there may be concentrations ("ghettos") of women in CRM and consulting and few women obtaining the Ph.D. degrees necessary for careers in universities. However, it is also clear that some change is coming about. A most encouraging sign is the 10 percent increase in Australian Ph.D.s gained by women over the last ten years, an increase from 26 percent in 1981 to 36 percent in 1990 (DEET 1992). I think similar increases could be expected for higher degrees in archaeology. There have been small increases in women's participation in other areas of archaeology as well. Equal representation may be a possibility in the mid- to long term. The prospects in academia will rely on changes in the university working environment. As Judith Allen (the first Chair in Women's Studies at Griffith University, Queensland) writes:

> The long term implications of changing faculty culture and enlarging the pool of women postgraduates (hence women qualified for faculty positions) would be an institution more accountable to women, more inclusive of them, in which constructive women's studies debate could safely flourish on the key topics of the curricula and on theoretical and political engagements with other positions. (Allen 1991: 10)

CRM and consulting may experience an increased amount of cross-fertilization with academic archaeology, where women as a group will benefit from the breaking down of the negative stereotypes of CRM practitioners and raising the status of archaeology in general. The first Australian Women in Archaeology Conference held in Albury, in early 1991, was certainly a fruitful one where women could discuss problems in all kinds of archaeological careers (duCros and Smith 1993). Projects evolved that will lead to greater intellectual interaction between archaeologists. For example, as a direct result of the conference discussions, our department engaged a consultant to investigate the setting up of an appropriate master's degree in applied archaeology, aimed at the CRM market. Such archaeology degrees are not usually undertaken by Australian cultural resource managers.

So practitioners of archaeology in Australia follow similar gender arrangements to those in other archaeological communities. While the proportion of women members of the Australian Archaeology Association is close to 50 percent, women make up only about one quarter of the Ph.D.s awarded in archaeology, publish fewer papers in journals, and are underrepresented in senior academic and government positions (Beck and Head 1989).

Thus, in its practice and in its aims, Australian archaeology has both similarities to and differences from archaeology as practised in the United States. It is a relatively new and small discipline and is focused on gatherer-hunter peoples.

Women as Writers of Australian Prehistory

The link between women as prehistorians and women as writers of prehistory has only recently become more obvious in the development of Australian archaeology. When Lesley Head and I reviewed Australian women's archaeological research in the late 1980s (Beck and Head 1989), we found that only very rarely was this research specifically related to feminism, gender, or sex-linked activities. The two exceptions were Betty Meehan's work on the economic roles of female hunter-gatherers and Sandra Bowdler's systematic study of the gendered division of labor in shell-fishing (e.g., Bowdler 1976; Meehan 1982). We concluded that although prehistoric women were more visible than they otherwise would have been, there was little evidence of a systematic feminist input by women prehistorians.

This situation is changing in the 1990s. The Australian Women in Archaeology Conference in February 1991 acted as a very important networking place and stimulus for a whole range of ideas about feminism, prehistory, and archaeologists. The papers and workshops included sessions on equity, biographies, personal experiences, and women in the archaeological record (duCros and Smith 1993). Here the functional links between the practitioners and the subject became obvious with added insights from our U.S. colleagues Meg Conkey, Joan Gero, and Alison Wylie. The personal and political experiences of women in the archaeological workplace often indirectly and directly lead us to reconsider the nature of gender, and then to consider the nature of existing accounts of the past.

The Coonabarabran Place Project

For the last five years, Margaret Somerville and I have been working with a small group of scholars on a project called the Coonabarabran Place Project, trying to approach the archaeology and material culture of this small region in Australia by experimenting with alternative and feminist ways of telling the past. Coonabarabran is a small rural town of 7000 people, about 600 kilometers northwest of Sydney, New South Wales, with cattle-grazing, grain cropping, and timber as the main industries. The Aboriginal population numbers several hundred people. I am an archaeologist with the Department of Archaeology and Palaeoanthropology, and Margaret is an adult educator now with the Department of Higher Education and Administrative Studies, both at the University of New England, Armidale, NSW. We initially met at a Women's Research Seminar in 1987 as a result of our common interests in, and experience of, women's studies, feminist theory, and Aboriginal women. For both of us, our research had been located in northern NSW. Both of us had also previously worked with Aboriginal people in northern Australia.

Teaching in women's studies courses, my experience and knowledge of equity issues for Australian women archaeologists (Beck and Head 1989), and working with a group of women researchers on a palaeoethnobotanical text book (Beck et al. 1989) have indirectly influenced the course of the Coonabarabran project (Wylie 1991a). The initial project directly developed out of Margaret's work with Aboriginal people in Armidale and my archaeological activities in Coonabarabran during the period 1986–88.

The Initiation of Multidisciplinary Research

Margaret and I talked about possibilities for combining our research interests, and the decision to pursue a joint research project was formally initiated by sending a research proposal at the beginning of 1988 to the Australian Research Council. This first attempt to write about an "integration of different knowledge bases in order to develop an understanding of Aboriginal relationship to place in the Coonabarabran area through time" (ARC 1988 application) was problematic. The difficulties were: (1) research based on different sources (archaeological field survey, archaeological excavation, recordings of Aboriginal people talking about places, environmental maps) had to be integrated in a way that did not simply appear to be a reconstruction of relationship to place chronologically ordered from prehistory to the present, as in the traditional archaeological report; (2) processes of conceptualization were as important a part of the project as the final report, making it a problem to specify the end products or results before the processes of creating them; and (3) the differences in language between the two fields of study made writing for a common audience difficult.

There have also been changes in focus as the research went on. The questions that we have been interested in throughout the project are how we can write a more inclusive view of the past, one that incorporates a diversity of viewpoints, that does not regard Aboriginal people or material culture as "objects of study" but that makes explicit the standpoint of the viewer. How can we incorporate verbal imagery, photographs, and drawings into this account? At the same time I did not want to reject totally the persuasive story of the "scientific" account. Much of our time during the six seasons of digging had been spent observing, sorting, and measuring archaeological features and finds. For example, stone artefact raw material did vary through time; fine-grained stones were more frequent in the middle part of the sequence and quartz rock was common at the top (Beck et al. 1992). Feminism allows for these conflicts and clashes, allows that within a single individual differences can be simultaneously held without disintegration (Haraway 1989:6). Throughout the project there has been a common focus on feminist ways of working, on politics of race and gender, focus on fieldwork, and on the concept of "place."

Feminist Ways of Writing and Working in Archaeology

It is only recently that the idea of writing as the central product of archaeology has really hit me, together with the notion that by analyzing the conventions of archaeological writing I could start to understand how to write differently myself.

The focus on story-telling is, of course, a position well known to feminists. "One story is not as good as another. . . . Attention to narrative is not instead of attention to science, but is emphasized in order to understand a particular kind of scientific practice that remains intrinsically story-laden as a condition of doing good science" (Haraway 1989: 331). The problem here is how to connect story and science, how to be objective, how to communicate with the diverse audience that might make up a feminist readership, how to bring together different perspectives without an infinite number of stories.

The writings of anthropologist Marilyn Strathern describe the perspective of feminist scholarship as that constructed by being partial, as

lying beyond the individual participants without necessarily being the object of a communal or corporate enterprise as a "body" itself. There is no agreed body of knowledge to which individuals must feel they are contributing. It meets on common ground-interest in promoting women's visibility-but scholars contribute their part by each being their own scholar. . . .

To be an anthropologist is to use feminist scholarship as a resource for or as an extension of anthropological insights, just as to be an organism rather than a machine is to extend organic possibilities. (Strathern 1991:33, 40)

Disjunctions between the stories, the types of knowledge, were seen as part of the whole process.

The Products of the Coonabarabran Place Project

The aim of the project in part is to present the fieldwork experience in a more inclusive way, one which incorporates a diversity of viewpoints, authors, and writing genres, one which does not regard Aboriginal people or material culture as "objects of study" (Figure 1). The books will contain essays about the process of fieldwork, interpretation of the finds, and Aboriginal people's talk and paintings at and of the sites. This type of writing is practically non-existent for field reporting in Australian prehistoric archaeology. The end products of the Coonabarabran Place project will be writing in different styles, arranged around subject themes.

The three main writing genres (Van Maanen 1988) will be:

(1) Realist stories (The Site Report, Beck et al. 1992). The archaeological stories told about place and the things of place. The structured parts will follow the pattern of the conventional site report, arranged by data categories and moving from the present to the past. Unlike conventional site reporting, we hope to make explicit the gender assumptions in interpreting the site and the ethnohistories. This is particularly important for the relationship between women and plants reflected by the unusually rich organic remains at these sites.

(2) Jointly told stories (stories told by Aboriginal women and Margaret Somerville about place). These stories fall into two groups, stories about the history and prehistory of the area and life histories of four Aboriginal women from Coonabarabran. These stories allow the Aboriginal women's talk to be the focus of the account, with commentary by Margaret. These stories also illustrate the political conflicts about constructions of the past, between black and white ownership and control of the past.

(3) Impressionistic stories (impressions of place). Accounts that present some of the fieldworkers' experience of place, in two categories, archaeological and written. They include imaginings of past lives, reactions of fieldworkers to archaeological finds, and writings about language and long-ago anthropological fieldwork. Much of this material will be written by women who are also students. It also includes a diary of fieldwork experience.

This list gives some idea of the range and diversity of archaeological writing that will be produced. The product should not be dull, distant, or lifeless, but will give a sense of the complexity and completeness of the field experience, and experiences of place, by an outside observer, an archaeologist, and an Aboriginal person.

At the end, the Coonabarabran Place Project is an experiment in doing feminist archaeology in Australia, and the precise configuration of the links between Australian women prehistorians and women in Australian prehistory is not always clear. The audience we want to appeal to includes both archaeologists and feminist scholars, but many of the former will say that "it doesn't read like a site report", and the latter may find implausible the very idea of knowing the prehistoric past, a comment made by one of my women's studies colleagues who is a sociologist!

Other feminist archaeologists are also experimenting with writing in different ways and accommodating other standpoints (Joyce, this volume; Spector 1991; Tringham and Stevanovic 1991), exposing androcentrism, arguing for the importance of women in archaeology, and demonstrating the significance of gender as a category for study (see papers in Claassen 1992; Gero and Conkey 1991b; Walde and Willows 1991). Articles in these books represent the first of many attempts to write from the viewpoint of feminist theory not just "women's issues" (Moore 1991: 410), although "women's issues" of employment, discrimination, and difference may be crucial but subtle links between the practice and theory of women scholars. Feminist theory is not a single entity; it is composed of contradictions and debates, and only through the increasing awareness of the politics of women and gender in archaeology and through the increasing participation of women archaeologists will this debate become more vocal and more comprehensive.

Acknowledgments

Parts of this article are derived from joint work with Lesley Head and Margaret Somerville, who are not responsible for any errors, however. I wish to thank the executive committee of the Australian Archaeological Association, especially John Appleton, for help with collecting membership data.

References Cited

Acker, S.
1977   "Sex Differences in Graduate Student Ambition: Do Men Publish While Women Perish?" *Sex Roles* 3(3): 285–313.
Aisenberg, Nodya and Mona Harrington
1988   *Women of Academe: Outsiders in the Sacred Grove.* Amherst: University of Massachusetts Press.
Alarcon, Norma
1990   "The Theoretical Subjects of This Bridge Called My Back and Anglo-American Feminism." In *Haciendo Caras: Making Face, Making Soul, Creative and Critical Perspectives by Women of Color*, edited by Gloria Anzaldúa, 356–369. San Francisco: Aunt Lute Foundation Books.
Allen, Judith A.
1991   "Women's Studies in the 1990s: Problems and Prospects." *Australian Universities' Review* 34(2): 8–11.
Allsebrook, Mary
1992   *Born to Rebel: The Life of Harriet Boyd Hawes.* Oxford: Oxbow Books.
American Anthropological Association
1988   *AAA Guide to Departments of Anthropology 1988–89.* Washington, D.C.
1989   *AAA Guide to Departments of Anthropology 1989–90.* Washington, D.C.
1991   *AAA Guide to Departments of Anthropology 1991–92.* Washington, D.C.
Andrews, E. Wyllys
1986   "Preface." In *Research and Reflections in Archaeology and History: Essays in Honor of Doris Stone*, edited by E. Andrews V, vii–viii. Middle American Research Institute, Publication 57. New Orleans: Tulane University.
Anonymous
1946   "Ann Axtell Morris." *American Antiquity* 12(1):117.
1955   "Dissertations in Anthropology." *Yearbook of Anthropology—1955*, edited by William L.Thomas, Jr., 701–752. New York: Wenner-Gren Foundation for Anthropological Research.
1971   "Board Welcomes Another Alumna." *Tulanian* 44:19.
1992   "Museum Fellow Katharine Bartlett is Honored by the Sharlot Society for Her Outstanding Work." *Museum Notes* 19(3 & 4):5.
Ashley, Margaret E.
1930   "On a Method of Making Rubbings." *American Anthropologist* 32: 578–579.

1932   "A Study of the Ceramic Art of the Etowans." *Etowah Papers*, III, 107–136. New Haven, CT: Yale University Press (for Phillips Academy).

Astin, Helen S. and A. E. Bayer
1979   "Pervasive Sex Differences in the Academic Reward System: Scholarship, Marriage, and What Else?" In *Academic Rewards in Higher Education*, edited by Darrel Lewis and William Becker, Jr., 211–219. Cambridge, MA.: Ballinger.

Babcock, Barbara A. and Nancy J. Parezo
1988   *Daughters of the Desert: Women Anthropologists and the Native American Southwest, 1880–1980*. Albuquerque: University of New Mexico Press.

Barbour, Thomas
1933   "Introduction." In *Santiago de los Caballeros de Guatemala*, by Dorothy H. Popenoe, vii–xii. Cambridge, MA: Harvard University Press.

Barker, Alex W. and Timothy R. Pauketat
1992   *Lords of the Southeast: Social Inequality and the Native Elites of Southeastern North America*. Archeological Papers of the American Anthropological Association, No. 3.

Bartlett, Katharine
1934   "Spanish Contact with the Hopi 1540–1823." *Museum Notes, Museum of Northern Arizona* 6(12):55–60.
1936   "Hopi History, No. 2: The Navajo Wars, 1823–1870." *Museum Notes, Museum of Northern Arizona* 8(7):33–37.
1943   "A Primitive Stone Industry of the Little Colorado Valley, Arizona." *American Antiquity* 8(3):266–268.

Bates, Ulku U., Florence L. Denmark, Virginia Held, Dorothy O. Helly, Susan H. Lees, Sarah B. Pomeroy, E. Dorsey Smith, and Sue R. Zalk
1983   *Women's Realities, Women's Choices*. New York: Oxford University Press.

Beck, Wendy, A. Clarke, and L. Head (editors)
1989   *Plants in Australian Archaeology*. Queensland Anthropological Museum, Tempus 1.

Beck, Wendy, C. Cooper, I. Davidson, P. Gaynor, and D. Murphy
1992   "Crazyman and Kawambarai, Two Dated Rockshelters near Coonabarabran, NSW." Unpublished paper, Department of Archaeology and Palaeoanthropology, University of New England, Armidale, NSW.

Beck, Wendy and L. Head
1989   "Women in Australian Prehistory." *Australian Feminist Studies* 11: 29–48.

Bender, Susan J.
1989   "Alternative Networks in the Career of Marian E. White." Paper presented at the annual meeting of the American Anthropological Association, Washington, D.C.
1991   "Towards a History of Women in Northeastern U. S. Archaeology." In *The Archaeology of Gender: Proceedings of the 22nd Annual Chacmool Conference*, edited by Dale Walde and Noreen D. Willows, 211–216. Calgary: Archaeological Association of the University of Calgary.

Bennett, John W.
1943   "Recent Developments in the Functional Interpretation of Archae-
        ological Data." *American Antiquity* 9:208–219.
Bernard, Jesse
1964   *Academic Women.* University Park, PA: Pennsylvania State Univer-
        sity Press.
Bernstein, Douglas, Edward Roy, Thomas Srull, and Christopher Wickens
1991   *Psychology.* Boston: Houghton Mifflin Company.
Bishop, Ronald L.
1991   "Anna O. Shepard: A Correspondence Portrait." In *The Ceramic
        Legacy of Anna O. Shepard,* edited by Ronald Bishop and Frederick
        Lange, 42–87. Niwot: University Press of Colorado.
Bishop, Ronald L. and Frederick W. Lange (editors)
1991   *The Ceramic Legacy of Anna O. Shepherd.* Niwot: University Press of
        Colorado.
Bonta, Marcia Myers
1991   *Women in the Field: America's Pioneering Women Naturalists.* College
        Station: Texas A&M University Press.
Bowdler, Sandra
1976   "Hook, Line and Dilly Bag: An Interpretation of an Australian
        Coastal Shell Midden." *Mankind* 10: 248–258.
Brennan, Louis A.
1976   "Marian, An Appreciation." *New York State Archeological Association,
        Bulletin* 66: 31–33.
Brook, Bill and Bob Clark
1937   Report on the Logan Museum-Chicago University Expedition to
        Shireland, Illinois. Ms. on file, Logan Museum of Anthropology,
        Beloit College, WI.
Brown, Dorothy M.
1987   *Setting a Course: American Women in the 1920s.* Boston: Twayne Pub-
        lishers.
Broyles, Bettye
1971   *Second Preliminary Report: The St. Albans Site, Kanawha County, West
        Virginia. Report of Archeological Investigations* No. 3, West Virginia
        Geological and Economic Survey, Morgantown, WV.
1992   Notes on telephone interview on file. Department of Anthropology,
        University of South Florida.
Brumfiel, Elizabeth
1992   "Distinguished Lecture in Archaeology: Breaking and Entering the
        Ecosystem—Gender, Class, and Faction Steal the Show." *American
        Anthropologist* 94:551–567.
Butler, Mary
1931   "Dress and Decoration of the Maya Old Empire." *University Museum
        Journal* 22(2).
1934   "A Note on Maya Cave Burials." *American Anthropologist* 36:223–
        225.
1935a   "Piedras Negras Pottery." *Piedras Negras Preliminary Papers,* No. 4.
1935b   "A Study of Maya Mouldmade Figurines." *American Anthropologist*
        37:636–672.

1936a   "Ethnological and Historical Implications of Certain Phases of Maya Pottery Decoration." *American Anthropologist* 38:452–461.

1936b   "Pottery Study in the Maya Area." *American Antiquity* 2:89–101.

1936c   "Archaeological Problems in Erie County, Pennsylvania." *Pennsylvania Archaeologist* 6(2):27–30.

1936d   "Recent Archaeological Work in Southwestern Pennsylvania." *Pennsylvania Archaeologist* 6(3):55–58.

1936e   "Archaeology in Western Pennsylvania." *University Museum Bulletin* 6(5):10–13.

1937   "Gods and Heroes on Maya Monuments." *Publications of the Philadelphia Anthropological Society, Twenty-Fifth Anniversary Studies* I:13–26.

1939–1940 Mary Lewis Butler Correspondence. Albany, NY: NYSM Archaeological Documentation Inventory.

1941   "Three Archaeological Sites in Somerset County, Pennsylvania." *Pennsylvania Historical Commission Bulletin* 753:1–79.

1947a   "Two Lenape Rock Shelters near Philadelphia." *American Antiquity* 12:246–255.

1947b   "Pottery Types in Pennsylvania." *Pennsylvania Archaeologist* 16(4):117–122.

Caldwell, Joseph R.
1958   *Trend and Tradition in the Prehistory of the Eastern United States*. American Anthropological Association, Memoir No. 88.

Caldwell, Joseph R. and Catherine McCann
1941   *Irene Mound Site, Chatham County, Georgia*. Athens: University of Georgia Press.

Campbell, Elizabeth W. Crozer
1929a   "A Museum in the Desert." *The Masterkey* 3:5–10.

1929b   "The Finding of the Five." *The Masterkey* 3:13–19.

1931a   "An Archeological Survey of the Twenty Nine Palms Region." Southwest Museum Papers 7.

1931b   "Cave Magic." *The Masterkey* 4:237–241.

1932   "Cremation in the Desert." *The Masterkey* 6:105–112.

1936   "Archaeological Problems in the Southern California Deserts." *American Antiquity* 1(4):295–300.

1949   "Two Ancient Archeological Sites in the Great Basin." *Science* 109:340.

Campbell, Elizabeth W. Crozer and William H. Campbell
1935   *The Pinto Basin Site*. Southwest Museum Papers 9.

1937   "The Mohave Site." In *The Archeology of Pleistocene Lake Mohave*, Southwest Museum Papers 11:6–44.

1940   "A Folsom Complex in the Great Basin." *The Masterkey* 14:7–11.

Ceram, C. W.
1951   *Gods, Graves, and Scholars: The Study of Archaeology*. New York: Knopf.

Chamberlain, Mariam K. (editor)
1988   *Women in Academe: Progress and Prospects*. New York: Russell Sage Foundation.

Chapman, Jefferson
1984   "A Buried Site Reconnaissance in the Tellico Reservoir, Eastern

Tennessee." National Geographic Society Research Reports 17: 273–280.

1988   "The Federal Archeological Program in Tennessee, 1966–1986: An Archeological Second Coming." In *Advances in Southeastern Archeology 1966–1986: Contributions of the Federal Archeological Program,* edited by Bennie C. Keel, 46–49. Southeastern Archeological Conference Special Publication No. 6.

Chester, Hilary, Nan A. Rothschild, and Diana diZerega Wall
1992   "Women in Historical Archaeology: The SHA Survey." Paper presented at the annual meeting of the American Anthropological Association, San Francisco.

Chilton, Elizabeth S.
1991   "The Goat Island Rockshelter: New Light from Old Legacies." M.A. thesis, University of Massachusetts.

Chiñas, Beverly Newbold
1988   "Zelia Maria Magdalena Nuttall (1857–1933)." In *Women Anthropologists: A Biographical Dictionary,* edited by Ute Gacs, Aisha Khan, Jerrie McIntyre, and Ruth Weinberg, 269–274. New York: Greenwood Press.

Chopin, Kate
1988   *The Awakening and Selected Short Stories.* Orig. 1899. New York: Bantam Books.

Christenson, Andrew L. (editor)
1989   *Tracing Archaeology's Past: The Historiography of Archaeology.* Carbondale: Southern Illinois University Press.

Claassen, Cheryl
1991   "Bibliography of Ethnoarchaeology and Archaeological Experiments in Mexico and Middle America since 1958." In *Annotated Bibliographies for Anthropologists* 1(1):167–214.
1993   "Black and White Women at Irene Mound." *Southeastern Archaeology* 12(2): 137–147.

Claassen, Cheryl (editor)
1992   *Exploring Gender Through Archaeology: Selected Papers of the 1991 Boone Conference.* Monographs in World Archaeology No. 11. Madison, WI: Prehistory Press.

Clarke, Ann
1993   "Cultural Resource Management as Archaeological Housework-Confining Women to the Ghetto of Management." In *Women in Archaeology: A Feminist Critique,* edited by Hillary duCros and Laurajane Smith. Department of Prehistory, Research School of Pacific Studies, Australian National University, Canberra. In press.

Cole, Jonathan R. and Harriet Zuckerman
1987   "Marriage, Motherhood and Research Performance in Science." *Scientific American,* February: 119–125.

Conant, Francis P.
1974   "Dorothy Cross Jensen, 1906–1972." *American Anthropologist* 76(1): 80–82.

Conkey, Margaret
1991   "Does It Make a Difference? Feminist Thinking and Archaeologies of Gender." In *The Archaeology of Gender,* edited by Dale Walde and

Noreen Willows, 24–34. Calgary: Archaeological Association of the University of Calgary.

Conkey, Margaret and Janet Spector
1984   "Archaeology and the Study of Gender." In *Advances in Archaeological Method and Theory*, vol. 7, edited by M. Schiffer, 1–38. Orlando, FL: Academic Press.

Conkey, Margaret and Sarah Williams
1991   "Original Narratives: The Political Economy of Gender in Archaeology." In *Gender at the Crossroads of Knowledge: Feminist Anthropology in the Postmodern Era*, edited by Micaela di Leonardo, 102–139. Berkeley: University of California Press.

Cordell, Linda S.
1991a   "Anna O. Shepard and Southwestern Archaeology: Ignoring a Cautious Heretic." In *The Ceramic Legacy of Anna O. Shepard*, edited by Ronald Bishop and Frederick Lange, 132–153. Niwot: University Press of Colorado.
1991b   "Sisters of Sun and Spade, Women Archaeologists in the Southwest." In *The Archaeology of Gender: Proceedings of the 22nd Annual Chacmool Conference*, edited by Dale Walde and Noreen Willows, 502–509. Calgary: Archaeological Association of the University of Calgary.

Costello, Julia G.
1992   Society for Historical Archaeology Membership Profile, 1987–1991. Manuscript report, 28 March 1992.

Cross, Dorothy
1937   "Movable Property in the Nuzi Documents." *American Oriental Society Series* 10.
1941   *Archaeology of New Jersey, Volume One*. Trenton: Archaeological Society of New Jersey.
1956   *Archaeology of New Jersey, Volume Two: The Abbott Farm*. Trenton: Archaeological Society of New Jersey.

Crown, Patricia L.
1991   "Appraising the Legacy: A Thematic Synthesis." In *The Ceramic Legacy of Anna O. Shepard*, edited by Ronald Bishop and Ferderick Lange, 383–393. Niwot: University Press of Colorado.

Culley, Margaret
1977   "Sob-Sisterhood: Dorothy Dix and the Feminist Origins of the Advice Column." *Southern Studies: An Interdisciplinary Journal of the South* 16(2):201–210.

Daniel, Glyn
1967   *The Origins and Growth of Archaeology*. Middlesex, England: Penguin.

Davis, Angela
1981   *Women, Race and Class*. New York: Random House.

Davis, Dave D.
1984   *Perspectives on Gulf Coast Prehistory*. Gainesville: University Presses of Florida. Davis, Hester
1957   "Social Interaction and Kinship in Big Cove Community, Cherokee, North Carolina." M.A. thesis. Department of Anthropology, University of North Carolina.
1992   Written interview on file. Department of Anthropology, University of South Florida, Tampa.

Davis, Hester
  1957   "Social Interaction and Kinship in Big Cove Community, Cherokee,
          North Carolina." M.A. thesis, Department of Anthropology, Uni-
          versity of North Carolina.
  1992   Written interview on file. Department of Anthropology, University
          of South Florida, Tampa.
de Laguna, Frederica
  1934   *The Archaeology of Cook Inlet, Alaska.* Philadelphia: University of
          Pennsylvania Press.
  1956   *Chugach Prehistory: The Archaeology of Prince William Sound, Alaska.*
          University of Washington, Publications in Anthropology 13. Seattle:
          University of Washington Press.
  1977   *Voyage to Greenland: A Personal Initiation into Anthropology.* New York:
          W. W. Norton.
de Lauretis, Teresa (editor)
  1986   *Feminist Studies, Critical Studies.* Bloomington: Indiana University
          Press.
Deagan, Kathleen
  1989   "Where Historical Archaeologists Are Publishing." Society for His-
          torical Archaeology *Newsletter* 22(2): 19–21.
Degler, Carl N.
  1981   "What the Women's Movement Has Done to American History." In
          A Feminist Perspective in the Academy: The Difference It Makes, edited by
          Elizabeth Langland and Walter Gove, 67–85. Chicago: University
          of Chicago Press.
Department of Education, Employment and Training, Australia (DEET)
  1992   *Higher Education Series.* Report No. 13. January.
Dill, Bonnie Thornton
  1983   "Race, Class, and Gender: Prospects for an All-Inclusive Sister-
          hood." *Feminist Studies* 9:131–150.
Dincauze, Dena F.
  1991   "Is Gender Still an Issue?" *Bulletin of the Society for American Archaeol-
          ogy* 9(1):10.
  1992   "Exploring Career Styles in Archaeology." In *Rediscovering Our Past:
          Essays on the History of American Archaeology,* edited by Jonathan E.
          Reyman, 131–136. Aldershot, England: Avebury/Ashgate Publish-
          ing Company.
Dohan, Edith Hall
  1942   *Italic Tomb Groups in the University Museum.* University Museum,
          University of Pennsylvania, Philadelphia.
Dormon, Caroline
  1931   "The Last of the Cane Basket Makers." *Holland's, The Magazine of the
          South* (October):13, 66.
  1934   "Caddo Pottery." *Art and Archaeology* 35(2):59–68.
  1967   *Southern Indian Boy.* Baton Rouge: Claitor's Book Store.
DuCros, Hillary and Laurajane Smith (editors)
  1993   *Women in Archaeology: A Feminist Critique.* Department of Prehistory,
          Research School of Pacific Studies, Australian National University,
          Canberra. In press
Dundy, Elaine
  1991   *Ferriday, Louisiana.* New York: Donald I. Fine.

Ehrich, Robert W.
1973   "Dorothy Cross Jensen, 1906–1972." *American Antiquity* 38(4):407–411.

El Palacio
1935   "New Pottery Found in Honduras." *El Palacio* 38 (21–22–23):124.

Engelbrecht, William and Donald Grayson
1978   *Essays in Honor of Marian E. White*. Occasional Publications in Northeastern Anthropology. No. 5. Peterborough, NH: Franklin Pierce College.

Engelstad, Erika
1991   "Feminist Theory and Post-Processual Archaeology." In *The Archaeology of Gender*, edited by Dale Walde and Noreen Willows, 116–120. Calgary: Archaeological Association of the University of Calgary.

England, Paula
1992a   *Comparable Worth: Theories and Evidence*. Hawthorne, New York: Aldine de Gruyter.
1992b   *Occupational Sex Segregation and the Sex Gap in Pay*. Initiative: The Udall Center for Studies in Public Policy 5:9–11. Tucson: University of Arizona.

Evans, Jo N.
1987   *Wings in the Night*. Jackson, MS: Cain Lithographers.

Fenton, William
1978   "Obituary: Marian E. White." *American Anthropologist* 80: 891–892.

Ferguson, Marjorie
1932   Report of Marjorie Ferguson, Research Fellow in Ethnology. Laboratory of Anthropology Archive 89ELH-011.
1933   "Preliminary Report on the Tecolote Ruin." *El Palacio* 34:196–197.

Ford, James A.
1936   *Analysis of Indian Village Site Collections from Louisiana and Mississippi*. Anthropological Study No. 2. New Orleans: Department of Conservation, Louisiana Geological Survey.

Fowler, Don D.
1986   "Conserving American Archaeological Resources." In *American Archaeology Past and Future: A Celebration of the Society for American Archaeology, 1935–1985*, edited by Donald Meltzer, Don D. Fowler, and Jeremy A. Sabloff, 35–162. Washington, DC: Smithsonian Institution Press.

Fox, Nancy
1976   "Marjorie Ferguson Lambert: A Brief Biography." In *Collected Papers in Honor of Marjorie Ferguson Lambert*, edited by Albert H. Schroeder, 1–18. Papers of the Archaeological Society of New Mexico 3.

French, Frances Crouser
1952   "The Morton Shell Heap on Weeks Island, Louisiana." M.A. thesis. Department of Geography and Anthropology, Louisiana State University.

Frisbie, Theodore R.
1974   "A Biography of Florence Hawley Ellis." In *Collected Papers in Honor of Florence Hawley Ellis*, edited by Theodore R. Frisbie, 1–11. Papers of the Archaeological Society of New Mexico 2.
1991   "Florence Hawley Ellis (1906–1991)." *Kiva* 57(1):93–97.

Gacs, Ute, Aisha Khan, Jerrie McIntyre, and Ruth Weinberg (editors)
  1989   *Women Anthropologists: Selected Biographies*. Urbana: University of
          Illinois Press.
Gale, Fay and S. Lindemann
  1989   "Women in the Academic Search for Excellence." *Australian Univer-
          sities' Review* 32(2): 2–6.
Galloway, Patricia
  1991   "Where Have All the Menstrual Huts Gone?" Paper presented at
          the Annual Meeting of the Southeastern Archaeological Confer-
          ence, Jackson, MS.
Gergen, Mary McCanney (editor)
  1988   *Feminist Thought and the Structure of Knowledge*. New York: New York
          University Press.
Gero, Joan M.
  1983   "Gender Bias in Archaeology: A Cross-Cultural Perspective." In *The
          Socio-Politics of Archaeology*, edited by Joan M. Gero, David M. Lacy,
          and Michael L. Blakey, 51–57. Research Report No. 23, Depart-
          ment of Anthropology, University of Massachusetts, Amherst.
  1985   "Socio-Politics and the Woman-At-Home Ideology." *American Antiq-
          uity* 50(2): 342–350.
  1991a   "Gender Divisions of Labor in the Construction of Archaeological
          Knowledge." In *The Archaeology of Gender, Proceedings of the Twenty-
          Second Annual Chacmool Conference*, edited by Dale Walde and Nor-
          een Willows, 96–102. Calgary: Archaeological Association of the
          University of Calgary.
  1991b   "The Social World of Prehistoric Facts: Gender and Power in Pre-
          historic Research." Paper presented at the "Women in Archaeology"
          Conference, Charles Sturt University, Albury, Australia.
Gero, Joan M. and Margaret W. Conkey
  1991a   Preface. In *Engendering Archaeology: Women and Prehistory*, edited by
          Joan Gero and Margaret Conkey, xi–xiii. Oxford: Basil Blackwell.
Gero, Joan M. and Margaret W. Conkey (editors)
  1991b   *Engendering Archaeology: Women and Prehistory*. Oxford: Basil Black-
          well.
Gero, Joan M., David M. Lacy, and Michael L. Blakey (editors)
  1983   *The Socio-Politics of Archaeology*. Research Report No. 23. Depart-
          ment of Anthropology, University of Massachusetts, Amherst.
Gibson, Jon L.
  1984a   "Margaret Elam Drew, 1919–1977." In *Louisiana Archaeology and the
          Society: Celebration of a Decade of Achievement*, edited by Jon L. Gibson,
          6–7, 9. Special Publication of the Louisiana Archaeological Society,
          No. 2.
  1988   Verbatim Transcription of Taped Conversation with Mrs. U. B. "Jo"
          Evans, at her Home at Haphazard Plantation, near Ferriday, Loui-
          siana, 18 August 1988.
Gibson, Jon L. (editor)
  1984b   *Louisiana Archaeology and the Society: Celebration of a Decade of Achieve-
          ment*. Special Publication of the Louisiana Archaeological Society,
          No. 2.
Giele, Janet Zollinger
  1978   *Women and the Future: Changing Sex Roles in Modern America*. New
          York: Free Press.

Gilchrist, Roberta
1991   "Women's Archaeology? Political Feminism, Gender Theory and Historical Revision." *Antiquity* 65: 495–501.

Glass, John B.
1966   "Archaeological Survey of Western Honduras." In *Handbook of Middle American Indians*, vol. 4, edited by G. Ekholm and Gordon Willey, 157–179. Austin: University of Texas Press.

Glazer, Penina Migdal and Miriam Slater (editors)
1987   *Unequal Colleagues: The Entrance of Women into the Professions, 1890–1940*. New Brunswick, NJ: Rutgers University Press.

Goldstein, Elyse
1979   "Effect of Same-sex and Cross-sex Role Models on the Subsequent Academic Productivity of Scholars." *American Psychologist* 34:407–410.

Golla, Victor (editor)
1984   *The Sapir-Kroeber Correspondence: Letters Between Edward Sapir and A. L. Kroeber 1905–1925*. Report No. 6. Survey of California and Other Indian Languages, University of California, Berkeley.

Golson, Jack
1986   "Old Guards and New Waves: Reflections on Antipodean Archaeology 1954–1975." *Archaeology in Oceania* 21(1): 2–12.

Gonzáles Torres, Yólotl (coordinadora)
1989   *Homenaje a Isabel Kelly*. Colección Científica. México, D.F.: Instituto Nacional de Antroplogía e Historia.

Gordon, George Byron
1898   *Researches in the Uloa Valley, Honduras*. Peabody Museum of Ethnology and Archaeology, Harvard University Memoirs 1 (4).

Goulding, M., Kathleen A. Buckley, and G. Brennan
1993   The Role of Gender in Archaeological Career Structures. In *Women in Archaeology: A Feminist Critique*, edited by Hillary duCros and Laurajane Smith. Department of Prehistory, Research School of Pacific Studies, Australian National University, Canberra, in press.

Graham, Ian
1990   "Tatiana Proskouriakoff: 1909–1985." *American Antiquity* 55(1):6–11.

Greenlee, Robert
1933   Archaeological Sites in the Chama Valley and Report on Excavations at Tsama, 1929–1933. Unpublished ms. Laboratory of Anthropology, Santa Fe, NM.

Griffin, James B.
1952   *Archaeology of Eastern United States*. Chicago: University of Chicago Press.
1985   "The Formation of the Society for American Archaeology." *American Antiquity* 50:261–271.

Guthe, Carl
1928   "Archaeological Field Work in North America." *American Anthropologist* 30:501–524.
1929   "Archaeological Field Work in North America." *American Anthropologist* 31:332–360.
1930   "Archaeological Field Work in North America." *American Anthropologist* 32:342–374.

1967   "Reflections on the Founding of the Society for American Archaeology." *American Antiquity* 32:433–440.

Hall, Edith
1907   *The Decorative Art of Crete in the Bronze Age*. Philadelphia: John C. Winston Co.
1912a   *Excavations in Eastern Crete: Sphoungaras*. Anthropological Publications, The University Museum, Philadelphia.
1912b   "The Cretan Expedition." *Museum Journal* 3(3):39–44.
1913   "The Greco-Roman Section." *Museum Journal* 4(4):117–167.
1914   *Excavations in Eastern Crete: Vrokastro*. Anthropological Publications, The University Museum, Philadelphia.

Hanfmann, George
1944   "Review of Edith Hall Dohan's Italic Tomb-Groups in the University Museum." *American Journal of Archaeology* 48(1):114–116.

Haraway, Donna
1989   *Primate Visions: Gender, Race and Nature in the World of Modern Science*. New York: Routledge.

Harding, Sandra
1991   *Whose Science? Whose Knowledge? Thinking from Women's Lives*. Ithaca, NY: Cornell University Press.

Harrold, C. C.
1934   (January 7). Letter to A. R. Kelly, Accession #122. Ms. on file, Southeast Archeological Center, National Park Service, Tallahassee, FL.

Hawes, Harriet Boyd
1908   *Gournia, Vasiliki and Other Prehistoric Sites on the Isthmus of Ierapetra, Crete*. Philadelphia: American Exploration Society.
1965a   "Memoirs of a Pioneer Excavator in Crete." *Archaeology* 18(2):94–101.
1965b   "Memoirs of a Pioneer Excavator in Crete: Part II." *Archaeology* 18(4):268–276.

Hawley, Florence M.
1930   "Prehistoric Pottery and Culture Relations in the Middle Gila." *American Anthropologist* 32:522–536.

Heilbrun, Carolyn
1988   *Writing a Woman's Life*. New York: Norton.

Heimlich, Marion Dunlevy
1952   Guntersville Basin Pottery. Geological Survey of Alabama, Museum Paper No. 32. University: Alabama Museum of Natural History.

Hodder, Ian
1986   *Reading the Past: Current Approaches to Interpretation in Archaeology*. Cambridge: Cambridge University Press.

Hodge, Frederick Webb
1935   "Foreword." In *The Pinto Basin Site*, 7–8. Southwest Museum Papers 9.

Hope, J.
1993   "Double Bind, Women Archaeologists in the New South Wales National Parks Service." In *Women in Archaeology: A Feminist Critique*, edited by Hillary duCros and Laurajane Smith. Department of Prehistory, Research School of Pacific Studies, Australian National University, Canberra. In press.

Hume, Ivor Noel
1987   *Historical Archaeology.* Orig. 1968. New York: Alfred A. Knopf.
Hunt, Eleazer D.
1986   "Marian E. White: Researching the Settlement Patterns of the Niagara Frontier." *North American Archaeologist* 7(4): 313–328.
Irwin-Williams, Cynthia
1990   "Women in the Field: The Role of Women in Archaeology before 1960." In *Women of Science: Righting the Record,* edited by G. Kass-Simon and Patricia Farnes, 1–41. Bloomington: Indiana University Press.
Itow, L.
1989   "Women and Minorities Face Uphill Battle in Academia." *UC Focus* 3(4):1, 8. University of California, Office of the President.
Jacobsthal, Paul
1943   "Review of Edith Dohan's Italic Tomb Groups in the University Museum." *Journal of Roman Studies* 33: 97–100.
James, Alice
1988   "Dorothy Louise Strouse Keur (1904–   )." In *Women Anthropologists: A Biographical Dictionary,* edited by Ute Gacs, Aisha Khan, Jerrie McIntyre, and Ruth Weinberg, 181–186. New York: Greenwood Press.
Jeter, Marvin, Jerome Rose, G. Ishmael Williams, Jr., and Anna M. Harmon
1989   *Archeology and Bioarcheology of the Lower Mississippi Valley and Trans-Mississippi South in Arkansas and Louisiana.* Arkansas Archeological Survey Research Series No. 37. Fayetteville: Arkansas Archeological Survey.
Johnson, Fran Holmon
1990   *"The Gift of the Wild Things": The Life of Caroline Dormon.* Lafayette: University of Southwestern Louisiana Press.
Johnson, Paula Patecek
1977   "The Spring of Abita Builds a Town." *St. Tammany Historical Society Gazette* 2:67–77.
Johnson, Paula Patecek and John Healy
1975   "Oral History: Lawrence Flot." *St. Tammany Historical Society Gazette* 1:41–48.
Jones, Jacquelin
1985   *Labor of Love, Labor of Sorrow.* New York: Vintage Books.
Joyce, Rosemary A.
1991   *Cerro Palenque: Power and Identity on the Southern Mesoamerican Periphery.* Austin: University of Texas Press.
Kehoe, Alice B.
1989   "Contextualizing Archaeology." In *Tracing Archaeology's Past: The Historiography of Archaeology,* edited by Andrew L. Christenson, 97–106. Carbondale: Southern Illinois Press.
Kelley, Jane H.
1992   "Being and Becoming." In *Rediscovering Our Past: Essays on the History of American Archaeology,* edited by Jonathan E. Reyman, 51–68. Aldershot, England: Avebury/Ashgate Publishing Company.
Kelley, Jane H. and Warren Hill
1991   "Relationships Between Graduate Training and Placement in Canadian Archaeology." In *The Archaeology of Gender,* edited by Dale

Walde and Noreen D. Willows, 195–200. Calgary: Archaeology Association of the University of Calgary.

Kelly, Arthur Randolph
1936   (April 5). Letter to A. M. Tozzer, Peabody Museum, Harvard University. Accession #122. Ms. on file, Southeast Archeological Center, National Park Service, Tallahassee, FL.
1938   (January 4). Letter to Dr. Donald Scott, Director, Peabody Museum, Harvard University. Accession #122. Ms. on file, Southeast Archeological Center, National Park Service, Tallahassee, FL.
1940   Archaeology in the National Park Service. *American Antiquity* 5:274–282.

Kelly, Arthur Randolph and Betty A. Smith
1975   The Swift Creek Site, 9Bi3, Macon, Georgia. Ms. on file, Department of Anthropology, University of Georgia, Athens.

Kelly, Isabel, Frances Watkins, and Eva Horner
1929a   Field Diary (7/18/29–8/14/29). Peabody Museum Archives 59-17.
1929b   Field Notes (7/23/29–8/6/29). Peabody Museum Archives 59-17.

Kennedy, Nedenia
1981   "The Formative Period Ceramic Sequence From Playa de los Muertos, Honduras." Ph.D. dissertation, Department of Anthropology, University of Illinois.

Keur, Dorothy
1941   *Big Bead Mesa: An Archaeological Study of Navaho Acculturation 1745–1812.* Society for American Archaeology Memoir 1.
1971   "Mary Butler Lewis: 1903–1970." *American Anthropologist* 73:255–256.

Kidder, Alfred. V.
1929   Letter to Elsie Clews Parsons, April 8, 1929. American Philisophical Association.
1930   "Phillips Academy." *El Palacio* 29:148–149.
1957   "Earl Halstead Morris—1889–1956." *American Antiquity* 22:390–397.

Kidder, Alfred V. and Charles A. Amsden
1931   *The Pottery of Pecos*, Vol. 1, *The Dull-Paint Wares.* Papers of the Phillips Academy, Southwestern Expedition 5.

Kneberg, Madeline D.
1945   "The Persistent Potsherd." *Tennessee Archaeologist* 1(4):4–5.
1952   "The Tennessee Area." In *Archaeology of Eastern United States*, edited by James B. Griffin, 190–198. Chicago: University of Chicago Press.
1954   "The Duration of the Archaic Tradition in the Lower Tennessee Valley." *Southern Indian Studies* 5:40–44.
1956   "Some Important Projectile Point Types Found in the Tennessee Area." *Tennessee Archaeologist* 12(1):17–28.
1957   "Chipped Stone Artifacts of the Tennessee Valley Area." *Tennessee Archaeologist* 13(1):55–65.
1959   "Engraved Shell Gorgets and Their Associations." *Tennessee Archaeologist* 15(1):1–39.
1962   "Woodland Fabric Marked Ceramic System." *Proceedings of the Sixteenth Southeastern Archaeological Conference* (Macon, GA 1959), Newsletter vol. 8:33–40.

Knobloch, Patricia J.
   1988   "Isabel Truesdell Kelly (1906–1983)." In *Women Anthropologists: A Biographical Dictionary*, edited by Ute Gacs, Aisha Khan, Jerrie McIntyre, and Ruth Weinberg, 175–180. New York: Greenwood Press.
Knudson, Ruthann
   1986   "Contemporary Cultural Resource Management." In *American Archaeology Past and Future*, edited by David J. Meltzer, Don D. Fowler and Jeremy A. Sabloff, 395–414. Washington, DC: Smithsonian Institution Press.
Kramer, Carol and Miriam Stark
   1988   "The Status of Women in Archaeology." *Anthropology Newsletter* 29(9):1, 11–12.
Krouse, Rita Moore
   1962   *Fragments of a Dream: The Story of Germantown*. Ruston, LA: Leader Press.
   1971   "Bayou Dauchite: The Ante-Bellum Lifeline of Claiborne Parish." *North Louisiana Historical Association Journal* 2(2):35–42.
   1972   "Two Old Claiborne Towns." *North Louisiana Historical Association Journal* 3(4):128–130.
   1973   "Communication: An Aspect of the Cultural Development of Early Claiborne Parish to 1860." *North Louisiana Historical Association Journal* 4(2):42–57.
Lazarus, Yulee W.
   1970   "Salvage Archaeology at Fort Walton Beach." *Florida Anthropologist* 23(1):29–42.
   1979   "The Buck Mound." Temple Mound Museum, Fort Walton Beach, FL.
   1992   Written interview on file. Department of Anthropology, University of South Florida, Tampa.
Lazarus, Yulee W. and Carolyn B. Hawkins
   1976   "Pottery of the Fort Walton Period." Temple Mound Museum, Fort Walton Beach, FL.
Lee, Richard B.
   1968   "What Hunters Do For a Living, Or, How to Make Out on Scarce Resources." In *Man the Hunter*, edited by Richard B. Lee and Irven DeVore, 30–48. Chicago: Aldine Publishing Company.
Leone, Mark P.
   1991   "Materialist Theory and the Formation of Questions in Archaeology." In *Processual and Postprocessual Archaeologists: Multiple Ways of Knowing the Past*, edited by Robert W. Preucel, 235–241. Carbondale: Center for Archaeological Investigations, Southern Illinois University, Carbondale, Occasional Paper 10.
Leone, Mark P. and Robert W. Preucel
   1992   "Archaeology in a Democratic Society: A Critical Theory Prespective." In *Americanist Archaeology Goals and Practice*, edited by LuAnn Wandsnider, 114–134. Carbondale: Center for Archaeological Investigations, Southern Illinois University, Occasional Paper 20.
Lerner, Gerda
   1977   *The Female Experience: An American Documentary*. Indianapolis, IN: Bobbs-Merrill.

Leslie, Vernon
    1949   "Let's Put Some Meat on the Bones." *Pennsylvania Archaeologist* 19:2.

Levine, Mary Ann
    1991   "An Historical Overview of Research on Women in Anthropology." In *The Archaeology of Gender*, Proceedings of the 22nd Annual Chacmool Conference, edited by Dale Walde and Noreen D. Willows, 177–186. Calgary: Archaeological Association of the University of Calgary.
    in preparation "Uncovering a Buried Past: Women in Americanist Archaeology Before the First World War." In *Mainstreams and Margins: Studies in the Professionalization of Archaeology*, edited by Alice B. Kehoe. Volume under review.

Lewis, Madeline Kneberg
    1992   Written interview on file. Department of Anthropology, University of South Florida, Tampa.

Lewis, Thomas M. N. and Madeline D. Kneberg
    1941   *Prehistory of the Chickamauga Basin in Tennessee*. University of Tennessee, Division of Anthropology, Tennessee Anthropological Papers No. 1 (Mimeographed).
    1946   *Hiwassee Island: An Archaeological Account of Four Tennessee Indian Peoples*. Knoxville: University of Tennessee Press.
    1947   *The Archaic Horizon in Western Tennessee*. Tennessee Anthropology Papers No. 2, University of Tennessee Record, Extension Series, vol. 23, No. 4.
    1954a   *Oconaluftee Indian Village: An Interpretation of a Cherokee Community of 1750*. Cherokee Historical Association. Cherokee, NC.
    1954b   (editors) *Ten Years of the Tennessee Archaeologist, Selected Subjects*. Chattanooga, TN: J. B. Graham.
    1956   "The Paleo-Indian Complex on the LeCroy Site." *Tennessee Archaeologist* 12(1):5–11.
    1957   "The Camp Creek Site." *Tennessee Archaeologist* 13(1):1–48.
    1958a   *Tribes That Slumber: Indians of the Tennessee Region*. Knoxville: University of Tennessee Press.
    1958b   "The Nuckolls Site." *Tennessee Archaeologist* 14(2):60–79.
    1959   "The Archaic Culture in the Middle South." *American Antiquity* 25: 161–183.
    1994   Appendix C. "Manual of Field and Laboratory Techniques Employed by the Division of Anthropology, University of Tennessee, Knoxville, Tennessee, in Connection with the Investigation of Archaeological Sites within the TVA Dam Reservoirs." In *The Prehistory of the Chickamauga Basin in Tennessee*, edited by L. Sullivan. Knoxville: University of Tennessee Press, in press.

Lewis, Thomas M. N. and Madeline Kneberg Lewis
    1961   *Eva: An Archaic Site*. Knoxville: University of Tennessee Press.

Licht, B. G. and Carol S. Dweck
    1984   "Determinants of Academic Achievement Orientations with Skill Area." *Developmental Psychology* 20: 628–636.

Lingua franca
    1991   "Where the Boys Are." *Lingua franca* 1(3): 6–7.

Lord, Louis E.
    1947   *A History of the American School of Classical Studies at Athens: 1882–1942*. Cambridge, MA: Harvard University Press.

Lurie, Nancy
  1966   "Women in Early American Anthropology." In *Pioneers of American Anthropology*, edited by June Helm, 31–81. Seattle: University of Washington Press.
Lutz, Catherine
  1990   "The Erasure of Women's Writing in Sociocultural Anthropology." *American Ethnologist* 17: 611–627.
Lyon, Edwin A.
  1991   New Deal Archaeology in the Southeast. Draft manuscript in possession of author.
Marcus, Joyce
  1988   "Tatiana Proskouriakoff (1909–1985)." In *Women Anthropologists: A Biographical Dictionary*, edited by Ute Gacs, Aisha Khan, Jerrie McIntyre, and Ruth Weinberg, 297–302. New York: Greenwood Press.
Mason, Carol I.
  1992   "From the Other Side of the Looking Glass: Women in American Archaeology in the 1950s." In *Rediscovering Our Past: Essays on the History of American Archaeology*, edited by Jonathan E. Reyman, 91–101. Aldershot, England: Avebury/Ashgate Publishing Company.
Mason, Ronald J.
  1985   *Great Lakes Archaeology.* Orlando, FL: Academic Press.
McBryde, I.
  1986   "Australia's Once and Future Archaeology." *Archaeology in Oceania* 21(1): 13–28.
McChesney, Lea S.
  1991   "Hemenway, Mary." In *International Dictionary of Anthropologists*, edited by Christopher Winters, 281–283. New York: Garland Publishing.
McClellan, Catharine
  1988   "Frederica de Laguna (1906–   )." In *Women Anthropologists: A Biographical Dictionary*, edited by Ute Gacs, Aisha Khan, Jerrie McIntyre, and Ruth Weinberg, 37–44. New York: Greenwood Press.
McGee, Anita Newcomb
  1989   "The Women's Anthropological Society of America." *Science* 13: 240–242.
McGowan, A.
  1991   Working Lives: the Career Prospects and Aspirations of Men and Women Cultural Resource Managers in Tasmania. Paper presented to the Australian Archaeological Association Annual Conference, Jindabyne, December.
McLemore, Denise and Linda Reynolds
  1979   "Employment of Female Archaeologists in the U.S. Forest Service." *National Women's Anthropology Newsletter* 4(1):6–9.
Meehan, Betty
  1982   *Shell Bed to Shell Midden.* Canberra: Australian Institute of Aboriginal Studies.
Menges, Robert J. and William H. Exum
  1983   "Barriers to the Progress of Women and Minority Faculty." *Journal of Higher Education* 54(2): 123–144.
Michael, Ronald L.
  1991   Letter to Mary C. Beaudry, March 27, 1991.

Milisauskas, Sarunas
1977 "Obituary: Marian Emily White, 1921–1975." *American Antiquity* 42:191–195.
Moore, Henrietta
1986 *Space, Text, and Gender: An Anthropological Study of the Marakwet of Kenya.* Cambridge: Cambridge University Press.
1991 Epilogue. In *Engendering Archaeology: Women and Prehistory,* edited by Joan Gero and Margaret W. Conkey, 407–411. Oxford: Basil Blackwell.
Moore, Kathryn M.
1982 "The Role of Mentors in Developing Leaders for Academe." *Educational Record* 63(1): 22–31.
Moorehead, Warren K.
1932 "Exploration of the Etowah Site in Georgia." In *Etowah Papers,* I. New Haven, CT: Yale University Press (for Phillips Academy).
Morris, Ann Axtell
1931 *Digging in the Yucatan.* New York: Junior Literary Guild.
1933 *Digging in the Southwest.* New York: Doubleday, Doran, and Co., Inc.
Morris Earl, H., Jean Charlot, and Ann Axtell Morris
1931 *The Temple of the Warriors.* 2 vols. Publication 406. Washington, DC: Carnegie Institution of Washington.
Morris, Elizabeth Ann
1974 "Anna O. Shepard, 1903–1973." *American Antiquity* 39:448–451.
Mott, Mildred
1938 "The Relation of Historic Indian Tribes to Archaeological Manifestations in Iowa." *Iowa Journal of History and Politics* 36(3):227–314.
Muller, Jon
1966 "Archaeological Analysis of Art Styles." *Tennessee Archaeologist* 22(1): 25–39.
1986 "Serpents and Dancers: Art of the Mud Glyph Cave." In *The Prehistoric Native American Art of Mud Glyph Cave,* edited by C. Faulkner, 36–80. Knoxville: University of Tennessee Press.
Nelson, Margaret C. and Deborah L. Crooks
1991 "Dual Anthropology Career Couples: Different Strategies and Different Success Rates." In *The Archaeology of Gender,* edited by Dale Walde and Noreen D. Willows, 220–225. Calgary: Archaeology Association of the University of Calgary.
Nelson, Sarah M.
1991 "Women Archaeologists in Asia and the Pacific." In *The Archaeology of Gender,* edited by Dale Walde and Noreen D. Willows, 217–219. Calgary: Archaeology Association of the University of Calgary.
Neuman, Robert W.
1984a *An Introduction to Louisiana Archaeology.* Baton Rouge: Louisiana State University Press.
1984b "Archaeology of the Louisiana Coastal Zone, 1970 to the Present." In *Perspectives on Gulf Coast Prehistory,* edited by Dave D. Davis, 156–164. Gainesville: University Presses of Florida.
Neuman, Robert W. and Lanier A. Simmons
1969 *A Bibliography Relative to Indians of the State of Louisiana.* Department of Conservation, Louisiana Geological Survey, Baton Rouge.

Nussbaum, Martha
  1990   *Love's Knowledge: Essays on Philosphy and Literature.* Oxford: Oxford University Press.
Ocmulgee Reading File
  1937   Letterhead of the Works Progress Administration, Atlanta, Georgia. Ms. on file, Southeast Archeological Center, National Park Service, Tallahassee, FL.
Ortner, Sherry B. and Harriet Whitehead
  1981   *Sexual Meanings: The Cultural Construction of Gender and Sexuality.* Cambridge: Cambridge University Press.
Parezo, Nancy
  1989   "Marginalized in Museums." Paper presented at the 22nd Annual Chacmool Conference, Calgary.
Patterson, Thomas C.
  1986   "The Last Sixty Years: Toward a Social History of Americanist Archeology in the United States." *American Anthropologist* 88:7–26.
Pearson, Charles E.
  1985   "Some Characteristics of the LAS Membership." *Louisiana Archaeological Society Newsletter* 12(2):13–14.
Perrigo, Lynn
  1982   *Gateway to Glorieta: A History of Las Vegas, New Mexico.* Boulder, CO: Pruett Publishing Co.
Pinkley, Jean M.
  1965   "The Pueblos and the Turkey: Who Domesticated Whom?" In *Contributions of the Wetherill Mesa Archaeology Project*, assembled by D. Osborn, 70–72. Society for American Archaeology, Memoir 19.
Popenoe, Dorothy
  1929   Letter to A. M. Tozzer, February 21. Harvard University, Peabody Museum of Archaeology and Ethnology, accession file 29-15.
  1930   "Two Expeditions in Search of Painted Pottery." Unpublished report, March 1930. Harvard University, Peabody Museum of Archaeology and Ethnology, accession file 30-46.
  1932   Letter to A. M. Tozzer, December 8. Harvard University, Peabody Museum of Archaeology and Ethnology, accession file 33-18.
  1934   ."Some Excavations at Playa de los Muertos, Ulua River, Honduras." *Maya Research* 1:62–86.
Popenoe, Wilson
  1933a Letter to A. M. Tozzer, January 20. Harvard University, Peabody Museum of Archaeology and Ethnology, accession file 33-18.
  1933b Letter to A. M. Tozzer, July 2. Harvard University, Peabody Museum of Archaeology and Ethnology, accession file 31-43.
Popenoe, Wilson and Dorothy Popenoe
  1931   "The Human Background of Lancetilla." *Unifruitco Magazine*, August: 6–10.
Proskouriakoff, Tatiana
  1946   *An Album of Maya Architecture.* Publication 558. Washington, DC: Carnegie Institution of Washington.
  1950   *A Study of Classic Maya Sculpture.* Publication 593. Washington, DC: Carnegie Institution of Washington.
  1960   "Historical Implications of a Pattern of Dates at Piedras Negras, Guatemala." *American Antiquity* 25:454–475.

1974   *Jades from the Cenote of Sacrifice, Chichén Itzá, Yucatán*. Harvard University, Peabody Museum of Archaeology and Ethnology Memoirs 10(1).

Quinn, Naomi
1985   "Culture, Gender, and Work." Paper Presented at the Spring Semester Colloquim in Feminist Theory and the Disciplines, Duke University Women's Study Program.

Rathje, William L. and Michael B. Schiffer
1982   *Archaeology*. New York: Harcourt, Brace, Jovanovich.

Reichard, Gladys
1929   Letter to Elsie Clews Parsons, August 25. Reprinted in "Past is Present" by Nathalie S. Woodbury, *Anthropology Newsletter*, September 1991.

Reskin, Barbara F. and Heidi I. Hartmann (editors)
1986   *Women's Work, Men's Work: Sex Segregation on the Job*. Committee on Women's Employment and Related Social Issues, Commission on Behavioral and Social Science and Education, and the National Research Council. Washington, DC: National Academy Press.

Reyman, Jonathan E.
1992b   "Women in American Archaeology: Some Historical Notes and Comments." In *Rediscovering Our Past: Essays on the History of American Archaeology*, edited by J. Reyman, 69–80. Aldershot, England: Avebury/Ashgate Publishing Company.

Reyman, Jonathan E.(editor)
1992a   *Rediscovering Our Past: Essays on the History of American Archaeology*. Aldershot, England: Avebury/Ashgate Publishing Company.

Rich, Adrienne
1986   "What Does a Woman Need to Know?" In *Blood, Bread, and Poetry: Selected Prose, 1979–1985*. New York: Norton.

Richter, Gisela and Mary H. Swindler
1943   "Edith Hall Dohan." *American Journal of Archaeology* 47(4):466.

Rick, John
1969   "Man and Superman." *Historical Archaeology* 3:1–2.

Ritchie, William A.
1985   "Archaeology in the Northeast." *American Antiquity* 50: 412–420.

Rolingson, Martha A.
1960   "A Study of the Paleo-Indian in Kentucky." M.A. thesis. Lexington: Department of Anthropology, University of Kentucky.
1964   "Paleo-Indian Culture in Kentucky." Studies in Anthropology No. 2, Lexington: University of Kentucky Press.
1967   "Temporal Perspective of the Archaic Cultures of the Middle Green River Region, Kentucky." Ph.D. dissertation. Chicago: Department of Anthropology, University of Chicago.
1992   Written interview on file. Department of Anthropology, University of South Florida, Tampa.

Rolingson, Martha A. and Douglas W. Schwartz
1966   *Late PaleoIndian and Early Archaic Manifestations in Western Kentucky*. Studies in Anthropology No. 3. Lexington: University of Kentucky Press.

Rosengarten, Frederic, Jr.
  1991   *Wilson Popenoe: Agricultural Explorer, Educator, and Friend of Latin America*. Lawai, Kauai, Hawaii: National Tropical Botanical Garden.
Rossiter, Margaret W.
  1982   *Women Scientists in America: Struggles and Strategies to 1940*. Baltimore: Johns Hopkins University Press.
Ryan, Mary P.
  1983   *Womanhood in America*. Baltimore: Franklin Watts, Inc.
Sacks, Karen Brodkin
  1989   "Toward a Unified Theory of Class, Race, and Gender." *American Ethnologist* 16:534–550.
Schroedl, Gerald F.
  1973   "Radiocarbon Dates from Three Burial Mounds at the McDonald Site in East Tennessee." *Tennessee Archaeologist* 29(1):3–11.
  1978   *Excavations of the Leuty and McDonald Site Mounds*. Report of Investigations No. 22, Department of Anthropology, University of Tennessee. Publications in Anthropology No. 15, Tennessee Valley Authority.
Scott, Joan
  1992   "Deconstructing Equality-Versus-Difference: or, The Uses of Post-Structuralist Theory for Feminism." In *Defining Women: Social Institutions and Gender Divisions*, edited by L. McDowell and R. Pringle, 253–264. Oxford: Polity Press.
Seifert, Donna J. (editor)
  1991   "Gender in Historical Archaeology." *Historical Archaeology* 25(4).
Shanks, Michael and Christopher Tilley
  1987   *Re-Constructing Archaeology: Theory and Practice*. Cambridge: Cambridge University Press.
Shenkel, J. Richard
  1984   "Early Woodland in Coastal Louisiana." In *Perspectives on Gulf Coast Prehistory*, edited by Dave D. Davis, 41–71. Gainesville: University Presses of Florida.
Shepard, Anna O.
  1936a   "'Cell-Tempered' Pottery." *American Antiquity* 2:137–139.
  1936b   "Metallographic Study of Copper Artifacts." *American Antiquity* 2:139–140.
  1939a   "Technology of La Plata Pottery." In *Archaeological Studies in the La Plata District: Southwestern Colorado and Northwestern New Mexico*, edited by E. Morris, 249–287. Publication 519. Washington, DC: Carnegie Institution of Washington.
  1939b   Technological Notes on the Pottery of San Jose. In *Excavations at San Jose, British Honduras*, by John Eric Thompson, 251–277. Publication 506. Washington, DC: Carnegie Institution of Washington.
  1948   *Plumbate: A Mesoamerican Tradeware*. Publication 573. Washington, DC: Carnegie Institution of Washington.
  1956   *Ceramics for the Archaeologist*. Publication 609. Washington, DC: Carnegie Institution of Washington.
  1971   "Ceramic Analysis: The Interrelations of Methods; the Relations of Analysts and Archaeologists." In *Science and Archaeology*, edited by R. Brill, 55–63. Cambridge, MA: MIT Press.

Simeone, Angela
1987   *Academic Women: Working Towards Equality.* Boston: Bergin and Garvey.

Simmons, Lanier A.
1978   "Additional Notes on the Archaeology of Little Pecan Island." *Codex Wauchope: A Tribute Roll,* edited by Marco Giardino, Barbara Edmonson, and Winifred Creamer, 13–17. Human Mosaic 12. New Orleans: Tulane University Press.

Smiley, T.L., S. Stubbs, and B. Bannister
1953   "A Foundation for the Dating of Some Late Archaeological Sites in the Rio Grande Area, New Mexico: Based on Studies in Tree-Ring Methods and Pottery Analysis." *University of Arizona Bulletin* 24 (3); *Laboratory of Tree-Ring Research Bulletin* 6.

Smith, Marvin T. and Julie Barnes Smith
1989   "Engraved Shell Masks in North America." *Southeastern Archaeolgy* 8(1):9–18.

Smith-Rosenberg, Carroll
1986   "Writing History: Language, Class and Gender." In *Feminist Studies, Critical Studies,* edited by Teresa de Lauretis, 31–54. Bloomington: Indiana University Press.

Society of Professional Archaeologists
1992   *Directory of Certified Professional Archaeologists.* Tampa, FL: The Society of Professional Archaeologists.

Solomon, Barbara Miller
1985   *In the Company of Educated Women: A History of Women and Higher Education in America.* New Haven, CT: Yale University Press.

South, Stanley A.
1969   "Wanted: An Historical Archaeologist." *Historical Archaeology* 3:75–84.

Spector, Janet
1983   "Male/Female Task Differentiation Among the Hidatsa: Toward the Development of an Archeological Approach to the Study of Gender." In *The Hidden Half: Studies of Plains Indian Women,* edited by Patricia Albers and Beatrice Medicine, 77–99. Washington, DC: University Press of America.
1991   "What This Awl Means." In *Engendering Archaeology: Women in Prehistory,* edited by Joan Gero and Margaret Conkey, 388–406. Oxford: Basil Blackwell.

Spector, Janet D. and Mary K. Whelan
1989   "Incorporating Gender into Archaeology Courses." In *Gender and Anthropology: Critical Reviews for Research and Teaching,* edited by Sandra Morgen, 65–94. Washington, DC: American Anthropological Association.

Speizer, J. J.
1981   "Role Models, Mentors, and Sponsors: The Elusive Concepts." *Signs: Journal of Women in Culture and Society* 6(4):692–712.

Stark, Miriam
1991   "A Perspective on Women's Status in American Archaeology." In *The Archaeology of Gender: Proceedings of the 22nd Annual Chacmool Conference,* edited by Dale Walde and Noreen D. Willows, 187–194. Calgary: Archaeological Association of the University of Calgary.

Stone, Doris Z.
1941   *Archaeology of the North Coast of Honduras*. Cambridge, MA: Memoirs of the Peabody Museum of Archaeology and Ethnology, IX (1).
1980   "A Fair Period for a Field Study." *Radcliffe Quarterly* 66(3):20–22.
Swanton, John R.
1985   *Final Report of the United States De Soto Expedition Commission*. Orig. 1939. Washington, DC: Smithsonian Institution Press.
1987   *The Indians of the Southeastern United States*. Orig. 1946. Washington, DC: Smithsonian Institution Press.
Strathern, Marilyn
1991   *Partial Connections*. New York: Rowman and Littlefield.
Sullivan, Lynne P. (editor)
1994   *The Prehistory of the Chickamauga Basin in Tennessee*, 2 vols. Knoxville: University of Tennessee Press.
Taos Working Conference
1990   "Save the Past for the Future: Actions for the '90s." Final Report of the Taos Working Conference on Preventing Archaeological Looting and Vandalism. Society for American Archaeology.
Taylor, Joe Gray
1984   *Louisiana: A History*. New York: W. W. Norton.
Taylor, Walter W.
1983   *A Study of Archeology*. Center for Archaeological Investigations, Southern Illinois University, Carbondale. (Originally published in 1948 as Memoir 69, American Anthropological Association.)
Thomas, Chester A.
1969   "Jean McWhirt Pinkley, 1910–1969." *American Antiquity* 34:471–473.
Thomas, Dorothy
1933   "Exploring the Museum Field." *Independent Woman* 12:238–239, 260.
Thompson, Dorothy Burr
1971   "Edith Hayward Hall Dohan." *Notable American Women, 1607–1950: A Biographical Dictionary*, edited by Edward T. James, Janet Wilson James, and Paul S. Boyer, 496–497. Cambridge, MA: Belknap Press of Harvard University Press.
Thompson, Raymond H.
1991   "Shepard, Kidder, and Carnegie." In *The Ceramic Legacy of Anna O. Shepard*, edited by Ronald L. Bishop and Frederick W. Lange, 11–41. Niwot: University Press of Colorado.
Tozzer, A. M.
1932a   Letter to Dorothy Popenoe, December 22. Harvard University, Peabody Museum of Archaeology and Ethnology, accession file 33-18.
1932b   Letter to Wilson Popenoe, January 22. Harvard University, Peabody Museum of Archaeology and Ethnology, accession file 31-43.
1933   Letter to Wilson Popenoe, January 10. Harvard University, Peabody Museum of Archaeology and Ethnology, accession file 33-18.
1934a   Letter to Wilson Popenoe, March 23. Harvard University, Peabody Museum of Archaeology and Ethnology, accession file 31-43.
1934b   "Obituary of Dorothy H. Popenoe." *Maya Research* 1:86.

Trigger, Bruce G.
1986   "Prehistoric Archaeology and American Society." In *American Archaeology Past and Future,* edited by D. Meltzer, D. Fowler and J. Sabloff, 187–216. Washington, DC: Smithsonian Institution Press.

Tringham, Ruth and M. Stevanovic
1991   "Vinca Domestic Architecture as Arenas of Household/Gender Tensions." Paper presented at the annual meeting of the Society for American Archaeology, New Orleans.

Tucker, Susan
1988   *Telling Memories Among Southern Women.* New York: Schocken Books.

Urban, Patricia A.
1988   "Book review of 'Research and Reflections in Archaeology and History: Essays in Honor of Doris Stone.'" *American Antiquity* 53: 887–888.

Vaillant, George C.
1934   "The Archaeological Setting of the Playa de los Muertos Culture." *Maya Research* 1:87–100.

Van Maanen, J.
1988   *Tales of the Field: On Writing Ethnography.* Chicago: University of Chicago Press.

Victor, Katharine L. and Mary C. Beaudry
1992   "Women's Participation in American Prehistoric and Historic Archaeology: A Comparative Look at the Journals *American Antiquity* and *Historical Archaeology.*" In *Exploring Gender Through Archaeology,* edited by Cheryl Claassen, 11–21. Madison, WI: Prehistory Press.

Villere, Keith J.
1980   "Historic Preservation of Abita Springs." Report produced for the St. Tammany Parish Planning Commission, Covington, and the Abita Springs Planning and Zoning Commission, Abita Springs.

Walde, Dale and Noreen D. Willows (editors)
1991   *The Archaeology of Gender, Proceedings of the 22nd Annual Chacmool Conference.* Calgary: Archaeological Association of the University of Calgary.

Ward, C. W. G.
1929   "Charming Young Archaeologists Rush Sheepherder to Las Vegas for Rattlesnake Bite Treatment." *Las Vegas Optic,* 27 August.

Ware, Susan
1981   *Beyond Suffrage: Women in the New Deal.* Cambridge, MA: Harvard University Press.

Warren, Claude N.
1970   "Time and Topography: Elizabeth W. C. Campbell's Approach to the Prehistory of the Californian Deserts." *Masterkey* 44(1):5–14.

Watkins, Frances E.
n.d.   "Seeking Archaeological Treasure." Unpublished manuscript. Southwest Museum ms. 50.
1930   "My Experiences as a Field Archaeologist." *Masterkey* 4:13–20.
1931   "Archaeology as a Profession for Women." *Masterkey* 4: 173–178.

Wauchope, Robert (editor)
1956   *Seminars in Archaeology: 1955.* Society for American Memoirs 11.

Webb, Clarence H. and Brian J. Duhe
1984   "The Louisiana Archaeological Society's First Decade, 1974–1984."
In *Louisiana Archaeology and the Society: Celebration of a Decade of Achievement*, edited by Jon L. Gibson, 55–87. Special Publication of the Louisiana Archaeological Society 2.

West, Frederick Hadleigh and Robert W. Neuman (editors)
1981   *Traces of Prehistory: Papers in Honor of William G. Haag*. Geoscience and Man XXII. Baton Rouge: School of Geoscience, Louisiana State University.

White, Jacqueline
1990   "'I Don't DO Faunal Analysis': A Review of the Publications by Women and Men in the Journal of *Historical Archaeology*." Research paper on file, Department of Archaeology, Boston University.

White, Marian E.
1958   "An Iroquois Sequence in New York's Niagara Frontier." *Pennsylvania Archaeologist* 28:145–150.
1961   *Iroquois Culture History in the Niagara Frontier Area of New York State*. Museum of Anthropology, University of Michigan, Anthropological Papers 16.
1965   "The Orchid Site Ossuary, Fort Erie, Ontario." *New York State Archeological Association Bulletin* 38: 1–35.
1967   "An Early Historic Niagara Frontier Iroquois Cemetery in Erie County, New York." *Researches and Transactions of the New York State Archaeological Association* 16(1): 1–36; 58–91.
1971   "Ethnic Identification and Iroquois Groups in Western New York and Ontario." *Ethnohistory* 18:19–38.
1972   The Crisis in Western New York Archaeology. Manuscript on file at the State University of New York at Buffalo.
1974   "NYAC—Friend or Foe?" *New York State Archeological Association Bulletin* 62: 1–4.

White, Marian E. and Elizabeth Tooker
1968   "Archaeological Evidence for Seventeenth Century Iroquoian Dream Fulfillment Rituals." *Pennsylvania Archaeologist* 35: 1–5.

White, Nancy Marie and Patricia S. Essenpreis
1989   Letter on Women in Field Archaeology. *Anthropology Newsletter* 30(8):3.

Whiteford, Andrew H.
1992   Interview on file. Department of Anthropology, University of South Florida, Tampa.

Whittlesey, Stephanie
1991   "Beyond Anatomy: The Sociology of Gender in Arizona Archaeology." In *The Archaeology of Gender*, edited by Dale Walde and Noreen D. Willows, 226–233. Calgary: Archaeology Association of the University of Calgary.

Widnall, S.
1988   "American Association for the Advancement of Science, Presidential Lecture: Voices from the Pipeline." *Science* 241:1740–1745.

Wildesen, Leslie
1980   "The Status of Women in Archaeology: Results of a Preliminary Survey." *Anthropology Newsletter* 21(5):5–8.

Willey, Gordon R. and Jeremy A. Sabloff
1974   *A History of American Archaeology.* London: Thames and Hudson.
1980   *A History of American Archaeology.* Second edition. San Francisco: W. H. Freeman.
Williams, Barbara
1981   *Breakthrough: Women in Archaeology.* New York: Walker & Co.
Williams, Stephen
1981   "Acknowledgments." In *Traces of Prehistory: Papers in Honor of William G. Haag,* edited by F. West and R. Neuman, xi. Baton Rouge: Geoscience and Man XXII. School of Geoscience, Louisiana State University.
1986a   "Bibliography of Doris Stone: Her Works from 1930 to 1984." In *Research and Reflections in Archaeology and History: Essays in Honor of Doris Stone,* edited by E. Andrews V, 203–209. Middle American Research Institute Publication 57. New Orleans: Tulane University.
1986b   "Doris Stone: The Pathways of a Middle American Scholar." *Research and Reflections in Archaeology and History: Essays in Honor of Doris Stone,* edited by E. Andrews V, 199–202. Middle American Research Institute Publication 57. New Orleans: Tulane University.
Williams, Stephen (editor)
1962   "Proceedings of the Sixteenth Southeastern Archaeological Conference" (Macon, GA 1959), *Newsletter* 8:33–40.
Williams, Theresa A.
1989   "Hudson Valley Archaeological Survey 1939–1940: Directed by Dr. Mary Butler Under a grant from the Carnegie Corporation Administered by Vassar College." Master's Project, Department of Anthropology, State University of New York at Albany.
Wolf, Eric R.
1982   *Europe and the People Without History.* Berkeley: University of California Press.
Woodall, J. Ned and Philip J. Perricone
1981   "The Archeologist as Cowboy: The Consequence of Professional Stereotype." *Journal of Field Archaeology* 8: 506–509.
Woodbury, Nathalie F. S.
1988   "Like Mother, Like Son, Like Father, Like Daughter: Generations in Anthropology." *Anthropology Newsletter* 29(5):4, 13.
Woodbury, Nathalie F. S. and Richard B. Woodbury
1988   "Women of Vision and Wealth: Their Impact on Southwestern Anthropology." In *Reflections: Papers on Southwestern Culture History in Honor of Charles H. Lange,* edited by Anne V. Poore, 45–56. Archaeological Society of New Mexico, Santa Fe.
Wray, Charles and Harry L. Schoff
1953   "A Preliminary Report on the Seneca Sequence in Western New York, 1550–1687." *Pennsylvania Archaeologist* 23(2): 53–63.
Wylie, Alison
1989   "Reasoning About Ourselves: Feminist Methodology and the Social Sciences." Paper presented at the Centre for Women's Study and Feminist Research, University of Western Ontario.
1991a   "Feminist Critiques and Archaeological Challenges." In *The Archaeology of Gender,* edited by Dale Walde and Noreen D. Willows, 17–21. Calgary: Archaeological Association of the University of Calgary.

1991b   "Gender Theory and the Archaeological Record: Why is There No Archaeology of Gender?" In *Engendering Archaeology: Women and Prehistory*, edited by Joan M. Gero and Margaret Conkey, 31–56. Oxford: Basil Blackwell.

1992   "The Interplay of Evidential Constraints and Political Interests: Recent Archaeological Research on Gender." *American Antiquity* 57:15–35.

Wylie, Alison and Constance Backhouse
1991   Prospectus for *The Chilly Climate for Women Faculty: Voices from the Sacred Grove*. Ms. in possession of authors.

Yellen, John
1983   "Women, Archaeology, and the National Science Foundation." In *The Socio-Politics of Archaeology*, edited by Joan Gero, David M. Lacy and Michael L. Blakey, 59–65. Anthropology Research Report No. 23, University of Massachusetts, Amherst.

1991   "Women, Archaeology, and the National Science Foundation: Án Analysis of Fiscal year 1989 Data." In *The Archaeology of Gender*, edited by Dale Walde and Noreen D. Willows, 201–210. Calgary: Archaeology Association of the University of Calgary.

Young-Brühl, Elisabeth
1991   "Pride and Prejudice: Feminist Scholars Reclaim the First Person." *Lingua franca* 1(3): 15–18.

Zinn, Maxine B., Lynn Weber Cannon, Elizabeth Higginbotham, and Bonnie T. Dill
1990   "The Costs of Exclusionary Practices in Women's Studies." In *Haciendo Caras: Making Face, Making Soul*, edited by Gloria Anzaldua, 29–41. San Francisco: Aunt Lute Foundation Books.

Index

Aborigines, 213–217
academic archaeology
  assistant professors, 160, 169
  attrition of women, 161–163, 165–166
  availability of jobs, 160, 162
  contract work, 182
  hiring, 169, 171
  networking, 172
  non-ladder affiliates, 163–164, 166–167
  number of Ph.D.s, 160, 163
  productivity, 161
  promotion, 160, 167, 169, 171
  proportion of women faculty, 161–161, 163, 168–169, 171
  publication, 161, 168, 170–171
  research institutions, 26, 39, 163
  status of women, 159, 162, 171
  teaching assistants, 169
  teaching colleges, 161, 168, 170
  tenured positions, 169
  visibility of women, 160–163, 165, 169
affirmative action, 2, 24, 159, 160, 171, 202, 208, 211
Alabama, 5, 107, 125, 130, 134
Alaska, 13, 194
amateur, 6, 103, 114, 122, 135. *See also* avocational
American Antiquity, 3, 30, 95, 114, 140, 170
American Anthropological Association, 12, 26, 96, 135, 158, 159
American Museum of Natural History, 15, 51
American School of Classical Studies, 42, 44
analogy, 63

archaeological theory, 1, 140, 145, 156. *See also* postmodern, postprocessual
Arizona, 3, 13, 19–20, 28, 33–34, 202–203
Arkansas, 104–106, 125, 151
artifact, 15, 16, 30, 31, 55, 80, 82, 87, 112, 114, 115, 117, 126, 132, 140, 144, 145–148, 151, 153–156, 178, 180, 197
Ashley, Margaret, 3, 98
Australia, 3, 149, 210–218
Australian Archaeological Association, 212
avocational, 83, 86, 89. *See also* amateur
Aztec, 51

Bartlett, Katharine, 3, 17, 19–21, 67
Brew, J. O., 7, 30, 105
Broyles, Bettye, 100, 106, 107
Bryn Mawr College, 12, 23, 42–44, 49
Bullen, Adelaide, 3, 100, 108
Butler, Mary (Lewis), 3, 23, 24, 36, 37, 87
burials, 56, 57, 63, 64, 73, 99, 116, 148, 149, 176

California, 17–18, 29, 33, 73, 136, 149, 151
Campbell, Elizabeth, 3, 17–18, 21, 38
Carnegie Institution, 24, 25, 29–31, 33
ceramics, 1, 30–32, 56, 57, 62, 64, 66, 73, 75, 98, 146–149, 151, 153, 155, 205
Chaco Canyon, 13, 30
children, 4, 17, 21, 24, 36–38, 48, 54, 59–61, 79, 103, 108, 127–131, 167, 200, 206
citation, 1, 9, 138, 140, 142, 144–147, 150, 152–154, 158

class, economic, social, 5–7, 43, 68, 71–72, 74, 80, 82–83, 123, 152, 199
Cole, Faye-Copper, 101–102, 111
Colorado, 21, 30–32, 105–106
Colton, Mary, 67
Columbia University, 12, 15, 98, 136
Conkey, Margaret, 69, 70, 96, 173–174, 198, 214, 218
Connecticut, 84
contract archaeology, 134–135, 182–183, 201. *See also* cultural resource management, salvage
Coonabarabran, 210, 214–215, 217
Cosgrove, Harriet, 67
Crete, 41–47, 50
Cross, Dorothy (Jensen), 3, 12, 14–17
cultural anthropology, 7, 12, 104, 130, 192, 198
cultural resource management (CRM), 3–4, 39, 174, 177, 180–182, 184, 193, 199, 202–203, 205, 207–208, 211–213. *See also* contract, salvage

Davis, Hester, 2–3, 96–97, 99, 103–104
de Laguna, Frederica, 2–3, 5, 12–13, 17, 39
discrimination, 21–22, 87–89, 102, 108–109, 120, 171–172
dissertation, 12–15, 23, 42–43, 58, 83, 87–88, 91, 106, 162, 165, 170, 197, 203
divorce, 14, 190
Dormon, Caroline, 3–4, 121, 124–126, 133
Dutton, Bertha, 67

ecological, 210
education, 6, 12, 15, 19, 21, 33, 43, 49, 77, 85, 89, 91, 93–96, 103, 105, 108, 114, 122–125, 129–130, 132, 135–136, 156, 160, 168, 183–185, 189, 191, 193, 204–206, 208–209, 215
Ellis, Florence, 3, 12–14, 16–17, 32, 67
Engendering Archaeology, 174
environment, 36, 63, 99, 107, 115, 124, 127, 151, 182, 199, 203, 205, 208, 210, 212–213, 215
ethnoarchaeology, 152
ethnography, 30, 33–34
ethnohistory, 36, 93, 112, 217
Evans, Arthur, 42, 44–45
Evans, Jo, 3, 121, 126–127, 133

excavation, 1, 5, 14, 19, 24, 31, 33, 35–36, 41–42, 44–45, 47, 50, 56, 66, 72, 74–76, 78, 82, 93–94, 98–101, 106–107, 114–115, 139, 145–146, 150, 174–177, 215. *See also* fieldwork
family, 3, 19–20, 24–25, 27, 36–38, 48, 61, 78, 80, 86, 101, 103–104, 124, 126–128, 131, 134–135, 157, 162, 167, 200, 206, 208
feminist theory, 69–71, 215, 218
field school, 30, 36, 68, 72–74, 82, 84, 104–105, 127–128
fieldwork, 1, 8, 11, 18–19, 23–24, 28–29, 37, 48, 50, 67–68, 74, 77, 83–84, 89–91, 98, 106–108, 111, 116, 121–122, 126, 129, 131–134, 139–140, 155–156, 170, 173, 176–177, 179, 197–198, 204, 216–217. *See also* excavation
Florida, 102–103, 107–108, 115, 125, 145, 147
French, Frances, 2–3, 121, 129–130, 133–134, 137

Gender
and archaeological specialty, 1, 204–205
and authorship, 7, 16, 144–158, 170
and bibliographies, 1–2, 8, 144, 147
and book reviews, 142, 145–146, 149–150, 152–154
and career choice, 1, 4, 202, 207–208
and education, 1, 6, 204, 206, 208
and employment, 4–5, 162, 203, 211–212, 218
and excavation skills, 1, 3, 97, 155, 173, 175–179
and job responsibilities, 1, 4, 203–204
and laboratory work, 1, 204–205
and marriage, 206, 208
and mentoring, 7, 109, 168, 170, 196, 198–199
and mobility, 4, 167, 202, 206
and personal responsibilities, 206, 208
and publication, 157
and the Past, 173–174, 180
and rank, 89, 135, 156, 161, 202, 205
and salary differences, 16, 99, 200, 202, 205–206, 208. *See also* salary
and tenure, 2, 8, 157, 167, 169, 205, 212
bias, 1–2, 68–69

equity, 200, 212, 214–215
influence on science, 1–2, 67, 69–70, 75, 83, 96–97, 157, 160–162, 197, 206, 208
Georgia, 5, 98, 100, 106–107, 147, 184
Gero, Joan, 84, 90, 96, 108, 121, 140, 153, 155, 170, 174, 197, 214, 218
Gesell, Geraldine, 50
Gladwin, Nora, 67
Gournia, 42–43, 45, 47–48
Griffin, James B., 14, 88, 106, 114, 116

Hall, Edith, 3–5, 41–45, 47–50
Harding, Sandra, 61, 71
Harvard University, 6–7, 11, 25–27, 36–37, 55, 73, 98–99. *See also* Peabody Museum
Hawaii, 176, 194
Hawes, Harriet Boyd, 3–5, 41–48, 50
Heimlich, Marion, 3, 107
Hemenway, Mary, 3, 11
Historical Archaeology, 3, 138, 142–153
historical archaeology, 140, 142, 145, 150, 153–155, 157–158, 194
Honduras, 4, 27–28, 31, 51–52, 54, 56–57, 59, 64
Horner, Eva, 3, 19, 68, 72–75, 77–78, 80–84
Hunter College, 15–16, 23

Illinois, 101, 107, 128
interwar years, 10, 12, 16, 21–22, 29, 37–39
Iowa, 35–36, 104
Iroquois, 88–89, 91–93

Johnson, Paula, 2–4, 121, 132–134, 137
Jones, Olive, 145, 147–149, 152

Kansas, 30, 36, 105
Kelly, Arthur R., 34, 99–100, 107
Kelly, Isabel, 3, 19, 28, 33–34, 36–37, 67–68, 72–84
Kentucky, 100, 105–106, 112, 114–115, 126
Keur, Dorothy, 3, 12, 15–16, 23–24, 67
Kidder, Alfred V., 19, 25–26, 28–30, 34, 56, 58, 72–77, 82–83
Kidder, Madeline, 67
Kincaid field school, 36
Kneberg, Madeline (Lewis), 2–3, 12, 100–102, 110–119

Kroeber, Alfred L., 33–34, 67–68, 120
Krouse, Rita, 121, 127–129, 134, 137

laboratory, 1, 6, 10, 15, 30–32, 37, 68, 77, 83, 93, 99, 102, 111, 121, 140, 170–171, 186–187, 192, 204
Lazarus, Yulee, 2–3, 102–103
Lambert, Marjorie, 3, 17, 20–21, 67, 84
Lewis, Mary. *See* Butler, Mary
Lewis, Madeline Kneberg. *See* Kneberg, Madeline
lithics, 1, 20, 108, 133, 205
Louisiana, 3–4, 120–137

marriage, 4, 17, 20, 24, 27, 38, 48, 51, 53, 59, 64, 78, 112, 129, 131–132, 161, 190, 208
Maryland, 150, 184
Mason, Carol, 23, 85, 107–108, 121, 145–146
Massachusetts, 30, 98, 103
Mathien, Frances, 148
McCann, Catherine, 3, 5, 107
mentor, 86, 109, 154, 168, 170, 196, 198–199. *See also* gender and mentoring
Mesoamerica, 3, 11, 23, 25, 28–31, 37, 56, 159–172, 197
Mexico, 7–8, 13, 33–34, 58, 81, 148, 150, 167
Michigan, 128. *See also* University of Michigan
Mississippi, 106, 125
Missouri, 32, 150–151
Mount Holyoke College, 43, 47
museum, 1, 3–5, 7, 10–13, 15, 17–23, 25–30, 34–38, 42–45, 47–49, 51, 55–57, 62, 64, 67–68, 70, 73, 77, 83, 87–88, 90–91, 95, 99, 102–107, 114, 131, 133, 140, 146, 197, 202–203, 205, 211

National Academy of Science, 12
National Geographic Society (NGS), 34
National Park Service, 34–35, 99, 109, 211
National Research Council (NRC), 33, 101, 125
National Science Foundation (NSF), 3, 91, 93, 106, 169–170, 197
National Youth Association (NYA), 6, 123

Nebraska, 29, 104, 107
Nevada, 150
New Deal, 5, 99, 110. *See also* Works
　Progress Administration
New Hampshire, 151, 184
New Mexico, 14–15, 20–21, 29, 31, 35–
　36, 67–68, 72, 78, 81–82, 99, 104–
　105, 203
New York, 15, 24, 30, 85–95, 107, 145,
　184
New York Archaeological Council, 94
New York State Museum, 87
North Carolina, 5, 104, 131
nursing, 44, 101, 113, 128
Nuttall, Zelia, 3, 11, 17

Ohio, 148
Oklahoma, 105, 147
Oregon, 104–105, 174

paleoethnobotany, 98, 153. *See also* plant
　remains
parent, 13, 86, 103, 105, 108, 160, 206
Peabody Museum, 1, 25–27, 55–57, 62,
　64, 73, 99, 104–105, 146. *See also*
　Harvard University
Pecos, 19, 30, 35, 58, 72–73, 75
Pennsylvania, 24–26, 36, 91, 107, 117.
　See also University of Pennsylvania
physical anthropology, 101, 108, 111, 198
Pinkley, Jean, 3, 28, 34–35, 37
plant remains, 59–60, 64, 156, 217. *See
　also* paleoethnobotany
Popenoe, Dorothy Hughes, 3–4, 51–66
postmodern, 69
postprocessual, 70, 158
Proskouriakoff, Tatiana, 3, 5, 23–26, 30,
　36–37
publication, 2–3, 8, 13–14, 16, 23–27,
　29–31, 33, 35, 42–43, 47, 49, 89, 91,
　93, 100–103, 105, 114–115, 117,
　121, 124–125, 138, 140, 142, 144–
　148, 151, 153–158, 161, 166, 168,
　170–171, 173–174, 183–185, 192–
　193, 212

race, 5, 62, 68, 71–72, 74, 82–83, 123,
　152, 216
Radcliffe College, 23, 26–27, 36, 101
research associate, 4, 10, 22–23, 25–30,
　33, 36–37, 88

Rhode Island, 148
Rolingson, Martha, 2–3, 100, 105–106
Roosevelt, Eleanor, 48
Rothschild, Nan, 147, 149, 152

salary, 14, 16, 20, 25, 112, 200, 206. *See
　also* gender and salary difference
salvage archaeology, 89, 91–92. *See also*
　contract archaeology
science. *See* gender and influence on sci-
　ence
sexism, 68, 70, 173
Shepard, Anna O., 3, 28–32, 37
Simmons, Lanier, 3–4, 121, 130–134
site report, 20, 74, 150, 217–218
site survey, 73, 75, 212
Smith College, 19, 28, 43–45, 48
Society for American Archaeology, 12,
　14–15, 88, 172
Society for Historical Archaeology, 140–
　142, 145, 150–151, 154, 156–158
Society of Professional Archaeologists,
　194–195
South Dakota, 36
Southeastern Archaeological Conference,
　97–98, 100–102, 106, 117
Spector, Janet, 70, 146, 173–174, 218
Stark, Barbara, 3, 90, 147, 166–167, 170,
　194–196, 198–199, 205, 212
Stone, Doris, 2–3, 5, 23, 26–28, 36–37,
　39, 53, 57
supervising, 4–5, 15, 19, 24, 35, 45, 98,
　102, 107, 110–111, 174–178, 180,
　204–205. *See also* gender and job re-
　sponsibilities

Tanner, Clara, 67
Tecolote ruin, 19, 67–68, 72–75, 77–80,
　82–84
Tennessee, 101–102, 106, 110–112,
　114–117, 125
Texas, 35–36, 127, 129, 140, 152
thesis, 13, 16, 30, 36, 104–105, 129–130,
　134. *See also* dissertation
Tozzer, A. M., 53, 55, 57, 60, 63–64, 66,
　99

undergraduate, 6–7, 16, 27, 29, 86, 90,
　101, 104–105, 133, 169, 191, 193,
　212

unemployment, 162
United States Forest Service, 3
University of Chicago, 13, 35–36, 73,
    101–102, 111, 115, 132, 136
University of Michigan, 6, 86–88, 90–91,
    106–107, 112
University of Pennsylvania, 14, 23, 25,
    36–37, 42, 136
unpaid, 11, 23, 30. *See also* volunteer

Vaillant, George, 51, 53, 55–58, 64, 66–
    67, 73
Vassar College, 23, 36
Vermont, 180, 184
Virginia, 147
volunteer, 42, 120. *See also* unpaid

Watkins, Frances, 3, 17–19, 21, 38, 67–
    68, 72–80, 83–84
Wedel, Mildred, 2–4, 28, 35–36, 38–39
West Virginia, 106–107
White, Marian, 2–4, 85–95
Wimberly, Christine, 2–3, 107
Wisconsin, 6, 146
Works Progress Administration (WPA), 5,
    16, 98–100, 102, 106–107, 109–115.
    See also New Deal
World War I, 10–11, 48, 54, 57, 59
World War II, 10, 14, 17, 24, 33, 43, 48,
    86, 109–110, 112–114, 128
writing, 1, 10, 15, 37, 39, 53–55, 58, 63,
    75, 108, 114, 116, 145, 147, 154,
    186, 204–205, 215–218
written histories, 9–10, 39, 53

Contributors

Mary Beaudry, Ph.D.
Associate Professor
Department of Archaeology
Boston University

Wendy Beck, Ph.D.
Department of Archaeology and
Palaeoanthropology
University of New England
New South Wales, Australia

Susan J. Bender, Ph.D.
Professor
Department of Sociology,
Anthropology, and Social Work
Skidmore College

Diane Bolger, Ph.D.
Lecturer in Archaeology
Overseas Program, European
Division
University of Maryland

Meredith S. Chesson
Graduate Student
Department of Anthropology
Harvard University

Cheryl Claassen, Ph.D.
Professor
Department of Anthropology
Appalachian State University

Hester A. Davis
Arkansas State Archaeologist
Arkansas Archaeological Survey

Anabel Ford, Ph.D.
Adjunct Researcher
MesoAmerican Research Center
Social Process Research Institute
University of California, Santa
Barbara

Barbara Avery Garrow, Ph.D.
Co-owner and Contract
Archaeologist
Garrow and Associates, Inc.
Atlanta, Georgia

Patrick Garrow, Ph.D.
Co-owner and Contract
Archaeologist
Garrow and Associates, Inc.
Atlanta Georgia

Rosemary Joyce, Ph.D.
Associate Professor
Department of Anthropology
Harvard University

Mary Ann Levine
Graduate student
Department of Anthropology
University of Massachusetts,
Amherst

Rochelle A. Marrinan, Ph.D.
Professor
Department of Anthropology
Florida State University

Robert W. Preucel, Ph.D.
Assistant Professor
Department of Anthropology
Harvard University

Lynne P. Sullivan, Ph.D.
Senior Archaeologist
New York State Museum

Tracy Sweely
Graduate Student
Department of Anthropology
University of Colorado

Pat A. Thomas, Ph.D.
Corporate Editor
Garrow and Associates, Inc.
Atlanta, Georgia

Jacquelyn White
3000 West Pointe #107
Pittsburgh, PA 15205

Nancy Marie White, Ph.D.
Associate Professor
Department of Anthropology
University of South Florida

Stephanie Whittlesey, Ph.D.
Contract Archaeologist
Statistical Research, Inc.
Tucson, Arizona

Susan Wurtzburg, Ph.D.
2060 Ferndale Ave.
Baton Rouge, La. 70808

This book was set in Baskerville and Eras typefaces. Baskerville was designed by John Baskerville at his private press in Birmingham, England, in the eighteenth century. The first typeface to depart from oldstyle typeface design, Baskerville has more variation between thick and thin strokes. In an effort to insure that the thick and thin strokes of his typeface reproduced well on paper, John Baskerville developed the first wove paper, the surface of which was much smoother than the laid paper of the time. The development of wove paper was partly responsible for the introduction of typefaces classified as modern, which have even more contrast between thick and thin strokes.

Eras was designed in 1969 by Studio Hollenstein in Paris for the Wagner Typefoundry. A contemporary script-like version of a sans-serif typeface, the letters of Eras have a monotone stroke and are slightly inclined.

Printed on acid-free paper.